S0-BYR-439

THE MIDDLE AGES
AFTER THE
MIDDLE AGES

IN THE ENGLISH-SPEAKING WORLD

The eleven essays in this volume are studies of specific instances of the influence and impact of the Middle Ages on western life and culture from the sixteenth century to the present day. They cover a wide range of topics – literature, stylistics, lexicography, art, the cinema, philosophy, history and myth-making, oral traditions, feminist issues – and reflect the enduring influence of the Middle Ages on European art and life.

Dr MARIE-FRANÇOISE ALAMICHEL is lecturer in English at the University of Paris IV-Sorbonne; Professor DEREK BREWER is Emeritus Professor of English, University of Cambridge.

THE MIDDLE AGES
AFTER THE
MIDDLE AGES
IN THE ENGLISH-SPEAKING WORLD

Edited by
Marie-Françoise Alamichel
and Derek Brewer

D. S. BREWER

© Contributors 1997

All Rights Reserved. Except as permitted under current legislation
no part of this work may be photocopied, stored in a retrieval system,
published, performed in public, adapted, broadcast,
transmitted, recorded or reproduced in any form or by any means,
without the prior permission of the copyright owner

First published 1997
D. S. Brewer, Cambridge

ISBN   0 85991 508 5

D. S. Brewer is an imprint of Boydell & Brewer Ltd
PO Box 9, Woodbridge, Suffolk IP12 3DF, UK
and of Boydell & Brewer Inc.
PO Box 41026, Rochester, NY 14604–4126, USA

A catalogue record of this publication is available
from the British Library

Library of Congress Cataloging-in-Publication data
The Middle Ages after the Middle Ages in the English-speaking world /
edited by Marie-Françoise Alamichel and Derek Brewer.
   p.   cm.
   Papers of a conference held at the Centre d'Etudes Médiévales
Anglaises of the University of Paris IV-Sorbonne, Sept. 15–17, 1994.
   Includes bibliographical references.
   ISBN 0–85991–508–5 (hc : alk. paper)
   1. English philology – Congresses.   2. Arthurian romances –
Adaptations – History and criticism – Congresses.   3. Medievalism –
English-speaking countries – History – Congresses.   4. English-
speaking countries – Civilization – Congresses.   5. Middle Ages in
literature – Congresses.   6. Middle Ages in art – Congresses.
   I. Alamichel, Marie-Françoise.   II. Brewer, Derek, 1923–   .
PE23.M53   1997
909'.097521 – dc21   96–54703
   GYA 5-01

This publication is printed on acid-free paper

Printed in Great Britain by
Boydell & Brewer Ltd, Woodbridge, Suffolk

CONTENTS

EDITORS' PREFACE

From 15 to 17 September 1994, the Centre d'Études Médiévales Anglaises of the University of Paris IV-Sorbonne hosted an international
conference on the theme of 'The Middle Ages after the Middle Ages'. It
enabled the members of the centre to go beyond the usual scope of their
research and studies as well as to meet specialists in other periods and
other fields: it was an exciting event for scholars who would not normally
have met, but who now were gathered together to listen to papers dealing
with various approaches to the Middle Ages taken during the last five
hundred years.

The opening article, by Claire Vial, is devoted to the Arthurian imagery
which inspired, to some extent, the celebration of the wedding of the son
of Henry VII of England, Prince Arthur, to Katherine of Aragon in 1501.
Her paper assesses the Malorian influence on the anonymous *Receyt of the
Ladie Kateryne* through a close study of cadence, vocabulary and stylistic
devices. Although she demonstrates that the chronicler of the *Receyt* was
partly inspired by literature, she insists that one must not jump to the
conclusion that the chronicle is simply a retelling of the *Morte d'Arthur*,
since the general mood of the *Receyt* differs significantly from that of
Malory's work.

The next two articles take us to the borders of the English-speaking
world with, first, D. S. Thomson's study of the influences of medieval
thinking upon the Gaelic world from the sixteenth to the nineteenth century. Bardic poetry is discussed first, then songs and ballads, followed by
medical and legal documents. The presentation of Christian writing (religious verse, lives of saints, religious prose and incantational verse) comes
next. Religious writing is shown either to look back to the Middle Ages
or, at least, to bear the marks of medieval stylistic devices and literary
language. Oral aspects also reveal that ways of life and attitudes from
much earlier times continued in the Gaelic world of the sixteenth to the
nineteenth centuries. Kees Dekker's interest lies in the tradition of Old
English scholarship in the Netherlands in the seventeenth century, which
he presents by way of a highly detailed analysis of Jan van Vliet's life and
works and his cooperation with Francis Junius. The article shows that the
study of Old English in the Netherlands was not a mere imitation of what
was being done in Great Britain at the time.

In his learned article, E. G. Stanley analyses what thinkers have meant
by their use of the term 'Dark Ages' and shows through numerous revealing quotations that, up to the twentieth century, historians have considered
part or all of the Middle Ages as a period of ignorance, superstition and

error. Historians of literature similarly condemned the earlier Middle Ages, Henry Hallam even going so far as to state that the medieval period had known 'nothing of original genius in the province of imagination'. A generation of more objective literary historians (starting with R. W. Chambers), praising the variety and excellence of Old English prose, felt it necessary to coin the more favourably styled 'Heroic Age'. E. G. Stanley, after explaining the reasons for this choice, goes on to say that though heroic verse is a reality, the 'Heroic Age' is no more than a myth.

Florence Bourgne focuses her attention on mirrors in sixteenth-and seventeenth-century pictorial art. It is her belief that *vanitas* was heralded in medieval art and literature, and she proves her point by studying the Wilton Diptych, Troilus's ascent to heaven at the end of Chaucer's *Troilus and Criseyde* and several manuscripts of Guillaume de Deguilleville's *Pèlerinage de vie humaine*.

The way Georgian England treated the Middle Ages is then discussed in two articles dealing with eighteenth-century adaptations of Chaucer's tales. Renate Haas' study is limited to the popular genre of old wives' fables, which she first defines and then illustrates with Chaucer's 'Wife of Bath's Tale'. Haas emphasises the role played by women writers in the development of the eighteenth-century vogue for fairy-tale, fable and riddle. She argues that such popular traditions formed the context for Dryden's reworking of Chaucer's old wives' fable, whose analysis brings her to the conclusion that Dryden used the old wives' tale 'to toy with it, parade his talent and wit'. Derek Brewer analyses the way modernisations of Chaucer both represented and misrepresented his poetry, showing the differences in treatments from Dryden to Wordsworth, and showing, too, how Chaucer acquired the reputation of being 'bawdy'. Interest in Chaucer focused during this period on *The Canterbury Tales*, in contrast to earlier centuries; translations tended to become more accurate, and questions of 'decency' began to be a consideration.

Laura Kendrick arouses our curiosity with a somewhat provocative title, 'The American Middle Ages'; but her sub-title, 'Eighteenth-Century Saxonist Myth-Making', immediately puts us at ease. And yet her article shows that there was a kind of Middle Ages in America. She shows how, for some Americans, the conquest of the New World led to a sort of revival of the early Middle Ages in Britain, and how these thinkers imaginatively transplanted the Middle Ages to the American continent. She continues with a presentation of the inventors of the myth, the Revolutionary forefathers (Thomas Jefferson and Ralph Waldo Emerson in particular), and reminds us that the British themselves had a long history of idealising the Saxon period, finally suggesting the reasons for this idealisation.

René Gallet was courageous enough to tackle the nineteenth century – that great century of medievalism and Gothic sympathy. He fills a gap with his study by showing that Coleridge was not merely dependent on

Kant and Schelling but also highly indebted to scholastic thinking. From 1801 onwards, Coleridge was deeply influenced by Duns Scotus, St Thomas Aquinas, Occam and St Anselm. Gallet argues that this influence ranged from terminology to ontology, and then sets out some important scholastic themes with which Coleridge was concerned.

The twentieth century is represented by two articles. James Noble reviews Marion Zimmer Bradley's best-seller, *The Mists of Avalon*, arguing that this feminist author is 'valorising the very belief system she thinks she is condemning', since the matriarchal culture which Bradley holds as an alternative to intolerant, oppressive patriarchal society is nothing but 'patriarchy in disguise . . . The two sexes remain in competition with one another for power and privilege.' Finally, Sandra Gorgievski also devotes her paper to the Arthurian legend, but makes us quit the field of literature for that of the cinema. She analyses two major films, both based on Malory but revealing divergent perspectives. She argues that *The Knights of the Round Table* by Richard Thorpe (1953) is a typical Hollywood portrayal of the Middle Ages, contaminated by the myth of the frontier and that of the lonesome cowboy. John Boorman's *Excalibur* (1981), on the other hand, is a heroic fantasy whose aesthetic universe is influenced by German, Celtic, Oriental and Byzantine mythology, with a renewed interest in magic and esoteric symbols: Boorman proves to have been highly 'personal in recapturing the great Arthurian motives while working from his own motivations'.

The Middle Ages are much studied and appreciated at the end of our own, twentieth century. This collection of essays will show that the medieval period has, in fact, always been considered, whether positively or negatively, as a fascinating one, inspiring all sorts of thinkers, writers and artists. It is hoped that the enthusiasm of the contributors will encourage the reader to return to the original works with renewed interest.

Marie-Françoise Alamichel
Derek Brewer

From Written Record to Legend:
The *Receyt of the Ladie Kateryne* as Retelling of the *Morte Darthur*

CLAIRE VIAL

On 14 November 1501 celebrations began to mark the wedding of Prince Arthur, Henry VII's eldest son, with Katherine of Aragon, daughter of Ferdinand and Isabella of Spain. The festivities were to last for several weeks. On the opening day Katherine was solemnly welcomed by the City of London, which devised in her honour a series of extraordinarily elaborate pageants – probably the most impressive in the whole of the reign of Henry VII – followed by a wedding ceremony at St Paul's, a royal banquet enlivened by masques, and three days of tournaments.

All these events have been much commented upon, owing to several testimonies which have proved extremely informative as regards the history of political propaganda, the history of drama and early masques, and the evolution of the tournament in England. The fullest account of the festivities was provided a few months afterwards by an anonymous author belonging to the circle of Henry VII. This author compiled an account which, although officially sanctioned, is in part that of an eyewitness. It includes Katherine's journey from Portsmouth to London as well as a report, composed by another hand, of Prince Arthur's death and funeral at Easter 1502.

This account, entitled *The Receyt of the Ladie Kateryne*[1] by its editor, Professor G. Kipling, has long been considered by scholars a historical gold mine for the early Tudor period. Yet the degree of Arthurian imagery which inspired the celebration, and consequently its anonymous chronicler, could not but lead Professor Kipling to draw a link, however superficial and incidental, between some literary features of the testimony and the most recent and famous Arthurian romance of the period, Malory's *Morte Darthur*. Kipling's statements regarding possible Malorian phraseology in the *Receyt* prove rather sweeping and non-committal. He

---

[1] G. Kipling, *The Receyt of the Ladie Kateryne* (EETS, Oxford, 1990). Hereafter referred to as *Receyt*.

explains, for instance, that 'it attempts to cast its historical materials into the form of a medieval romance, occasionally borrowing prose cadences from Malory or Lord Berners to describe the actions of Katherine, Arthur and Henry VII' (*Receyt*, p. xiii).

The purpose of this paper is to dig a little deeper into these assumptions, to assess Malory's influence on the style rather than on the content of the *Receyt*, and, in more general terms, to determine whether it really is part of this umpteenth period of Arthurian revival.

I will first give a brief survey of the concrete elements of the festivities actually based on an Arthurian background, so as to put into perspective the impression of pervasive Arthurian propaganda one tends to form when dealing with this period. Then I will try to assess the degree of stylistic imitation of Malory, before examining the numerous reservations undermining the suggested parallel between the *Receyt* and the *Morte Darthur*. In conclusion we shall see if the *Receyt*, as a literary piece, can be inscribed within the broader frame of the romance genre.

As Professor Sidney Anglo showed some thirty years ago, the modern assumption of an all-pervading Arthurian vein specific to early Tudor propaganda should be considerably played down.[2] On the one hand, the myth of King Arthur's rebirth as a prominent member of the royal dynasty was not specific to the court of Henry VII, although this particular attempt was a little more successful than previous ones. On the other hand, the Arthurian revival proper concentrated on the person of Prince Arthur during his short life only, while the main concern of the propaganda was aimed at asserting Tudor legitimacy by emphasising their British descent. This is why such a character as Cadwallader, the last British king, was just as much honoured during the wedding festivities as King Arthur himself.

Thus, starting with Katherine's entry into London, it appears that only one pageant out of the six held explicitly associated the figure of King Arthur with that of Prince Arthur. This pageant featured SS Ursula and Catherine of Siena, who admonished Katherine with speeches about the virtues she was to acquire before reaching the throne of honour where the bridegroom awaited her. The moral journey she was to undertake partly announced the other pageants she was to ride by. St Ursula's speech contains an explicit reference associating the two figures of Arthur:

> As Arthure, your spouse, than the secund nowe
> Succedith the furst Arthure in dignite. (*Receyt*, ii. ll. 114–15).[3]

Other less explicit references included that in the third pageant, of the Moon, which featured the Archangel Raphael, King Alphonse the Wise of Spain, Job and Boethius; it was decorated with a number of devices

---

2 S. Anglo, *Spectacle, Pageantry, and Early Tudor Policy* (Oxford, 1969).
3 References are to book and line numbers.

including a green and white check pattern, identified at the time as King Arthur's colours. The final association of King Arthur with Prince Arthur was expressed in the fourth pageant, that of the Sun. This contained numerous references to the constellation Arcturus,[4] considered to be the place to which King Arthur's soul had been taken after his death (rather than the Isle of Avalon) and from which it had descended to incarnate in the person of Prince Arthur.[5] As regards the rest of the celebrations, the only other presence of the 'Arthurian way of life' was found in the tournaments held at the end of the festivities, although this time the sphere of reference was not King Arthur especially, but rather the chivalrous world in general.

It is thus quite clear that, on the level of historical facts and performances, the characters of King Arthur and his knights featured very infrequently. We therefore have to concentrate on another domain, that of the literary rendering of the events, to find a consistent set of 'Malorianisms' and other references to the Arthurian matter.

As Kipling points out, but without trying to support his point, some sentences in the *Receyt* seem strongly reminiscent of Malory in their general tone and wording. This is the case in several singular episodes; for instance, when an event is officially announced:

> And in the aftirnon towards the nyght, the Kynges grace lete warne and monysshe in generall all the nobles of the realme and estates that were within the Cytie of London to be redy in the mornyng at ix of the clock.
>
> (*Receyt*, iii. ll. 350–4)

> So in every goode towne and castell off this londe was made a crye that in the contrey of Surluse sir Galahalte shulde make a justis that shulde last seven dayes (. . .). Whan this crye was knowyn, kynges and pryncces, deukes, erlys and barownes and noble knyghtes made them redy to be at that justis. (*Malory*, p. 399, ll. 20–6)[6]

Such resemblances are also apparent in the *Receyt*, when spectators display their astonishment,[7] or during tournaments.[8]

Apart from these elusive echoes, Malory's influence on the author can be classified in three categories, ranging from the closest to the remotest

---

4 *Receyt*, ii. ll. 496–500; 513–15.
5 See Kipling's commentary on these lines, *Receyt*, pp. 132, 134.
6 References to page and line numbers may be found in E. Vinaver, ed., *Thomas Malory: Works* (Oxford, 1971). Hereafter referred to as *Malory*.
7 'that wondre hit was and joye to here that goodly and plesaunt noyse' (*Receyt*, iii. ll. 425–6); 'Thereat the courte had much mervayle whens com all that gere' (*Malory*, p. 180, ll. 22–3); 'Than sir Galahad . . . began to breke spearys mervaylously, that all men had wondyr of hym' (*Malory*, p. 521, ll. 13–14).
8 'Aftir that the othir couples in like wise faught egrely, and meny strokes were betwene theim' (*Receyt*, iv. ll. 465–6); 'and aythir mette other so harde and so fersely that both their horsis felle to the erthe' (*Malory*, p. 645, ll. 27–8).

type of imitation. I will therefore examine the various devices of term-to-term imitations, rhetorical similarities and, finally, transpositions of narrative sections.

A series of common features between the two works draws the reader's attention at first glance towards there being a conscious model for the *Receyt*: that is, its overall structure, which is divided, exactly as the *Morte* is, into books and short chapters. As a matter of fact, however, the source in this case would be Caxton rather than Malory, taking into account the presence of a prologue featuring the historical characters of King Ferdinand of Spain, and above all, of Henry VII. They are introduced as *exempla*, whose behaviour must become a model for future generations, and who surpass the worth of former sovereigns, however famous these may be:

> The moost noble and prudent kynges in the world, as well our excellent Suffrayn and Prince of Englond, Kyng Henry the vijth, as the worthy and famous Prince, Fardinand, by provysion of God, King of Espayn, in likewise have allowid the sentence of unite and peax to be moost expedient.
> (*Receyt*, Prologue, ll. 73–7)

The same prologue, just like Caxton's Preface, stresses the veracity of the account:

> the Lady Katheryn, of whois arryving, receite, mariage, with the circumstans, this pusant and litle tretes folowing is drawen and compiled, conteyning truly and withowt fables the very gest and fourme of the mater, nothing being in his dedes abreviat, neither by eny superfluous addicions fayn thinges representing . . . (*Receyt*, Prologue, ll. 90–5)

> To whom I answerd that dyvers men holde oppynyon that there was no such Arthur and that ale suche bookes as been maad of hym ben but faynes and fables, . . . that in hym that shold say or thynke that there was never suche a kyng callyd Arthur myghte wel be aretted grete folye and blyndenesse, for [I] sayd that there were many evydences of the contrarye.
> (*Malory*, Caxton's Preface)

The chapter headings in the *Receyt* also echo both Malory's and Caxton's phraseology:

> The furste chapter: how the Princese departid from her fathre and mothre, beyng in Hispayne, and what wiendes and jeopardies she suffred in her passage. (*Receyt*, i. ch. 1)

> Chapter 1: How Sir Tristram de Liones was born, and how his mother died at his birth, wherefore she named him Tristram.
> (Caxton's edition, viii. ch. 1)

Secondly, the tournament theme is particularly illustrative of the mimetic effect between the *Receyt* and the *Morte*. Though the *Receyt*-writer is more explanatory, both writers cherish the same stylistic hobby-horses. They both repeatedly use a hyperbolised periphrasis instead of the simple terms *joust* or *tournament*; where Malory consistently mentions *dedis of armys* (p. 15, ll. 36, 39; p. 149, l. 7; p. 646, l. 39), the *Receyt* speaks of *feates of werre* (iv. l. 368) or *dedes of armys* (iv. l. 373), or a mixture of the two, *noble feates of armys and werre* (iv. l. 44) or *noble dedys of werrys* (iv. l. 65).

When it comes to sentence-structure in descriptions of fights, both authors tend to simplify the coordination of independent clauses, and depict the rapid succession of sequences with sentences introduced by the smallest link-word, 'and':[9]

> and annon they chargid and ranne toguyder at the large . . . and brake their stavys right noble ij or iij course. . . . and after them every othere couple of Chalengeours and Defendours ich unto othir made ther cursys full nobly . . . and aftir them therl of Essex and the Dukes brothir did theis like goodly dedys . . . and in the same maner the Lord Barners and the Lord Wiliam of Devenshire. (*Receyt*, iv. ll. 537–55)

A passage of similar action would read in Malory:

> Than cam therein sir Gaherys, and there encountyrd with hym sir Ossayse of Surluse, and sir Gaherys smote hym over his horse croupe. And than ayther party encountyrd with othir, and there were many speres broken and many knyghtes caste under fyete. (*Malory*, p. 408, ll. 19–23)

The way of describing the assaults proper is extremely repetitive in both cases, the sentences following the order 'verb, manner, result'. Phrasing in the *Receyt* typically runs as follows:

> And so furst the Duke and the Lord marques runne toguyders egerly and with great currage . . . and brake dyvers stavis right valiauntly.
> (*Receyt*, iv. ll. 408–11)

> And secundly, therl of Essex and the Lord Henry of Bukkyngham rane toguyders . . . and did full nobly, . . . brekyng uppon ich othir dyvers and many sperys. (*Receyt*, iv. ll. 411–15)

> The residue copled and ranne iche to othir and nobly brake their stavys.
> (*Receyt*, iv. ll. 418–19)

Malory uses similar word-order and vocabulary:

> and than ayther party encountryd with ithir, and there were many speres broken and many knyghtes caste undir fyete. (*Malory*, p. 408, ll. 21–3)

---

9 Occasionally, the *Receyt* uses the same coordinator in circumstances other than the description of tournaments: see i. ll. 45–57.

And so they began grete dedys of armys and many spearys were brokyn and many knyghtes were caste to the erthe. (*Malory*, p. 409, ll. 39–41)

Thirdly, several lexical and grammatical devices sound like echoes of Malorian *topoi* in the *Receyt*. One thinks above all of the homeric adjective *noble* used in Caxton's Preface, qualifying *gentylmen, hystorye, crysten men, Arthur*, of course, *actes, memorye, feates, volumes, knyghtes, lordes*, and so on. This adjective is also a recurrent one in the *Receyt*, to mention the Royals: the *noble kynges* (i. ll. 5, 112), the *noble lady Katherine* (i. ll. 169, 202), the *noble Princes* (i. ll. 37, 57, 224; iii. l. 257), their *noble seatis* (iv. l. 151), and *noble and prudent audiens* (i. l. 198). The author uses in the same way the adjective *goodly* (*so goodly a lady and princess*, i. l. 16; *the goodly prince and princes*, iii. l. 180).

Then, when Malory deals with a celebration of some kind, be it a wedding, a banquet or a royal entry, he generally uses a single word, the term *solempnité*, or its adjectival form:

for there was never a solempner metyng in one cité togedyrs, for all maner of rychesse they brought with hem at the full.

(*Malory*, p. 146, ll. 14–17)

So they brought hym to his lodgynge with grete solempnyté, and there al the people becam his men. (*Malory*, p. 438, ll. 18–20)

And uppon Myghelmas day, the bysshop of Caunterbyry made the weddyng betwene sir Gareth and dame Lyonesse with grete solempnyté.

(*Malory*, p. 224, ll. 29–30)

The term *solempnité* thus covers a wide range of meanings, from the event itself to the way it is devised. The *Receyt* uses exactly the same variation on the same word, for the celebration (*the solempnyte of mariage*, iii. l. 171; *this great, goodly solempneties*, iii. ll. 316–17), but in most cases the term is part of a couplet and its meaning becomes redundant:

solempnely with honour (*Receyt*, ii. l. 821)

solempnely with moost honoure and behavour (*Receyt*, ii. l. 911)

this solempne and ordinat entrance (*Receyt*, ii. l. 653)

Both accounts also aim from time to time at shortening a description by using a sweeping and generalising expression such as *all maner of*:

all maners of matters (*Receyt*, i. l. 198)

with all maner of taclynges and marinurs (*Receyt*, iv. l. 453)

all maner of plenté . . . all maner revels and games . . . all maner of mynstralcy (*Malory*, p. 225, ll. 26–8)

Another summarising technique consists in using over and over again a descriptive phrasing that can apply to people, animals and elements of setting. Such is the case with the vague expression *richely beseyne*, meaning *equipped* as well as *good-looking*: the *Receyt* uses it for the Princess (i. l. 120) and noble members of the cortège (ii. l. 21), for men of honour (iv. ll. 317, 328) and for a whole pageant (ii. ll. 498, 907), as well as for a horse-litter (ii. l. 739). Malory inserts the same phrase for material (*a clothe leyde rychely beseyne of all that longed to a table*, p. 82, l. 22), rooms (p. 82, ll. 27, 29–30), men of honour (p. 177, l. 23) and knights (p. 282, l. 6). Both expressions denote a set of details that the narrator does not feel like examining at close range, as well as an abundance of goods on display.

A fourth category of borrowings from Malory involves the same stylistic figures in similar circumstances. The most obvious case is perhaps figures linked with hyperbole. The *Receyt* often piles up adverbs or adjectives with redundant meaning:

> uppon their goodly cursours right well and plesauntly trappid and garnysshid (*Receyt*, iv. ll. 76–7)

> the treasure right goodly and riche (*Receyt*, iv. ll. 970–1)

Or it describes fights whose outcome is much more spectacular than realistic:

> sumtyme bothe the partys of theim were borne to the grounde, bothe hors and man (*Receyt*, iv. ll. 422–3)[10] .

This kind of description is recurrent in Malory, often carried a step further:

> they so sore fought that hir shyldis felle on pecis and both horse and man felle to the erthe. (*Malory*, p. 15, ll. 31–2)

> at the last sir Galahalte smote a stroke of myght unto sir Palomydes sore upon the helme; but the helme was so hard that the swerde myght nat byghte, but slipped and smote of the hede of his horse.
> (*Malory*, p. 401, ll. 24–6)

Both Malory and the *Receyt*-author display a particular fondness for the superlative. Furthermore, they make the same hyperbolic use of the double superlative. When Malory speaks of the *moste honorablyst* (p. 60, l. 27) or *moste shamfyllyste wyse* (p. 100, l. 37), of the *moste mervayloust and moste adventurest man* (p. 557, ll. 2–3), or of the *moste nobelyste knyght* (p. 666, l. 4), the *Receyt* echoes with the *most excellent princes* (i.

---

[10] Cf. Kipling's note on these lines, *Receyt*, p. 156; and another, rather comical hyperbole, in iv. ll. 59–63.

l. 256), the *moost lengest desired season* (ii. ll. 3–4), the *moost purest water* (iv. l. 795) and numerous others.

A recurrent way for Malory of expressing an absolute superlative lies in the abundant use of the modifier *passing*; thus, people as well as situations are *passynge wyse* (p. 3, l. 6), *passynge well* (p. 15, l. 41), *passyngly sore* (p. 53, l. 39), *passynge good* (p. 70, l. 39), *passynge fayre* (p. 70, l. 39), *passynge lyght* (p. 86, l. 15), *passyng hardy* (p. 86, l. 18), *passyng faste* (p. 151, l. 30) and so on. The *Receyt* does not use the adverb *passing*, but resorts to two other adverbs, *goodly* and *right*, so often mentioned that they completely lose their semantic value, and remain only as undetermined intensifiers. These globally appreciative formulae may not be directly inspired by Malory, but they play the same role in the *Receyt* as similar formulae used in the *Morte* to allude to something in a positive way, without having to provide a fully detailed description: hence such phrasings as *goodly wrought* (ii. ll. 510–11), *goodly ordred* (iv. l. 6), *goodly appreparid* (iv. l. 573), *goodly barred and besett* (iv. l. 772) and *goodly beseen* (iv. l. 931).

Even when used as a qualifier, *goodly* as an adjective is applied to so many different substantives that it almost becomes a Homeric adjective, inseparable from any royal object, person, location or activity.[11] The use of *right* is exactly the same, sometimes with an emphasis, absent from the Malorian *passing* formula, on the appropriate aspect of the objects thus described: *right goodly behaviour and maner* (*Receyt*, i. ll. 150–1; iii. ll. 345, 419), *right great ryalty* (ii. l. 219), *right semely company* (ii. ll. 10–11), *right worshipfull chier and parleyaunce* (iii. l. 349), *right crafty buyldyng* (iv. ll. 133–4), or *right freshly disguysid* (iv. l. 223). Sometimes the two intensifiers are associated, as in *right goodly and pleasauntly* (iv. ll. 361–2).

Another tool common to both writers consists in suggesting the magnificence of a particular festive scene on the pattern of a negative comparison. This reads in the *Receyt*:

> So great a nombre and multitude [of knights] have not been seretofore in Englond at oon season made. (*Receyt*, iii. ll. 454–6)

> this goodly ryaltie and devyce and behavor have not beseen in like in verey long remembraunce. (*Receyt*, iv. ll. 109–10)

> [a banquet] excedyng the prayse of any othir usid in great seasons bifore.
> (*Receyt*, iv. ll. 246–7)[12]

---

[11] In *Receyt*, see 'all goodlie maner and haste' (i. l. 35), 'a goodly company' (i. ll. 55, 204; ii. l. 120; iii. l. 105; iv. ll. 25, 738), 'goodly mountain' (iii. l. 217), 'goodly disportes' (iii. l. 301), 'goodly numbre' (iii. l. 125; iv. l. 684), 'goodly tre' (iv. l. 12), 'goodly ryaltie' (iv. l. 110), 'goodly disguysyng' (iv. l. 142), 'goodly knight' (iv. l. 209) and so on.
[12] See also *Receyt*, iv. ll. 331–2, 399–402, 605–6.

In Malory the same situation is described in the following way:

> and wyte you well there was never seyne in kynge Arthurs dayes one
> knyght that ded so muche dedys of armys as sir Launcelot.
>
> (*Malory*, p. 502, ll. 20–2)[13]

To complete this stylistic survey, a whole set of narrative transpositions must be noted between the Arthurian author and his would-be imitator.

Let us first examine Malory's *Book of the Grail* and Book II of the *Receyt*, which is entirely devoted to the description of civic pageants. The reader is put in the position of the heroine of the day, Lady Katherine, so that the development of the entry is perceived as a series of beautiful pageants, adorned with an abundance of more or less cryptic allusions containing numerous levels of understanding, which the beholders may or may not be able to decipher. It is up to the pageants' actors to explain their identity and status, as well as the meaning of the setting in which they appear, and to allude to the forthcoming stages – pageants – on the bride's geographical and moral itinerary.[14] Though there is no pageantry in Malory, we do find several episodes in which protagonists are in the situation of beholding a spectacle – not a performance, of course, but some puzzling scene – whose meaning they cannot grasp without external help. These passages are essentially located in the Grail story, when Arthur's knights seem suddenly unable to find a meaning to their adventures, and miraculously come across a guide, generally a hermit, who enlightens them by explicating the connections between the objective content of the adventure and its moral equivalent. My point is that just as the versified speeches of the pageants' actors form a separate part of the main text, the hermits' explanatory discourses build a kind of clearly identifiable subtext, giving knights the historical background they lack (p. 543, ll. 1–23), deciphering the symbolic meaning of dreams (p. 547, l. 31–p. 548, l. 4), or announcing their degree of success in the holy quest (p. 554, l. 38–p. 555, l. 13).

In the same way, the author of the *Receyt* manages to describe Katherine's journey through London as though she met each pageant almost by chance:

> they cam to the enteraunce of the great bridge of London, whereuppon
> was the furst pagent in maner and fourme folowyng: that so to sey, there
> was on the myddes of the bridge erecte a tabernacle of two flowers, assem-
> blaunt unto tweyne rodeloftes, in whoes lougher floure and particion there
> was a sete. And within the sete a faire yong lady with a wheel in hir hand in
> liknes of Seint Kateryne, with right many virgyns in every side of her.
>
> (*Receyt*, ii. ll. 28–35)

---

13 Also *Malory*, p. 146, ll. 15–17.
14 The speeches were not all heard by the author of the account, who, as a follower of the king, could not watch all six pageants in person. However, he integrated the speeches

This introduction of the pageant, especially with the reference to the bridge and the young virgin, two strategic elements of chivalrous adventure, can easily be compared with the way Malory stages the suddenness of adventure, whether at court, in a forest or in a castle. Knights seem to ride from enchanted castles to anonymous pavilions, with only very brief intervals in between devoted to a quick summary of their move from one point of the forest to another. Since the narrator of the *Receyt* chooses to describe the civic pageants from the point of view of the main protagonist of the day rather than listing them as mere designer's projects,[15] and since he inserts them in the actual itinerary covered by Katherine, I think we may legitimately speak again here of transposition of a recurrent Malorian narrative device.

There also exists another type of characteristic passage, whose focus is the listing of the members of a procession. In the *Receyt* this concerns first the king's suite, with characters spiritual and temporal (i. ch. 6); we also have the full list of people forming Katherine's welcoming procession on her arrival in London (ii. ll. 14–23); and symmetrically the members of the princess's own cortège (ii. ll. 675–750).[16] Similar passages in Malory are set during the description of tournaments, when – in contrast to his somewhat sloppy method with processions – Malory carefully records the names of knights joining in the game, as well as the emblems they display.[17] Tedious as these lists may seem to the modern reader, from the chronicler's perspective they provide one more piece of evidence for the veracity of the account of Arthur's power. Above all, by their very number these knights represent the far-ranging domination of Arthur, which is constantly extending through the dubbing of new knights or the overcoming of former enemies, who either die or join Arthur's forces.

In the *Receyt*, I think the listings have exactly the same function, beyond the historical precision required from the chronicler.[18] The richness of the procession in terms of number and ornaments reflects the grandeur of the sovereign. It is not by chance that the description of the procession on the king's side is just a bit longer than that on the Spanish side: what is at stake here is the public image of the king, supported by the number and ranks of his followers. And it is not by chance either that, among such a display of magnificence, the only jarring note comes from the remarkable ugliness of some Spanish ladies-in-waiting, carefully noted by the author as well!

---

corresponding to all of them, probably thanks to a copy of the actors' parts circulated at court at the time.

[15] Although he most probably resorted to such documents for the description of the pageants he did not actually see.

[16] See also *Receyt*, iii. ll. 374–91.

[17] See *Malory*, p. 239, ll. 37–44; p. 404, ll. 22–38; p. 644, ll. 21–35.

[18] See also Kipling's note about *Receyt*, ii. ll. 14–23.

And aftir thoes v charys came ij other charys not so richely beseen, in which ij charys were Spanyssh women apparellyd aftir the Spanysshe fachion. Ther apparell was busteous and marvelous, and they were not the fairest women of the company. (ii. ll. 741–5)

All that being said, the critic must allow for the fact that these stylistic borrowings or influences cannot hide the essentially differing perspectives of the *Morte* and the *Receyt*. A closer look at the Preface of the *Morte* and the Prologue of the *Receyt* may reveal the opposed standpoints of the writers, which make their narrations irretrievably alien in content, although closely comparable in style. Caxton's Preface to the *Morte* insists on the bellicose qualities of King Arthur by replacing him in the lineage of Alexander the Great. Arthur thus appears not as a king of peace but as one of conquest, alongside Charlemagne and Julius Caesar. On the other hand, when the *Receyt* evokes the Romans or Alexander, they are used as counter-models, not to be followed, for the sake of peace and unity:

How long had Alexander the clere possession of the realmes and straunge countreis of the worlde, that with his great labour, payne and losse of his people he conquerid and subdued to his dominion? A small while, whiles he lyved, and straight after his descease every prince had his londes and kyngdoms forthwith in peax. (ll. 63–7)

On the contrary, Ferdinand and Henry VII have followed for several years the wiser course of peace, beneficial for both lands and peoples, for the microcosm as for the macrocosm. They are related not to the tradition of war-captains, but to that of peace-warrants:

The moost noble and prudent kynges in the world, as well our excellent Suffrayn and Prince of Englond, Kyng henry the vijth, as the worthy and famous Prince, Fardinand, by provysion of God, King of Espayn, in likewise have allowid the sentence of unite and peax to be moost expedient.

(ll. 73–7)

Similarly, the original aims of the works have little in common: the *Receyt* was almost certainly composed on official request. Consequently, and whatever his precise status, there are several events to which the author was bound to pay particular attention, a constraint which Malory was not obliged to heed. If one takes, for instance, all the particulars of dates and locations, Malory's calendar follows the main liturgical feasts, without the need of any further precision: anything happening during the twelve days of Christmas comes under the chronological reference to 'Christmas'. The other temporal notations constitute a self-referring set such as *on the morne*, *on the next day*, and so on. The *Receyt* is logically concerned by dates and times, and also evolves within a much shorter span.

It is therefore natural that the *Receyt* should keep a very close record not only of countries and towns, but also of precise locations in towns, providing information about the Princess's itinerary to London, and then on the places where festivities were held, particularly royal residences in and around London. The description of the royal entry also integrates the strategic role played by selected urban sites. The precise description of Richmond Palace in Book IV (1–885) is clearly motivated by the fact that the Palace had just been rebuilt and redecorated for the occasion. Malory, on the contrary, relies on a selective geography including the main landmarks only, such as Winchester, Camelot, Tintagel, Brittany or Rome: his scale is utterly different. He is certainly not interested in describing a hall all hung with festive ornaments, for instance. More generally speaking, Malory follows the tradition of Arthurian romances in passing from castles to palaces through forests, and totally omitting the urban world and its inhabitants. He is not concerned with the notion of town life; so that, even on the rare occasions when royal entries appear in the *Morte*, he concentrates on royal and noble members of the cortège, occasionally on knights, but never on ordinary spectators of and participants in civic performance.

This is where we come to the core of the difference of perspective, and consequently of literary focusing, between the *Morte* and the *Receyt*: all the *solempnytes* revived in minute detail by the *Receyt*, whose general style attempts, as we have seen, to recreate a Malorian atmosphere, are precisely the episodes which Malory consistently leaves out. Malory is not interested in festivals for their own sake and especially not in gratuitous displays of royal splendour – that is, the kind of shows that do not provide occasions for knightly deeds.[19] The only festivals in which he shows interest are tournaments. In fact, all courtly celebrations, even liturgical feasts, serve as settings for jousts and tournaments. Details concerning colour, emblems, materials, members of processions and the food at banquets are of no interest to him when they are part of passages of mere passive entertainment; so that public occasions like royal entries, as well as more private ones like the wedding banquet and the accompanying masques, are considered as superfluous episodes. This does not mean that they do not exist in the *Morte*: they are simply disposed of as quickly as possible by the narrator, in favour of tournaments. If one turns, for instance, to Malory's descriptions of wedding banquets, it is clear that he systematically assumes the reader's knowledge of the events, piling up generalising expressions:

> So than the kynges, quenys, pryncis, erlys, barouns, and many bolde knyghtes wente to mete; and well may ye wete that there was all maner of plenté and all maner revels and game, with all maner of mynstralcy that was used tho dayes. (*Malory*, p. 225, ll. 25–8)

---

[19] For more details see C. Vial, 'Feasts and Festivals in Malory's *Morte Darthur*', in *Bulletin des Anglicistes Médiévistes* (Paris, 1993).

When the author of the *Receyt* makes a pretence not to describe at whole length a royal banquet, he may use the same kind of expression, but as a paralipsis, and continue to describe the various courses (iii. ll. 263–71).

It is therefore clear that the *Morte Darthur* and the *Receyt* display two totally different ways of apprehending the very notion of festival, on the one hand that of a knight, and on the other that of a member of the Tudor court. The official account of the 1501 wedding festivities is aimed at supporting the elaborate diplomacy which led to this fortunate alliance, and the splendour of a court whose king managed to conclude such a treaty: hence the general mood of admiration and approbation of the spectacle. This is why the *Receyt* draws on such words or phrases from Malory as mostly express either a positive judgement, or more generally, a tendency to hyperbole. The nuance introduced by the *Receyt* is that when Malory uses, say, a double superlative to convey the idea of worthiness, the *Receyt* uses the same rhetorical figure to emphasise the magnificence of the performance and, indirectly, the glory of the Tudor dynasty. Another relevant piece of evidence for this is that, when it comes to entertainments that are not so aesthetically impressive, like tournaments, the author of the *Receyt* in his turn uses generalising expressions as if he did not want to bother with paying attention to the fights:

> the which goodly feates and therof the hool description appieryth weell pleynner and more opyn in the bokys of the haroldes of armys.
>
> (Receyt, iv. ll. 124–6)[20]

When examining the ceremony of dubbing, present in both accounts, these divergent perspectives appear all the more clearly: in the only dubbing described at length by Malory, the narrator insists on the formal gestures and spoken formulae of the ritual (see Torre's dubbing, p. 61, ll. 39–62, 6). On the contrary, the narrator of the *Receyt* glosses over the ritual (iii. ch. 7) and insists on the mundane side of the ceremony, as part of the magnificence displayed on such special occasions as weddings or coronations. In Malory, new knights are knights of war; in the *Receyt*, they are knights of honour.

In other words, the writers have radically different interests: performance and spectacle for the *Receyt*-author, active entertainment for Malory. It is quite a paradox that the narrator of Prince Arthur's wedding should draw most of his style from one who is not interested in festivals. It is clear that, though the author of the *Receyt* borrows not only cadences but vocabulary and stylistic devices from Malory, the general mood of his account has nothing to do with the *Morte*. And this is the case even if the unfortunate and untimely death of Prince Arthur at Easter following the wedding, which constitutes the fifth and last book of the *Receyt*, increases

---

[20] See also *Receyt*, iv. ll. 350–7.

the parallelism in the overall structure of the two works.[21] The author of the *Receyt* shows in his account a complete distortion, or at least revision, of the Arthurian heroes and of the general understanding of the world portrayed by Malory.

Does this therefore mean that the *Receyt* fails in its attempt at reviving the romance-world? I do not think so. Considering the *Receyt* not purely as a historical account but as a piece of literature in its own right, albeit perhaps not always a consistent one, we can find in it features of the chivalric romance. If we take the definition of this genre[22] item by item, it appears that the conventionally high degree of civility to be found in medieval romances is undoubtedly present in the *Receyt*, not only in the complexity of the various festivities forming the celebration but also in the way the author minutely records details of ceremonial garments, room-decoration and combinations of emblems. The theme of the quest is amply present in the journey of the heroine, first from her native country to her adoptive one, then from the gates of London to the throne, during which she acquires the essential virtues of the good ruler. The representation of courtly love in the civic pageants in Book II is aptly balanced with the description of jousts and tournaments in Book IV, while the wedding ceremony and reuniting banquet constitute the third and central book of the account. Wonders and marvels are present both in the intricate symbolism and devices of the civic pageants and in the description of courtly masques, all of them written from the point of view of a spectator discovering and admiring the performance.

The reader should also take into account the *Receyt*-author's sense of drama when dealing with Katherine's journey to England, threatened and then delayed by the *wiendes and jeopardies she suffred in her passage*;[23] this is introduced deliberately in order to induce a sense of relief at her safe arrival. A similar dramatic sense is shown in the last chapter of Book IV (originally the last chapter of the whole account), where the author emphasises Katherine's sorrow at the departure of her fellow countrymen after the festivities. We should also note the almost supernatural abundance observed in royal halls, which gives the impression of a secular version of the permanent plenty provided by the Holy Grail.[24]

---

[21] Kipling explains that this last book was added afterwards. It is very different in style and vocabulary, and was probably composed by another writer; the main author went only as far as to reshape the end of Book IV so as to integrate what became Book V. Though there is no point in comparing in this paper the manner of Book V with the Malorian model, it is interesting to note that the death and burials of Prince Arthur resemble very much the last pages of the *Morte*, especially Guinevere's funeral, organised by Launcelot (*Malory*, p. 723, ll. 1–31).

[22] Based on M. H. Abrams' *Glossary of Literary Terms* (Orlando, 1988).

[23] The title and object of the very first chapter.

[24] 'There was a stondyng cuppbord with plate of clene gold very precious and riche and also of right great plentie' (*Receyt*, iii. ll. 252–4); 'The numbre of the spice plates and

Most of the time, the relationships between history and fiction work in two ways: either a writer of fiction makes a pretence of telling a true, historical account, or literary sources inspire the devising of historical spectacles. This is what happens, for example, in pageantry. What is remarkable about the *Receyt of the Ladie Kateryne* is that an official chronicler, while recording a series of historical events partly inspired by literature, manages to turn his account into a literary work very much resembling the sources of the events in question. What we have with the *Receyt* is an instance of early modern history successfully transposing a typically medieval literary genre.

cuppis were goodly and marvellous and yet the more to be wondred, for that the cuppbord was nothyng towchid but stode complet, garnysshid, and fulfillyd, not oonys dimynysshid' (iv. ll. 255–9).

Influences of Medieval Thinking on the Gaelic World in Scotland, in the Sixteenth Century and Later

DERICK S. THOMSON

The Gaelic-speaking areas of Scotland were not, of course, a part of the English-speaking world until relatively recent times, and for the main part of this paper what we shall be dealing with is a situation parallel to those with which English medievalists are directly concerned. There will be points of contact between the two subject areas at many stages, and the differences between them may be as interesting as the similarities. Occasionally I shall venture across linguistic borders, particularly with Scots and English (which in Scotland we regard as separate linguistic and literary traditions).

The pace of societal change mirrors the extent of conservatism in a culture, and remoteness has a bearing on such change. Gaelic Scotland in some senses was on the edge of the world in earlier times, an outer edge of the European world, no longer invaded from the Norse area and not yet spilling into the American one. That Gaelic world had grown from an Irish base, from the third and especially the fifth century AD onwards; but it had been grafted on to (and had supplanted) a Pictish- and Ancient-Welsh-speaking world, and had had intermittent contacts with Norse, Saxon, Norman, French and Flemish culture from the seventh century to early modern times. For a lengthy period, say from the Middle Ages to the eighteenth century, the Gaelic-speaking islands off the west coast were somewhat isolated from the outside world, and retained ways of life and attitudes from much earlier times, some of which survived well into the twentieth century.

As in other societies, Gaelic society contained different sectors showing varying degrees of conservatism or change. Some of these sectors may be said to have a class connotation, others a cultural one not specifically tied to class. The impact of religion, including the conflicts of the Reformation, and the survival of a certain kind of paganism, are important factors. We have to look at both the literate and the oral aspects of Gaelic society, and will find links in both with the Middle Ages.

Literate and literary orders had a secure place in earlier Gaelic society in both Scotland and Ireland. They were part of society's power structure, affirming the legitimacy of the ruling families and providing a range of services. The literary orders, the poets in particular, are very prominent in this system, developing and maintaining a standard literary language that changed little from about 1200 to 1600 AD. Hereditary dynasties developed, often running their own bardic schools with their own textbooks of style and metrics. Among the most prominent of these families were the O'Dalys in Ireland and the MacMhuirichs in Scotland, families which were themselves related. Some of the basic functions of these poets were, firstly, to maintain and publicise the historical importance of their patrons, making sure that their genealogies were kept in view, and linking them to a heroic past; secondly, to record current events in these families in verse (whether births, marriages, deaths or victories); and thirdly, to maintain their own literary traditions, which were strongly linked to saga, history and legend.

A few examples from the work of MacMhuirich poets illustrate these aims and practices. One poet, Lachlann MacMhuirich, composed a battle-incitement before the battle of Harlaw in 1411, using an ancient basic metre, and setting his praise and encouragement of the MacDonald warriors in an alphabetic structure which must surely have links with such secular Latin poetry of the Middle Ages as the poem on the Hawk and the Peacock (*De Accipitre et Pavone*). The Harlaw poem is relatively simple in structure, giving two lines and four praise epithets to each letter of the alphabet, as follows:

> Gu h-àirneach, gu h-arranta,
> Gu h-athlamh, gu h-allanta,
> Gu beòdha, gu barramhail,
> Gu brìoghmhor, gu buan-fheargach.[1]

This particular technique did not continue to be popular, though there exists an eighteenth-century gross extension of this very poem which sometimes gives as many as forty epithets for one alphabetic category. But the central idea of praise for warriors continues well beyond the classical bardic era, for example with elaborate praise and incitement poems addressed to a range of clans expected to take part in Jacobite Risings of 1715 and 1745.

A favourite strategy of the professional bards is to link their patron to heroes of earlier history and legend. The strong influence of ancient Irish tradition shows up here, as where Cathal MacMhuirich, a seventeenth-century poet, links his praise of a MacDonald chief to the Irish court-centre of Tara, and to heroes of early legend such as Guaire and Niall of the

---

[1] See D. S. Thomson, 'The Harlaw Brosnachadh: An Early Fifteenth-Century Literary Curio', in *Celtic Studies*, ed. J. Carney and D. Greene (London, 1968), pp. 147–69.

Nine Hostages. A little of this technique spills over into the work of later vernacular poets, as when John MacCodrum, in the eighteenth century, refers to heroic characters of legend such as Diarmad and Goll. In the case of professional bards a favourite device is to develop such an analogue, which implicitly compares the patron to a hero of legend and in which the legend itself is recounted at some length.

In a similar way, some similes and metaphors become standard clichés in praise poetry. The tree-metaphor is one of the most popular, with all the names for trunk, branch, twig and foliage being brought into play. Murdo Mackenzie of Achilty has a poem dated 1643 in which he applies the tree-metaphor six times to the chief, as well as using an even older metaphor, that of the battle-pillar, which is also popular in Irish verse. Calvert Watkins traces this particular metaphor back to Pindar.[2]

The professional poets were also involved to some extent in compiling the large body of heroic verse or balladry relating to such legendary figures as Cú Chulainn, Ossian, Finn and Oscar. We can trace this type of verse back to the twelfth century, though it was based then on legends that were very much older. This kind of verse was widely popular in Ireland and Scotland. In Scotland it surfaces in considerable detail in a manuscript from the first half of the sixteenth century, the *Book of the Dean of Lismore*. Large collections were made from oral recitation in the eighteenth and nineteenth centuries, while the eighteenth century saw the enormous impact of certain aspects of this tradition on European literature and the arts through James Macpherson's slightly genuine, largely spurious 'translations' of the ballads. There were still a good number of traditional bearers of these ballads, in recited and sung form, in the present century, and I have personally recorded some of these. A short version of the ancient saga, the *Táin* (the 'Cattle Raid of Cooley') was recorded in the Hebrides in the 1950s.

These literary orders operated in different ways. Some of the poets were also expert genealogists, and have left detailed records of various clan genealogies, as in a manuscript of 1467. Others wrote more extended clan histories, as the seventeenth- to eighteenth-century Niall Mac-Mhuirich did for the Clan Donald. Other branches of the literate establishment specialised in different areas; thus we have a sizable collection of Gaelic medical manuscripts and a range of hereditary lines of medical professionals, the most prominent of these being the MacBeths/ Beatons/Bethunes, who first came to prominence in Scotland early in the fourteenth century and were still holding hereditary office in 1700. Some of these held office in the courts of Scottish kings, others with the chiefs of such clans as the MacDonalds and the Macleans. Branches of this family operated widely in Scotland, and in their post-literate phase

---

2   See C. Watkins, 'Some Celtic Phrasal Echoes', in *Celtic Language, Celtic Culture*, eds Matonis and Melia (California, 1990).

continued to pass on traditions of herbal medicine. I had one great-great-grandmother who was a Beaton and who still retained some of this expertise in the nineteenth century. The tradition of the manuscripts goes back to Continental schools such as that of Montpellier, and the core of medical expertise to Greek and Muslim medicinal writers such as Hippocrates (*c.* 460–370 BC), Galen (2nd c. AD) and Avicenna (AD 980–1037). The language of these medicinal manuscripts is the classical Gaelic used by the literary orders generally.

In contrast, there are few survivals of legal manuscripts, although a small range of Gaelic legal terms survives in such Scots legal writings as the *Regiam Majestatem*, and in common usage until the eighteenth century (*cudeichs*, that is, *cuid-oidhche's*, or 'price of a night's refection', were paid in corn and straw in Atholl, and so named in records, as late as 1720). Yet there are hereditary legal families also, with titles such as *judex* and *dempster*, which appear in records of the twelfth and thirteenth centuries and which apparently represent an older Gaelic system. The Gaelic word for 'judge' is *britheamh*, Scotticised and Irished as *brehon* or *breve*. The earliest such to appear in a Gaelic manuscript in Scotland dates from *c.* 1132 (*Book of Deer*), but a family of Morrisons who had acted as legal experts for the MacDonald Lords of the Isles was prominent in Lewis as late as the eighteenth century, and has identifiable descendants to this day.

Close connections between clerics and members of the Gaelic learned orders go back to the distant past, and Gaelic literacy must be linked at a very early stage to Christian literacy. In medieval times we see these connections maintained, and a hereditary line frequently branches into poetry and medicine as well as maintaining the clerical calling. The sixteenth-century Dean of Lismore, perhaps more a lawyer than a cleric, was the main collector of a remarkable Gaelic verse anthology, and he includes a poem by a John MacMhuirich, Dean of Knoydart in the early years of the sixteenth century, and doubtless closely related to another John Mac-Mhuirich, the head of that bardic family in Kintyre in the 1530s. Beatons and MacLachlans surface as prominent medics as well as clerics. These are natural movements across professional borders. It is natural also that clerics and medics would find it easier to move into more cosmopolitan areas than the poets and literati would; and they, along with the chiefs of clans, take advantage of university education, while the poets remain thirled to their bardic schools, and the schools and the poets go down together.

We can probably make a connection between the decline of the old order and the emergence of a new literacy, prominently encouraged by Gaelic clerics in the sixteenth, seventeenth and eighteenth centuries. The movement seems to come to a head in the eighteenth century, when we find a succession of clerics appearing as dedicated collectors of Gaelic verse, from the Rev. John Pope in the 1730s to James McLagan throughout the second half of the century, and Donald MacNicol, who had a sparring match with Dr Johnson. These men, and others of their kind, rescued a large body of verse of sixteenth- to eighteenth-century dating from the oral tradition, together with the sometimes older balladry. The most remarkable of the eighteenth-century poets, Alasdair Mac Mhaighstir Alasdair, had acquired Gaelic literacy from his clerical father, including a degree of classical Gaelic literacy; but he had access also to some Latin and Greek literature, and is influenced by the Scots poetry of Gavin Douglas and the English poetry of James Thomson. An eighteenth-century successor, Ewen MacLachlan, was to extend the literary bounds by translating much of the *Iliad* into Gaelic. Several other eighteenth-century Gaelic poets, although illiterate, were deeply steeped in the oral tradition, and in two prominent instances (those of Duncan Bàn Macintyre and Rob Donn) their work was written down by churchmen and their families.

One would expect a significant degree of continuity in religious practices and literature, despite the Reformation. There was an old tradition of religious verse. The occasional verse of Dark Age clerics, on Nature and the seasons, is perhaps a fringe activity, but we may be justified in seeing links between such verse and some late-sixteenth-century poems by John Stewart of Appin, while seasonal verse was to be greatly developed in the eighteenth century. There was also a substantial body of more doctrinal writing which shows up especially in Ireland from the early thirteenth century. Examples of this, and of prose writings such as saints' lives, are prominent in surviving Scottish manuscripts from late medieval and early modern times. A more clearly Scottish Gaelic tradition of religious writing may be discerned from the sixteenth century onwards, and late in the seventeenth century Duncan MacRae's Fernaig manuscript includes a large collection of religious poems. One poem by MacRae himself consists of a series of confessions covering the Seven Deadly Sins; and it has been suggested that the specific nature of this list of confessions retains a Catholic emphasis. MacRae also has a poem which is a debate between the body and the soul. This was a popular type of dialogue in Catholic Ireland, especially Munster, but one which the Reformed Scottish Gaelic writers did not greatly favour.[3] Later, emphasis comes to rest specifically on the Bible story, with Alexander Munro of Strathnaver, for example, versifying many parts of it during the first half of the seventeenth century, over a hundred years before there was a full Gaelic translation of the New Testament. The emphasis in later Gaelic spiritual verse is on the Bible story and evangelical interpretations of it, but a tradition of Catholic hymnology survived.

The transition from old to new in religious prose took a rather different form from that of verse, and raises some interesting questions. The first Gaelic printed book in either Scotland or Ireland was John Carswell's

---

3   Rev. John Macinnes, in *Trans. Gaelic Soc. of Inverness*, 46, p. 318.

translation of the *Book of Common Order*, which was itself a revision of the *Geneva Book* or John Knox's *Liturgy*, printed in Edinburgh in 1562. Carswell's translation, with some original matter by himself, appeared in 1567. His connections were with Argyll, and he became ecclesiastical superintendent for Argyll and the Isles after the Reformation. His translation is basically in classical Common Gaelic, and this choice may have been made to make the book accessible in both Scotland and Ireland. But it could be accessible only to certain classes – the literate classes discussed already, including the Gaelic clergy, or some of these. There could have been little intention of making direct contact with the commonality. In one of Carswell's personal additions to the text he deplores the lack of a Gaelic translation of the Bible, and then goes on to castigate the Gaels for their inordinate interest in vain and worldly stories about the Tuatha Dé Danaan and Fionn Mac Cumhaill. This seems to anticipate remarkably the later evangelical dogmas associated with the Free Church, as well as most of the modern Highland sects. Yet Carswell does not turn his back on the stylistic devices that go with the old storytelling, using alliterative pairing extensively.

The decision on language underlines the dominance of the old literary language at this stage, and probably underlines a class prejudice also. We see these attitudes continuing with the translation of Calvin's Catechism, probably published in 1631, and probably translated by a member of one of the literary dynasties. It was not until 1653 that a more frankly vernacular translation of the Shorter Catechism appeared.

It was only in the middle of the eighteenth century that religious Gaelic prose threw off the yoke of the classical literary language. Even the 1767 New Testament translation carried a few influences from that source despite being clearly aimed at a new, still very constricted, but growing literate public.

It may be, however, that the strength of the old literate tradition saved the traditional orthography of Gaelic from a fate such as befell Manx. The Dean of Lismore in the early sixteenth century seemed to be heading away from the tradition, using the 'secretary hand' and an orthography more in tune with Scots usage, although he must have been able to handle traditional Gaelic manuscript sources. This Scotticised Gaelic continued to appear, for example, in the citing of Gaelic patronymics and place-names in documents relating to the Highlands, so that in Perthshire documents of the eighteenth century we find entries such as 'John Mc Onochkian' (for *Mac Dhonnchaidh 'ic Iain*, 'son of Duncan son of John').[4]

Another, and more remarkable, survival was that of ancient incantational verse, some of it with pagan undertones, but with a very strong emphasis on the saints of the early Celtic Church. A much larger body of

---

[4]   W. A. Gillies, 'Extracts from the Baron Court Books of Menzies', in *Trans. Gaelic Soc. of Inverness*, 39–40, p. 113.

such work survived in Scotland than in Ireland, and it was mainly collected in the nineteenth century by Alexander Carmichael and published under the title *Carmina Gadelica*. The verses, which can be hymns, incantations, spells or accompaniments to a wide range of activities, include items such as an Invocation for Justice, a Sleep Prayer, a Baptism Blessing, a salute to the New Moon, a Song of Hogmanay, lays used when kindling or smooring the fire, Quern Blessings, Milking Croons, a Hatching Blessing, charms and exorcisms (many involving the use of special plants), with frequent invocations of Michael, Mary, Bride, Columba and so on. It is likely that a good many of these go back into the Middle Ages. Although a large number survived best in the Catholic Western Isles they clearly belonged to Gaelic Scotland more generally, and a significant number were recovered from areas which had long been Protestant. As a footnote to this brief discussion, I recall hearing old people in one particular area of Lewis, which had not been Catholic for centuries, using the expression *Moire!* (Gaelic for Mary, the Virgin Mary) as an asseveration, while there was general use of the expression *Ma-ruibhe*, a deformation of *Maol-ruibhe*, the name of an early saint associated with mainland Ross-shire and still commemorated in the place-name Loch Maree. But to us *Ma-ruibhe* meant something like 'Don't bother'.

Scottish Gaelic also has a large body of so-called 'folk-song', some written down from the eighteenth century onwards, some published in book form from the later eighteenth century, and much circulating orally until the present century, with a wide range of melodies. This tradition has been reinforced from time to time from printed sources, and now from mechanical recording. The origins of part of this body of song certainly go back to before the sixteenth century, although that is the earliest century to yield a crop of datable songs. The range of styles and metres in the sixteenth-century crop strongly suggests a much older tradition, in some cases possibly going back many centuries. Some of the heroic icons survive here too. A MacDonald chief is praised round about the year 1600 by his foster-nurse, who invokes for him the strength of Cù Chulainn and of the elements: this passage is credibly regarded as echoing a medieval Gaelic prayer and, beyond that, a much earlier composition, perhaps of the eighth century, known as 'St Patrick's Breastplate'.[5]

I cannot venture convincingly into discussion of the melodies of these songs. Many of them use a basic pentatonic scale which is likely to be archaic and conservative. The earlier songs usually have choruses composed apparently of meaningless vocables, sometimes consisting of one line but frequently of several. It has been suggested that some of these choruses originated in dance sequences; and also that the melodies to which the heroic ballads were sung may relate to melodies used for

5   John Macinnes, 'Religion in Gaelic Society', in *Trans. Gaelic Soc. of Inverness*, 52, pp. 223–6.

classical or *dán díreach* poems of the Middle Ages.[6] In recent times there has been conjecture that the idiosyncratic style of Gaelic psalm-singing may relate somehow to Coptic melody. And we have just as little convincing evidence to suggest that the elaborate classical pipe music known as *ceòl mòr* had a long lineage before the sixteenth and seventeenth centuries, when it came into prominence, gradually supplanting the traditional harp music which must certainly have ancient origins.

The undermining of old Gaelic society which followed the political and cultural upheavals of the sixteenth, seventeenth and eighteenth centuries was in some parts of society a very gradual process, but in others it probably had a more immediate effect. The ancient ornamental stone-carving associated with stone crosses and ecclesiastical buildings survives marginally, with an occasional efflorescence, as in the sixteenth-century church at Rodil, Harris, and as in its stylised use for modern gravestones. Decorative metalwork continued to flourish, especially as part of the art and craft of weapon-makers, and there are many modern developments of medieval patterns in jewellery and silverware. In other forms of art, especially painting, there does not seem to have been a developed tradition on which to build, and the post-medieval art which is associated with the Highland area, whether portraiture, landscape or other, has basically non-Gaelic origins.

The most persistent detritus of the Middle Ages is language-based and linked to the survival of indigenous communities, usually in an isolated and conservative society. It would be possible to trace through literature the gradual shedding of earlier linguistic usages, such as the retention of the old negative *ni* rather than the spreading Scottish negative *cha*, in the seventeenth century; and certain verbal forms, such as *thugais* for the first singular past, survive into the eighteenth century. There are, too, occasional twentieth-century usages – surviving archaisms – which sometimes mark a dialect or even an ideolect. At one time there were four distinct forms of the consonantal phoneme which we denote by *l*. By the early twentieth century these had usually been reduced to three, but I recall old people from the 1920s and 1930s who regularly used four. The highly industrious Gaelic lexicographer Edward Dwelly was able to rescue many ancient words and usages in the early decades of this century, including names for early-morning libations of whisky, largely subsumed now in the universal *drama*. Gaelic, like other languages, has a detritus of obsolete items of vocabulary, with particular items or areas retained by individuals or small communities.

Seasonal rituals and superstitions also died hard in isolated and conservative communities. The Hallowe'en and Hogmanay rituals were still healthy this century, and the Hogmanay one survives in the Glasgow Gaelic community in the form of a popular annual stage presentation.

---

6 Terence P. McCaughay, in *Eriu*, 35, pp. 39–57.

Witches were still identifiable this century, and the warning cry of the *caointeag* (a black weeping woman) is still referred to in Kintyre, while instances of the second sight are still coming up. I have just experienced one such instance: in the early years of the twenty-first century I see Cù Chulainn and Fionn Mac Cumhaill leading an assault on the Westminster Parliament and bringing seventy-two hang-dog MPs back to Parliament Square in Edinburgh.

Much as I wish to shock the English fraternity by relating this vision, I should end on a more sober note. The medieval and conservative influences that have retained some of their power over succeeding centuries have often been supported by an isolation or ghetto scenario, but have frequently been buttressed also by a more positive cultural nationalism, such as pride in language and literary tradition. The signs at present are that few of these various buttresses or fencings will work effectively for much longer.

Works Cited

John Bannerman, *The Beatons* (Edinburgh, 1986)

J. L. Campbell, *Highland Songs of the Forty-Five* (Edinburgh, 1984)

Alexander Carmichael, *Carmina Gadelica* (Edinburgh, 1900–71)

W. A. Gillies, 'Extracts from the Baron Court Books of Menzies', *Trans. Gaelic Soc. of Inverness*, 39–40, (1963), p. 113

John Macinnes, 'Religion in Gaelic Society', *Trans. Gaelic Soc. of Inverness*, 52 (1983), pp. 222–42

Rev. John Macinnes, 'Gaelic Spiritual Verse', *Trans. Gaelic Soc. of Inverness*, 46 (1971), pp. 308–52

T. P. McCaughey, 'The Performing of Dán', *Eriu*, 35 (1984)

W. D. H. Sellar, 'Celtic Law and Scots Law: Survival and Integration', *Scottish Studies*, 29 (1989), pp. 1–27

D. S. Thomson, *An Introduction to Gaelic Poetry* (London, 1974; Edinburgh, 1990)

———, 'Gaelic Learned Orders and Literati in Medieval Scotland', *Scottish Studies*, 12 (1968), pp. 57–78

———, 'Gaelic Literature', in *Scotland: A Concise Cultural History*, ed. P. H. Scott (Edinburgh, 1993), pp. 127–43

———, *The Companion to Gaelic Scotland* (Oxford, 1983; Glasgow, 1994)

———, 'The Earliest Scottish Gaelic Non-Classical Verse Texts', in *Proceedings of the Fourth International Conference on Scottish Language and Literature* (Frankfurt am Main, 1986), pp. 533–46

———, 'The Harlaw Brosnachadh: An Early Fifteenth-Century Literary

Curio', in *Celtic Studies*, ed. J. Carney and D. Greene (London, 1968), pp. 147–69

———, 'The MacMhuirich Bardic Family', *Trans. Gaelic Soc. of Inverness*, 43 (1966), pp. 276–304

———, 'The Seventeenth-Century Crucible of Scottish Gaelic Poetry', *Studia Celtica*, 26–7 (1993), pp. 155–62

R. L. Thomson, Adtimchiol an Chreidimh: *The Gaelic Version of John Calvin's* Catechismus Ecclesiae Genevensis (Edinburgh, 1962)

———, Foirm na n-Urrnuidheadh: *John Carswell's Gaelic Translation of the* Book of Common Order (Edinburgh, 1970)

Calvert Watkins, 'Some Celtic Phrasal Echoes', in *Celtic Language, Celtic Culture*, ed. Matonis and Melia (California, 1990), pp. 47–56

W. J. Watson, *Scottish Verse from the Book of the Dean of Lismore* (Edinburgh, 1937, 1978)

Jan van Vliet (1620–1666) and the Study of Old English in the Low Countries

KEES DEKKER

The Dutch philologist Francis Junius (1591–1677) has rightly been called the founding father of early Germanic studies (Lucas, 1997). In 1664, at the venerable age of 73, Junius finished his final publication, the edition of the Gospels in Gothic and Anglo-Saxon together with the *Glossarium Gothicum*. The work was published the following year. It crowned his career as a scholar of Germanic languages, and although he continued his work for another twelve years, he was to leave further publication to posterity. In 1621, after his studies at Leiden and Middelburg and a short but unsuccessful career as a minister, Junius entered the service of Thomas Howard, the Earl of Arundel (1585–1646) as librarian and tutor to his youngest son (Aldrich *et al.*, 1991, p. xxxi). Arundel's library gave him an opportunity to expand his knowledge and develop his remarkable lexicographical skills, although exactly when and why he became involved in Old Germanic studies remains largely obscure. Aided by his knowledge of his mother tongue, Dutch, Junius became expert not just in Old English but also in Old High German and Old Frisian, and he worked hard to arrive at the same proficiency in the older Scandinavian languages (Bennett, 1938, pp. 217–21).

Unfortunately, most of Junius's achievements in the field of Old English have remained in manuscript: throughout his career he made thirty-seven transcripts of parts of original manuscripts, including several Old English glossaries. These transcripts and glossaries provided the material for his Old English–Latin dictionary in MSS Junius 2 and part of 3, in all over 700 folios. MSS Junius 4 and 5 contain the *Etymologicum Anglicanum*, an etymological dictionary of the English language, which was ready for press when he died and was posthumously edited and published by Edward Lye in 1743.

In 1652 Junius received the Caedmon manuscript from James Ussher (1581–1656), Archbishop of Armagh, of which he produced an edition in 1655. Earlier that year he had published his *Observationes in Willerami*, a collection of philological comments on Paullus Merula's 1598 edition of

Abbot Willeram's Old High German paraphrase of the Song of Songs. When in 1654 he received the Codex Argenteus, the fifth-century manuscript of part of the New Testament in Gothic, from his nephew Isaac Vossius (1618–89), he set out to unravel the mystery of this ancient language. After ten years of study he produced his edition side by side with an Anglo-Saxon version and accompanied by an elaborate glossary, in which many of the words were explained and given etymologies.

Junius's masterpiece was more than just a personal triumph. It gave evidence of his collaboration with two of his friends, the English clergyman Thomas Marshall (1621–85) and the Dutch lawyer Jan van Vliet (1620–66). But what is perhaps most important of all, the work also marked the culmination of a prolonged period of significant interest in the Old English language in the Netherlands. Much more than this essay would be required to deal with the vast achievements of Francis Junius with regard to the study of Old English.[1] Instead, I intend to present a survey of the tradition of Old English scholarship in the Netherlands in the seventeenth century, and to go into further detail about the cooperation between Francis Junius and his admirer and friend, Jan van Vliet, whose brief but well-documented career provides an illustration of the motivation and purpose of Dutch attention to Old English. I will demonstrate that the study of Old English in the Netherlands was in no way an imitation of what was being done in England at the time. Rather, it incorporated an important contribution to the understanding of the Old Germanic languages in general and of Old English in particular.

The sixteenth century showed very little interest in the Old English language in the Netherlands, although the history of the English people and its migration from Northern Germany to Britain, derived from medieval sources like Procopius and Bede, had attracted due scholarly attention. The Brabander Johannes Goropius Becanus (1518–73) discussed the language, although he had probably seen very little or none of it. In his *Origines Antwerpianae* (1569, p. 760) Becanus claimed an early relation between English, Danish and Swedish, and asserted that the Germanic words in the English language were not Saxon, with which the language would have little in common, but mainly Danish in origin. His ideas on the antiquity of the Dutch language and its relation to other languages provided a frequent starting-point for later scholars to work on the same subject (Metcalf, 1974, p. 239).

The lack of early medieval sources formed an impediment to the aspirations of many a scholar who wished to contribute to the establishment of the identity of the Dutch language, and it forced scholars to seek beyond the confines of the Dutch language to find material to support their assumptions. The Flemish lexicographer Cornelis van Kiel, better known as

---

[1] See Bremmer (1990a); Breuker (1990); Aldrich *et al.* (1991); Voorwinden (1992); Lucas (1997).

Kiliaan (1528–1607), who worked as a corrector in Antwerp at the Plantin Press, compiled the first etymological dictionary of the Dutch language, the *Etymologicum Teutonicae Linguae* (Antwerp, 1599). In his book Kiliaan included some Old English place-names from William Camden's *Britannia*, as well as a few miscellaneous words from William Lambarde's *Archaionomia*, the first edition of the Old English laws. Although the number of Old English words was very limited, Kiliaan's autograph annotations to his private copy of the book[2] reveal that he intended to include more Old English in a subsequent edition (Claes, 1981, pp. 39–40, 48–51).

Antwerp was also the home of the English expatriate of Dutch origin, Richard Rowlands Verstegen (*c.* 1550–1640), who had received his education at Oxford (*DNB* 49, pp. 352–53).[3] However, as a Catholic activist he was exiled soon after 1576 and spent most of his days in Antwerp, where he wrote the first history of the English language, *A Restitution of Decayed Intelligence in Antiquities Concerning the Most Noble and Renowned English Nation* (Antwerp, 1605). The book includes a glossary of some 900 Old English words as well as a chapter on the etymology of English names (pp. 207–338). Written in the English language, which hardly anybody outside England was able to read in those days, the book was clearly intended for the English market. Soon after this, Verstegen reworked much of the material he had used for *A Restitution* into a Dutch book named *Nederlantse Antiquiteiten*, 'Dutch Antiquities', in which he openly propagated the promotion of the Roman-Catholic faith. He omitted the lengthy glossaries, but in his discussion of the role of Willibrord in the Anglo-Saxon mission he presented the Lord's Prayer, Hail Mary, and the first chapter of the Gospel of St John in Old English, Modern English and Dutch (Bremmer, 1990a, p. 183). The resemblance between Old English and Dutch was quickly noted by Verstegen, who was fluent in both languages, and he stated:

> So then St Willibrord preached in these countries, in the same language as he preached in England, which beyond doubt was thus the natural language of these two countries at the time. (Verstegen, 1613, 36–7)[4]

Willibrord's importance as an Anglo-Saxon missionary in the Netherlands remained popular in the Catholic south, and was mentioned again in 1649 by a Flemish lawyer from Bruges, Olivier de Vree (1578–1652), in

---

2 The Hague, Royal Library 393 F 10.

3 That Verstegen's education in Oxford did not include Old English will be demonstrated by Rolf H. Bremmer, Jr., 'The Anglo-Saxon Pantheon according to Richard Verstegen (1605)', *Anglo-Saxon Studies 1550–1720*, ed. Timothy Graham (forthcoming).

4 'So heeft dan S. Willebrort in dese landen gepreeckt in de selve taele / daer hij in Engeland in preeckte, hetwelck sonder twijfel de natuerlijcke taele van alle beyde desen landen aldoens gheweest is.'

his *Historia Comitum Flandriae*. De Vree, in an attempt to establish the identity of Flanders by relating its origin and language to the court of Charlemagne, presented a glossary on the Salic Laws and illustrated his commentary with specimens from various Old Germanic languages. Old English was included in the form of a passage dealing with the mission of Willibrord, which he had taken from Wheloc's edition of the Old English translation of Bede's *Historia Ecclesiastica Gentis Anglorum* (De Vree, 1650, App. lxx; Wheloc, 1644, pp. 408–9).

For a more scholarly approach to philology we have to turn to the newly founded university at Leiden, where, in the late sixteenth century, a broad philological tradition was taking shape. This tradition bore the stamp of one of the most important scholars of the time, the Frenchman Joseph Justus Scaliger (1540–1609), who had come to Leiden in 1593. Scaliger occupied himself with a wide variety of subjects, which, as well as the usual Latin, Greek and Hebrew, also included Arabic, Geography, Geometry, Theology, History and comparative language studies. He broadened the scope of Humanism by transcending the formal distinction between Biblical, Classical, Barbaric (Medieval) and Greek, and stated that the description of world history required all aspects of that history to be considered in their proper perspective and cohesion (Bruehl, 1960, p. 213).

Scaliger inspired a group of Leiden scholars who displayed a remarkable interest in languages other than Latin, Greek and Hebrew, both for antiquarian reasons and because they were interested in the comparison of languages. In the Netherlands they had been confronted with the popular tradition of comparative linguistics as started by Goropius Becanus (Van de Velde, 1966, pp. 66–7). Scaliger himself possessed excerpts from the Codex Argenteus[5] and had written on Gothic (Van de Velde, 1966, p. 81), while he had also produced an influential treatise on the relations between languages (Scaliger, 1610, pp. 119–22). Towards the end of his life Scaliger even learnt some Old English, which he considered to be a 'primitive' language (L'Isle, 1623, Preface; Kendrick, 1950, p. 118). Justus Lipsius (1547–1606) had unearthed a psalter with Old Dutch glosses, which he published as part of his scholarly correspondence (Lipsius, 1605, pp. 41–62). Paullus Merula (1558–1607) provided an edition of the Leiden text of the Old High German paraphrase of the Song of Songs by Abbot Willeram, while Janus Dousa (1545–1604) participated in the publication of an early Middle Dutch rhyming chronicle. The first to publish a sample of Old English was the Leiden Professor of Greek, Bonaventura Vulcanius (1538–1614). In his treatise *De Literis et Linguae Getarum Sive Gothorum* (Leiden, 1597), Vulcanius presented specimens of Gothic, Crimean Gothic, Old High German, Old English, Frisian, Persian and runes. The Old English passage consisted of part of King Alfred's preface to the

5   Leiden, University Library Codices Scaligeri, 61, pp. 145–8.

Old English translation of Pope Gregory's *Pastoral Care*, with an interlinear modern English translation followed by one in Latin (Vulcanius, 1597, pp. 70–86). Vulcanius derived his text from the *Aelfredi Regis Res Gestae*, published at the instigation of Archbishop Parker in 1574 (Stanley, 1987, p. 50). He was also familiar with William Lambarde's *Archaionomia*.

Scaliger and his school produced a generation of scholars characterised by a remarkable degree of versatility and open-mindedness as regards the study of philology. One of these, Johannes de Laet (1581–1649), had shown an interest in Old English as early as 1616, and had become acquainted with various English scholars, including the antiquarian William Camden (1551–1623) and the Saxonists Sir Simonds D'Ewes (1602–1650), Sir Henry Spelman (1564–1641) and Abraham Wheloc (1593–1653) (Bremmer, 1990a, p. 176).

In 1638 De Laet openly proclaimed that he was engaged in compiling an Anglo-Saxon dictionary (Bekkers, 1970, p. xix). At first his English friends took an interest in the project and supplied him with any material he asked for, but by 1640 interest turned into envy with some of the English Saxonists, who deemed it improper that an Anglo-Saxon dictionary should be produced by a foreigner. In an intricate intrigue Spelman, d'Ewes and Wheloc tried to dissuade both each other and De Laet from the project, but failed in every respect. The 1640s did not see the production of an Anglo-Saxon dictionary in England, and Jan de Laet continued his work, borrowing manuscripts from Patrick Young (1584–1652), the keeper of the Royal Library, and James Ussher, who even lent him the Caedmon manuscript.[6] In 1641 De Laet went to England, where he secretly managed to borrow the Old English *Herbarium Apuleii* (Bekkers, 1970, pp. xx–xxi),[7] a collection of recipes and names of plants, which he found hard to understand.[8] Feeling somewhat abandoned by his English colleagues, De Laet turned for help to another Leiden alumnus, the Danish philologist Olaus Wormius (1588–1654), with whom he also corresponded on Old Norse and runes.

In 1643 De Laet received an edition of Norwegian laws from Wormius, which may have been related to his plans to revise and enlarge Lambarde's edition of the Old English laws (Bekkers, 1970, pp. xxv–xxvii). Presumably De Laet wanted not only to add more Old English laws to the collection, but also to provide a new Latin translation of them with philological comments, as well as collations with Old Frisian and other Old Germanic laws. Lambeth Palace MS 1742 contains De Laet's translations of the laws of King Aethelberht, with marginal annotations, and British Library MS Harley 3321 is De Laet's *Glossarium Latino-Barbarum*, in

---

6   Now MS Bodleian Junius 11.
7   Now MS BL Cotton Vitellius C. III. Bekkers (1970, pp. xix–xxi) presents a list of the De Laet's sources.
8   MS BL Cotton Vitellius C. III.

which he explains a large number of vernacular words from various Latin Germanic laws. These elucidations, in which he refers to a wide variety of sources (including Lambarde's *Archaionomia*, Otfrid's Old High German Gospels, unspecified works by Marquard Freher and William of Malmesbury and Sibrandus Siccama's edition of Old Frisian Laws), give evidence of his wide reading. De Laet took a similar approach towards his dictionary. In a letter to Sir Simonds D'Ewes he indicated that he would not restrict himself to Old English and Latin, but also intended to enrich it with Middle English, Dutch and especially Frisian (Bremmer, 1990a, pp. 176–9). Because of De Laet's sudden death in 1649 the dictionary, although ready for the press, remained unpublished. It was entrusted to the Leiden historian, Marcus Zuerius van Boxhorn (1602–1653), who, instead of publishing it, passed it on to a Danish student at Leiden, Peder J. Resen. In 1685 the manuscript was given to the Royal Academy in Copenhagen, where the first significant Dutch contribution to Old English studies was destroyed in a fire in 1728 (Bekkers, 1970, p. xxv).

Boxhorn was more than marginally interested in languages. He repeatedly referred to De Laet and his Anglo-Saxon lexicon as his source of information on Old English (Boxhorn, 1662, pp. 226, 228). In the *Prima Religionis Christianae Rudimenta* (Leiden, 1650) Boxhorn not only presented the Lord's Prayer, the Creed and the Ten Commandments in Old English, but also a part of the laws of King Alfred (Stanley, 1987, p. 50). In his *Historia Universalis* (Leiden, 1652) he included the Old English Creed in a version which had been printed earlier by the German Marquard Freher (Boxhorn, 1652, p. 101). In the same work he added a list of the Anglo-Saxon kings and stressed the importance of the study of the Germanic languages, promising the reader that, God willing, he would publish something on this subject (Boxhorn, 1652, pp. 362–8). Divine reluctance released him from his promise when he died in 1653.

Other former Leiden students who referred to the Old English language in their works were Hugo Grotius (1583–1645) and Gerardus Johannes Vossius (1577–1649). In his *Historia Gothorum Vandalorum et Langobardorum* (Amsterdam, 1655) Grotius included a glossary of proper names, in which he sometimes added Old English cognates for comparative purposes (Grotius, 1655, pp. 583–604). Vossius made more extensive use of Old English in his *De Vitiis Sermonis et Glossematis Latino-Barbaris Libri Quatuor* (Amsterdam, 1645). In Book II he provided the etymologies of those words that had entered Latin from the Germanic languages, including Old English (Vossius, 1645, pp. 161–347). Most of his information can be traced to Lambarde's *Archaionomia*.

As guardian of the orphan Francis Junius, Gerardus Vossius formed a major influence on the education and career of his promising ward (Hetherington, 1980, p. 223). Vossius's son, Isaac, to whom I referred in relation to his role in the first edition of the Gothic Bible, became a renowned classicist and bibliophile, whose library included various Anglo-Saxon manuscripts. In 1659 the same Isaac Vossius established the contact between his uncle, Francis Junius, and his friend and former fellow-student, Jan van Vliet.

Like many of his predecessors, Jan van Vliet (1620–66) had also studied at Leiden, where his professors included Boxhorn, mentioned above, and the renowned Daniel Heinsius. His education, which had taken place along the same broad Humanist lines as that of De Laet, Vossius, Grotius, Olaus Wormius, Boxhorn and Junius, had initially directed his attentions to the study of Latin and Greek; but his travels to England and France in 1641 had also provided him with an adequate knowledge of the languages of these countries, and he also seems to have picked up German and Italian on the way. He became a lawyer by profession, first in The Hague, and after 1649 in Breda, a town in the Dutch part of Brabant.

In the 1650s Van Vliet was appointed Town Clerk of Breda, which gave him access to the medieval town records. That it did not take long for him to develop an interest in these documents is widely visible from the traces he left on them. He provided the earliest statute-books of Breda with title pages and annotations, and collated them with medieval charters from the town archives, often unscrupulously adding dates and other characteristics in the margins. He aptly noted variations between spellings in his collations of the two oldest statute-books,[9] showing for the first time his interest in the history of the Dutch language, which he publicly vented in his scholarly correspondence after 1655.

In the middle of the 1650s Van Vliet voiced his plans to write a history of Breda, which was to include a section on the town's ancient laws and statutes. He took a philological approach to the study of law, which had been popularised in the sixteenth century by Guillaume Budé (1467–1540) and Andrea Alciati (1492–1550) and was known as *mos Gallicus* (Gilbert, 1960, pp. 94–5). Legal texts were studied according to Humanist principles, which argued in favour of a philological examination of the earliest and most original texts. Thus, Van Vliet inevitably came in contact with the capitularies. Although these laws were written in Latin, most of them contained a fair number of vernacular terms, often explained in the Humanist editions, such as the *Historia Comitum Flandriae* by Olivier de Vree mentioned above, and the *Codex Legum Antiquarum*, a comprehensive collection of Germanic laws published in 1613 by the German scholar Friedrich Lindenbrog (1573–1648), another Leiden alumnus. Even closer to home was the Carolingian *Lex Frisionum*, which had been edited by Sibrandus Siccama (1570–1622) in 1617, but whose laws were also known to exist in related Old Frisian texts. As we have seen, it is but a small step from the Old Frisian to the Anglo-Saxon laws, which were recorded in their earliest form only in the Old English

9   Breda, Municipal Archives Hi. 2.

language. In his 1663 edition of part of the Breda Statutes Van Vliet quoted from Middle Dutch, Old Frisian and Old English laws as well as from Latin capitularies, illustrating the importance of law in Germanic studies in the Netherlands. Besides Van Vliet, Gerardus Vossius and De Laet had also been occupied with the Anglo-Saxon laws, and even Francis Junius, a theologian by training, provided collations of the Old English laws on various occasions.[10] It is not exactly known when Jan van Vliet applied himself to Old English, but the first evidence of his interest in it dates from the beginning of 1659, when he excerpted a medieval English manuscript that belonged to the relatives of an English refugee in Breda, Thomas Aylesbury. The manuscript in question is that of the twelfth-century *Ormulum*,[11] which he had managed to purchase on 6 February 1659 for the substantial sum of eighteen guilders.[12] In the same period Van Vliet also copied an unusual transcript of Aelfric's *Glossary*.[13] Some time during spring 1659 Isaac Vossius presented Van Vliet with a copy of Francis Junius's *Observationes in Willerami*, which supplied a wealth of information on the Old Germanic languages and frequently referred to Junius's forthcoming lexicographical works, including his edition of the Gothic Bible. Van Vliet was deeply impressed by the book, and wrote to Isaac Vossius in July 1659 that he hoped to learn more from his uncle and his work in progress:

> I ask you, if Minerva [i.e. Junius] will receive a swine [i.e. Van Vliet], to ask him if sometime I can communicate with him and I will gladly put at his disposal my own Anglo-Saxon manuscript, which contains the Gospels written in the manner of Otfrid. Although it is more recent than all others that exist, it is not yet mixed with the Romance or present-day French language.[14]

In September the two men had met.

Encouraged by his contacts with Junius, Van Vliet continued his work on the *Ormulum*. Unlike English scholars, who had directed their energy

---

[10] See MSS Bodleian Junius 10, 52 and MSS BL Harley 307, 374, 464.

[11] Now MS Bodleian Junius 1.

[12] According to Van Vliet's personal annotations in MS Junius 1, fol. 1r.

[13] London, MS Lambeth Palace 783, fols 248r–253v. The exemplar, which belonged to Van Vliet's friend, Johannes Fredericus Gronovius (1611–1671), was itself a transcript by Heinrich Lindenbrog. It is preserved in Leeuwarden, Provincial Library 149 Hs. For the provenance of this text see Ronald E. Buckalew, 'Nowell, Lambarde and Leland: The Significance of Laurence Nowell's Transcript of "Aelfric's Grammar and Glossary" ', in *Anglo-Saxon Scholarship: The First Three Centuries*, ed. Carl T. Berkhout and Milton McC. Gatch (Boston, Mass.: G. K. Hall, 1982), pp. 19–50.

[14] 'rogo: et, si suem Minerva admittit, me quaedam percupere cum eo communicare, et Anglosaxonicum cod. meum, Otfridi paene modo Evangelia conscripta continentem, libenter suppeditaturum. Est autem recentior omnibus quae extant; nihil tamen Romanici sive hodierni Gallici sermonis admixtum habens' (Amsterdam, University Library III E 9, 29).

mainly at the editing of Old English texts, Van Vliet, like his Dutch fellow-philologists, was especially concerned with lexicography and etymology. In a considerable part of MS Junius 1 he separated the words by small vertical lines and added the corresponding references to the Bible to facilitate his understanding of the text. Apart from a number of fragmentary transcripts, Van Vliet compiled a glossary to which he added words and translations as he read along. In addition, he made a list of what he called 'homonyma', in which he noted many of Orm's typical, often alliterating, synonyms, which make up an important aspect of the verse. Van Vliet's *Ormulum* excerpts, which have been preserved as part of Lambeth Palace MS 783, are significant in that they contain material from a part of the manuscript now lost and therefore provide words and forms that have no other attestation. In 1962 Robert Burchfield compiled a list of these words, and in 1992 I discovered yet another list on a loose sheet preserved in Van Vliet's copy of William Somner's *Dictionarium Saxonico-Latino-Anglicum*.[15]

The fact that the language of the *Ormulum* is not Old English but Early Middle English, lacking many of the essential qualities of the earlier texts, was apparently a distinction that Van Vliet did not make; nor did Francis Junius, for that matter. Van Vliet was well aware of the age of the manuscript, which he indicated in his letter to Isaac Vossius; but he saw no reason to make the distinction, which was later made by George Hickes (1642–1715). Hickes classified the language on a more structural basis, and coined the phrase 'Semi-Saxon' to distinguish the language of the *Ormulum* and other Early Middle English texts from classical Old English (Bennett, 1938, pp. 106b–12). Instead, Van Vliet identified the language on the basis of vocabulary, which was the aspect that mattered most to him.

As Old English manuscripts were hard to come by outside England, printed books formed the prime source of information for students of the Old English language in the Netherlands. Even Francis Junius, who had the opportunity to transcribe a wide variety of manuscript material, frequently used printed books for his studies, and he annotated books belonging to others too. Van Vliet, who possessed a substantial library of well over 1,200 titles, also used a range of printed books. In various smaller studies preserved in Lambeth Palace MS 783 he gives evidence of having studied works by William Camden, William Dugdale and Richard Verstegen. Moreover, he owned Wheloc's combined edition of Bede's *Historia Ecclesiastica* and Lambarde's *Archaionomia* with parts of the *Anglo-Saxon Chronicle* (1644), as well as John Spelman's Old English *Psalterium Davidis* (1640) and William Somner's *Dictionarium Saxonico-Latino-Anglicum* (1659).

---

15 Leiden University Library 766 A 5. To be published.

Van Vliet's copy of Somner's dictionary shows the nature of his co-operation with Francis Junius. Apart from the additions from the *Ormulum*, Van Vliet collated his copy of Somner's dictionary with Junius's autograph Old English–Latin dictionary.[16] The collation must have been a difficult and time-consuming process, for Junius's gatherings consist of originally loose sheets on which he listed his findings. He did not always use the same sheets to list similar forms, obviously intending further editorial work, and this practice has resulted in sometimes triple occurrences of the same word. Moreover, Junius interspersed his Old English lexicon with Gothic entries from the *Codex Argenteus*, and cognates in runes derived from the works of Olaus Wormius. Van Vliet managed to add 210 spelling variants and entirely new words to Somner's dictionary, mostly in the sections A–F. No doubt he was one of the first to subject the dictionary to a critical scrutiny.

A further example of Van Vliet's use of Junius's library is his glossary to the *Canons of King Edgar*, as produced by John Selden in his edition of *Eadmer*. That he used Junius's copy, now MS Junius 18, can be concluded from the fact that he copied some of the numerous corrections that Junius had made in his book. Van Vliet also transcribed five Latin hymns with Old English glosses from MS Junius 107.

Van Vliet's researches were not confined to Old English alone. Throughout his work he tended to widen the scope by collating Old English with as many other Germanic languages as he could. In so doing, he placed himself in the tradition of his Dutch predecessors; but he modelled his Old Germanic studies predominantly on Junius's commentary in the *Observationes in Willerami* and his similar works in manuscript. Apart from the Old English additions, Van Vliet supplied his copy of Somner's dictionary with Gothic, Old High German, Old Frisian and 'Runic'[17] cognates, and added a considerable number of Dutch translations. It should be noted, however, that Van Vliet mostly restricted himself to the Germanic languages, and only rarely attempted to extend his etymologies to Latin, Greek and even Hebrew, as his fellow-philologists often did. Whereas Junius frequently traced the etymology of Old English words to Greek roots on speculative grounds, this is one of the rare occasions where Van Vliet did not follow in Junius's footsteps.

Van Vliet produced only one small book devoted solely to the Old Germanic languages. In *'t Vader Ons in XX Oude Noordse en Duytse Taelen met d'uytleggingen*, 'The Lord's Prayer in Twenty Old Northern and Germanic Languages, with Explanations', he presented versions of the Lord's Prayer in Gothic, Old and Middle English, Old and Middle

---

[16] MSS Bodleian Junius 2 and part of 3.

[17] Van Vliet and Junius used this term to denote the oldest forms of the Scandinavian languages, which they supposed to have been written exclusively in runes (Bennett, 1938, p. 219).

High German, Frisian, Middle Dutch, 'Runic', Swedish, Danish, Norwegian, Icelandic and Finnish, and supplied etymological comments to many of the words. The book was to serve as a curtain raiser for Junius's Gothic – the Anglo-Saxon Gospels and the *Glossarium Gothicum* – and the commentary is mainly based upon Junius's lexicographical works. Van Vliet included four Old English specimens of the Lord's Prayer: the first, originating from Cambridge University Library MS Gg 3.28, was copied from Wheloc's edition of Bede (Van Vliet, 1664, pp. 11–12); two collated specimens were taken from the Gothic/Anglo-Saxon Gospels by Junius and Marshall (Van Vliet, 1664, p. 12); while the fourth, which was copied from Camden's *Remaines of a Greater Work Concerning England* (Dunn, 1984, pp. 25–6), ultimately derives from the Lindisfarne Gospels (Van Vliet, 1664, p. 33).[18]

In the preface to the book, Van Vliet elaborated on his studies and presented his ideas of the history of the Germanic peoples and languages. Again, he largely used as a model Junius's preface to the *Observationes in Willerami*; but his claim that all Germanic languages descended directly from Gothic, whose offspring consisted of Runic, Old German and Anglo-Saxon, is original. His views of Dutch, English and Frisian are more in line with tradition. He counted English, Old Frisian and also part of the Dutch language as children of the Anglo-Saxon language, and explained this as follows:

> Runic and Old Teutonic were born in their own countries, but Anglo-Saxon has been passed to us by the Frisians (when they ruled over these provinces from the Elbe and Lauwers as far as the Rhine), and in the year 449 it was shipped to England with Horsa and Hengist, and although after the year 1060 much oppressed by William the Norman and corrupted by his Norman Romance, it has been preserved in its entirety by a multitude of old books, and especially through the exemplary supervision and labour of the wise King Alfred. (Van Vliet, 1664, fols a3[r] and [v])[19]

Van Vliet set out from the traditional assumption that there is a close relationship between Dutch, Frisian and Old English. This assumption was based on a well-established opinion, which existed in Frisia and Holland, that the Anglo-Saxon invaders had actually been Frisians, a belief which was supported by the many resemblances between the two languages (Bremmer, 1990a, 1990b). However, the Frisian language was

---

18 MS BL Cotton Nero D. IV.

19 'De Runisse en Oude Teutse hebben hun geboorte in eijgen land genomen; maer de Engels-Saxe, is door de Friesen (doen zij over dese gewesten van den Elve en Lauwers aen tot op den Rijn geheerst hebben) ons aengekomen, ende in 't jaer 449. met Horsus en Hengistus in England overgescheept; en hoewel door Willem den Normander nae den jaere 1060 seer verdruckt, en met zijn Normands Romaijn verbastert, door menighte van oude boecken, insonderheijt door de even voorgaende toesicht en arbeijd van den Wijsen Coningh Alvrede noch in sijn geheel behouden.'

also often regarded as an older form or remote dialect of Dutch, an idea that was used by Verstegen and shared by philologists at Leiden University, including Bonaventura Vulcanius (Feitsma, 1978, p. 8) and Justus Lipsius, who remarked:

> At the same time when the Angles and the Saxons migrated to Britain, and the old inhabitants were expelled, they brought in their, that is our, language. Clearly ours as it once was, for afterwards it was changed by the Normans who came from France. (Lipsius, 1605, pp. 55–6)[20]

Johan de Laet explained in a letter to Sir Simonds d'Ewes that Frisian was a Dutch dialect,[21] and in his preface to the *Observationes* Franciscus Junius claimed that the entire Dutch language, including Frisian, descended from Anglo-Saxon. That Frisian was often unintelligible to Dutchmen he attributed to its being closer to Anglo-Saxon than Dutch[22] (Junius, 1655, p. xii; Feitsma, 1978, pp. 9, 22). Consequently, despite their slightly different approaches, both Van Vliet and Junius claimed that the study of Old English and other Old Germanic languages could be used to enrich the vernacular Dutch tongue. This argument had originated in the sixteenth century, and fitted in well with the Humanist principle of using the oldest available sources to arrive at the purest reading of, in this case, a language.

Materially, any lasting effects of the study of Old English in the Low Countries should be accredited to Francis Junius, whose works formed an inspiration and source of material to future Saxonists from George Hickes to Joseph Bosworth (1789–1876). Most of De Laet's work was lost; Boxhorn died before he could fulfil his promise; while Jan van Vliet died in miserable circumstances in 1666, too young to have accomplished anything of lasting significance. The output of original text editions had remained limited to Junius's edition of Caedmon (1655) and the edition of the West Saxon Gospels (1665). After Van Vliet had died and Junius had moved to Oxford, the study of Old English in the Low Countries waned until, in the eighteenth century, it flared up again with the works of Lambertus ten Kate (1674–1731) and Balthasar Huydekoper (1695–1778). However, the tradition of Old English scholarship in the Netherlands in the seventeenth century, and its international character, had changed the nature of Old English studies for good. Its lasting effect was

---

[20] 'Simile in Britannia, quam Angli è Saxonia immigrarunt, & veteri pulsa, suam, id est nostram linguam intulerunt. Planè nostram, ut olim quidem fuit nam postea Normannorum è Gallia superventu mutavit.'

[21] MS BL Harley 374, fol. 154.

[22] 'Ex Anglo-Saxonicâ verò promanavit magna pars Anglicae & Scoticae, totaquoque Belgica, praecipuè tamen Frisica illa vetus, reliquis universi Belgii incolis vix intellecta, propterea quòd in plurimis vocibus, atque in ipsâ quoque plurimorum vocabulorum orthographiâ & pronuntiatione manifestissima Anglo-Saxonicae vestigia usque in hunc diem retinuerit.'

that the Old English language was no longer seen as merely an exotic remnant of a distant past, to be used only in England by a limited group of initiates for antiquarian or polemic reasons. Instead, by placing the study of Old English in the broader context of cognate Germanic languages, it could be used as a means to enrich the existing knowledge of the common Germanic past, and could thus help establish the identity of the Anglo-Saxons and their language within the Germanic continuum.[23]

Works Cited

Aldrich, Keith, Ph. Fehl and R. Fehl (1991), *Franciscus Junius, The Literature of Classical Art. I: The Painting of the Ancients/De Pictura Veterum. II: A Lexicon of Artists and their Work/Catalogus Architectorum.* . . (Berkeley: University of California Press)

Becanus, Johannes Goropius (1569), *Origines Antwerpianae, sive Cimmeriorum Becceselana Novem Libros Complexa* . . . (Antwerp: Chr. Plantijn)

Bekkers, J. A. F. (1970), *Correspondence of John Morris with Johannes de Laet (1634–1649)* (Assen: Van Gorcum)

Bennett, J. A. W. (1938), 'The History of Old English and Old Norse Studies in England from the Time of Franciscus Junius till the End of the Eighteenth Century' (unpubl. diss., Oxford)

Boxhorn, Marcus Zuerius (1650), *Primae Religionis Christianae Rudimenta* . . . (Leiden: David Lopez de Haro)

——, (1652), *Historia Universalis Sacra et Profana* . . . (Leiden)

——, (1662), *Marci Zuerii Boxhornii Epistolae et Poematae*, ed. J. Baselius (Amsterdam)

Bremmer Jr., Rolf H. (1990a), 'Late Medieval and Early Modern Opinions on the Affinity between English and Frisian: The Growth of a Commonplace', *Folia Linguistica Historica*, 9, pp. 167–91

——, (1990b), 'The Nature of the Evidence for a Frisian Participation in the Adventus Saxonum', in *Britain 400–600: Language and History*, ed. A. Bammesberger and A. Wollmann (Heidelberg: Carl Winter, Universitätsverlag), pp. 353–71

Breuker, Philippus H. (1991), 'On the Course of Franciscus Junius's Germanic Studies, with Special Reference to Frisian', in *Aspecst of Old Frisian Philology*, ed. R. H. Bremmer, Jr., G. van der Meer and O. Vries (Amsterdamer Beiträgen zur älteren Germanistik, 31; Estrikken, 69), pp. 42–68

[23] I am much indebted to Rolf Bremmer for his suggestions and comments on a draft of this paper. This publication is part of a project funded by the Netherlands Organization for Scientific Research (NWO).

Bruehl, Clemens M. (1960–1), 'Josef Justus Scaliger, Beitrag zur geistes-geschichtliche Bedeutung der Altertumswissenschaft', *Zeitschrift für Religions- und Geistesgeschichte*, 3, pp. 201–18; 4, pp. 46–65

Buckalew, Ronald E. 'Nowell, Lambarde and Leland: The Significance of Laurence Nowell's Transcript of "Aelfric's Grammar and Glossary" ', in *Anglo-Saxon Scholarship: The First Three Centuries*, ed. Carl T. Berkhout and Milton McC. Gatch (Boston, Mass.: G. K. Hall, 1982), pp. 19–50

Burchfield, R. W. (1962), 'Ormulum: Words Copied by Jan van Vliet from Parts Now Lost', in *English and Medieval Studies Presented to J. R. R. Tolkien*, ed. Norman Davis and C. L. Wrenn (London: George Allen & Unwin), pp. 94–111

Camden, William (1594), *Britannia* . . . (London: George Bishop)

————, (1607; 1984), *Remaines of a Greater Work Concerning Britaine* . . ., ed. R. D. Dunn (Toronto: Toronto University Press)

Claes, F. (1981), *De Vierde Kiliaan* (Oude Nederlandse Woordenboeken, ser. III, pt. 2; 's-Gravenhage: Martinus Nijhoff)

The Dictionary of National Biography (London, 1885–1912)

[Dousa, Janus] (1591), *Hollandtse Rijmkronijk Inhoudende de Geschiedenissen* . . . (Amsterdam)

Feitsma, A. (1978), *Tussen Volkstaal en Schrijftaal, Meningen van Filo-logen over het Fries* (Leeuwarden: Koperative Utjowerij)

Gilbert, N. W. (1960), *Renaissance Concepts of Method* (New York: Columbia University Press)

Grotius, Hugo (1655), *Historia Gothorum, Vandalorum et Langobar-dorum* . . . (Amsterdam: Elzeviers)

Hetherington, M. Sue (1980), *The Beginnings of Old English Lexicogra-phy* (Spicewood, Tex.; privately printed)

Junius, Franciscus F. F. (1655a; 1997), *Caedmonis Monachi Paraphrasis Poetica Genesios ac Praecipuarum Sacrae Paginae Historiarum* . . . ed. Peter J. Lucas (Early Studies in Germanic Philology, 3; Amsterdam, 1655; Atlanta, Ga.: Rodopi, 1997)

————, (1655b; 1992), *Observationes in Willerami Abbatis Cantici Can-ticorum*, ed. N. Voorwinden (Early Studies in Germanic Philology, 1; Amsterdam, 1655; Atlanta, Ga.: Rodopi, 1992)

————, (1665), *Quatuor D.N.J.C. Evangeliorum Versiones Perantiquae duae, Gothica Scil. et Anglo-Saxonica* . . . (Dordrecht: Van Esch)

————, (1665), *Gothicum Glossarium* . . . (Dordrecht: Van Esch)

————, (1743), *Etymologicum Anglicanum* . . . ed. Edward Lye (Oxford: Sheldonian Theatre)

Kendrick, T. D. (1950), *British Antiquity* (London: Methuen)

Ker, N. R. (1957), *A Catalogue of Manuscripts Containing Anglo-Saxon* (Oxford: Oxford University Press)

Kiliaan, C. (1599), *Etymologicum Teutonicae Linguae* . . . (Antwerp: Plantijn)

Lambarde, William (1568), *Archaionomia* . . . (London: John Day)

Lem, G. A. C. van der and C. S. M. Rademaker (1993), *Inventory of the Correspondence of Gerardus Johannes Vossius (1577–1649)* (Assen/ Maastricht: Van Gorcum)

Lindenbrog, Friedrich (1613), *Codex Legum Antiquarum* . . . (Frankfurt: J. & A. Marne)

Lipsius, Justus (1605), *Epistolarum Selectarum Centuria Tertia ad Belgas* (Antwerp: Joh. Moretus)

L'Isle, William (1623), *A Saxon Treatise Concerning the Old and New Testament* . . . (London: John Haviland)

Lucas, Peter J. (1997) see Junius 1655a

Marckwardt, Albert H. (1952), *Laurence Nowell's Vocabularium Saxonicum* (Ann Arbor, Mich.: University of Michigan Press)

Metcalf, George J. (1974),'The Indo-European Hypothesis in the Sixteenth and Seventeenth Centuries', in *Studies in the History of Linguistics*, ed. Dell Hymes (Bloomington, Ind.: Indiana University Press), pp. 223–58

Merula, Paulus (1598), *Willerami Abbatis in Canticum Canticorum Paraphrasis Gemina* . . . (Leiden: Plantijn)

Scaliger, Joseph Justus (1610), *J.J. Scaligeri J.C.F. Opuscula Varia Antehac non Edita* . . . (Paris: Hier. Drouart)

Selden, John (1623), *Eadmer* . . . (London: W. Stansby)

Siccama, Sibrandus (1617), *Lex Frisionum sive Antiquae Frisiorum Leges* . . . (Franeker: Johannes Lamrinck)

Somner, William (1659), *Dictionarium Saxonico-Latino-Anglicum* . . . (Oxford: William Hall)

Spelman, John (1640), *Psalterium Davidis Latino-Saxonicum Vetus* . . . (London: R. Badger)

Stanley, Eric G. (1987), 'Continental Contributions to the Study of Anglo-Saxon Writings', in his *A Collection of Papers with Emphasis on Old English Literature* (Toronto: Pontifical Institute of Medieval Studies), pp. 49–74

———, (1997), 'The Sources of Junius's Learning as Revealed in the Junius Manuscripts in the Bodleian Library', *Franciscus Junius and his Circle*, ed. R. H. Bremmer, Jr. (Amsterdam and Atlanta, Ga.: Rodopi)

Velde, R.G. van de (1966), *De Studie van het Gotisch in de Nederlanden* (Gent: Koninklijke Vlaamse Academie)

Verstegen, Richard (1605), *A Restitution of Decayed Intelligence* . . . (Antwerp: Robert Bruney)

———, (1613), *Nederlantsche Antiquiteiten* . . . (Antwerp: Caspar Bellerus)

Vliet, Jan van (1663), *'t Recht van Successie volgens de Costumen der Stad en Lande van Breda* (Dordrecht: Van Esch)

[———], ([1664]),*'T Vader Ons in XX Oude Duijtse en Noordse Taelen, met d'Uijtleggingen &c* (Dordrecht: Van Esch)

Voorwinden, N. (1992) see Junius 1655b

Vossius, Gerardus Johannes (1645), *De Vitiis Sermonis et Glossematis Latino-Barbaris, Libri IV* . . . (Amsterdam: Elzeviers)

Vree, Olivier de (Vredius) (1650), *Historia Comitum Flandriae* . . . (Bruges: Lucas Kerckhove)

Vulcanius, Bonaventura (1597), *De Literis et Linguis Getarum sive Gothorum* . . . (Leiden: Plantijn)

Wheloc, Abraham (1644), *Historiae Ecclesiasticae Gentis Anglorum Libri V.* . . . *Quibus in Calce Operis Saxonicam Chronologicam Seriem . . ., quibus Accesserunt Anglo-Saxonicae Leges: et ultimo Leges Henrici I* . . . (Cambridge: Roger Daniel)

Wormius, Olaus (1636), *RUNER, seu Danica Literatura Antiquissima* . . . (Amsterdam: Johannes Jansonius)

The Early Middle Ages = The Dark Ages = The Heroic Age of England and in English

E. G. STANLEY

1. *The terms:* the Middle Ages, medium aevum, middle-aged; *and* the Dark Ages

It is a fact, a sad fact, that the period to which Anglo-Saxonists devote their labour is in Modern English often called the Dark Ages. The terms *the Middle Ages* and *the Dark Ages* form the subject of Fred C. Robinson's Presidential Address to the Medieval Academy of America in 1984, and there are other, variously substantial works on the terms, works that shed a little light on the inspissated gloom on which – rather than, I hope, in which – we labour.[1]

The recognition came only slowly that the period after the decline of the Roman Empire was an age in the middle between Antiquity, the end of which was symbolised in the victorious Christianity of the Emperor Constantine the Great, and the modern world. The view mocked by Godefroid Joseph F. Kurth as *une puérile tautologie* seems right, *le moyen âge est un âge moyen*: it is, as an early historian of the Middle Ages expressed it in the very title of his book,[2] *medii aevi a temporibus Constantini Magni ad*

---

[1] For valuable earlier discussions, see Fred C. Robinson, '*Medieval*, the *Middle Ages*', *Speculum*, 59 (1984), pp. 745–56; reprinted in F. C. Robinson, *The Tomb of Beowulf* (Oxford, 1993), pp. 304–15; G. Kurth, *Qu'est-ce que le Moyen Âge?*, Questions historiques (Paris, 1910), quotation at p. 29; P. Lehmann, *Vom Mittelalter und von der lateinischen Philologie des Mittelalters*, Quellen und Untersuchungen zur lateinischen Philologie des Mittelalters, 5/1 (1914), and the same author's 'Mittelalter und Küchenlatein', *Historische Zeitschrift*, 137 (1928), pp. 200–6, repr. in P. Lehmann, *Erforschung des Mittelalters*, i (Leipzig, 1941; Stuttgart, 1959), pp. 49–56; G. S. Gordon, 'Medium Aevum and the Middle Ages', *S.P.E. Tract* No. xix (1925); L. Varga, *Das Schlagwort vom "finsteren Mittelalter"* (Baden, 1932); and O. Lauffer, *Die Begriffe "Mittelalter" und "Neuzeit" im Verhältnis zur deutschen Altertumskunde* (Berlin, 1936) who repeats (pp. 7–8), without acknowledgement, some of the bibliographical information in Kurth's work. I have, of course, made use of the references given in these works.

[2] C. Cellarius, *Historia medii aevi a temporibus Constantini Magni ad Constantinopolim a Turcis captam* (Zeitz, 1688; 2nd edn, Jena, 1698).

Constantinopolim a Turcis captam: a middle age before Constantinople
fell to the Turks, before printing with movable type, before the great
advances in the sciences, not least those in astronomy, before the accession of the Tudors to the throne of England, before the discovery of the
New World, before the Reformation, and before the glories of Classical
Antiquity itself were, as it seemed, reborn in a new sensibility based both
on better Greek and Latin philological competence: glories to be emulated
in vernacular eloquence, and based also on the recognition of Classical
mastery of form triumphantly symbolised by the finding in 1506 of the
Laocoön Group. That the age in the middle, between Antiquity and the
new age in which they lived, was over may have been clear early south of
the Alps to scholars, writers and artists with a sense of history, but north of
the Alps it did not become clear before the sixteenth century had run for
some time, and in England and in English the age between was not
distinguished terminologically till the seventeenth century. Terms like
medium aevum were at first nowhere applied to delimit exactly the period
in the middle, though general characteristics were associated with it.[3] In
English, as appears from the quotations in the *Supplement* to *The Oxford
English Dictionary*, Sir Henry Spelman and John Donne were using

---

[3]   It appears that *media tempestas* is first recorded in a dedicatory letter to Pope Paul II by
Giovanni Andrea, Bishop of Aleria, in his edition of Apuleius [fol. 4v], published in Rome
in 1469 [*Gesamtkatalog der Wiegendrucke*, no. 2301; *Catalogue of Books Printed in the
XVth Century now in the British Museum*, iv (London, 1916), p. 6, IB. 17116]; paying
tribute to Nicolaus Cusanus, the German cardinal who had died at Todi in 1464, Andrea
says, 'Vir ipse: quod rarum est in germanis: supra opinionem eloquens. et latinus. historias
idem omnis non priscas modo: medie tempestatis: tum ueteres: tum recentiores: usque ad
nostra tempora retinebat.' ['The man himself was, as is rare among Germans, beyond
expectation eloquent and a Latinist, who could recall alike all historical events not only
ancient, and of the age in the middle, as also more recent events right through to our
times.']
    It also appears that *medium aevum* is first recorded in Melchior Haiminsfeld Goldast's
Paraeneticorum veterum, (Insulæ, 1604) i. p. 380, in a phonological absurdity which
Goldast, with considerable acquaintance of Old High German from the eighth century
onwards, must have put at some period between the founding of Rome and a considerable
time, impossible to say how long, before the earliest Old High German; writing on Middle
High German *schilt* 'shield', for which he suggests a Greek origin, he says, with numerous
examples, that in that middle period the sound represented by Roman letter <c> had
become /ʃ/ in the language from which German is derived: 'C. mutare in SCH. medij æui
consuetudo coepit' ['Usage of the middle age began to alter *c* into *sch*']. Referring to
Ratpertus of St Gall who died *c.* 890 [cf. M. Manitius, *Geschichte der lateinischen
Literatur des Mittelalters*, i. 'Von Justinian bis zur Mitte des zehnten Jahrhunderts', in I.
von Müller (ed.), Handbuch der klassischen Altertums-Wissenschaft, IX, ii, 1 (Munich,
1911), p. 606], Goldast's use of the term *media aetas*, in an attempt to identify etymologi-
cally the Thuringians with the people of Zürich, is similarly vague: see his *Alamannicarum
Rerum Scriptores aliquot vetusti* (Frankfurt, 1606), I, ii. p. 2: 'Illustri & generosa familia
natus in pago Tigurino, qui media aetate Thuregiensis appellari coepit' ['born of a distinguished and noble family in the canton of Zürich which in the middle age began to be
called Thuringian'].

middle ages and *middle age* for the period when the Church Fathers and Scholastic theologians were writing, rather than more generally for the period between Roman Antiquity and the Renaissance. They also used the now-obsolete adjectival *middle-aged* 'medieval' and this was recorded a little earlier. All three are used from 1611 to 1621 (though Donne's use only got into print considerably later).[4]

The monastic and religious preoccupations of most medieval writers – they were devout and moral men and women, commendable yet unfashionable qualities both in later ages – were felt to be distracting from enjoyment by the first users in English of the term *the Dark Ages*, and *mutatis mutandis* in the other modern languages, long before the term was applied to literature. Professional readers and perhaps even historians of medieval literature, may view that age more favourably than the rest of the world; to us it is light and brightly coloured when seen, as far as we can see it, from within medieval literature, including, of course, the vernacular literature of the Anglo-Saxons in the early Middle Ages. As early as the eighteenth century the act of writing a history of the Middle Ages was seen as throwing light on the darkness of those times, as a book title proclaims,[5] *Ein Licht Aus der Finsternüß*; for, on the whole, and with a few honourable exceptions, the historians of the Middle Ages (including historians of Anglo-Saxon England) are not at ease when reading medieval vernacular writings, for them therefore the darkest source material of the Dark Ages. Some historians seem to be puzzled, not surprisingly, by the poetic kinds of obscure vernacular literatures and, more surprisingly,

---

4   See R. W. Burchfield (ed.), *Supplement to the Oxford English Dictionary*, ii (Oxford, 1976), s.vv. (there is no hyphen in *middle aged* as used by Thomas James in 1611). Credit for first drawing attention to James's use of the word belongs to P. Lehmann, *Vom Mittelalter* (1914; see n. 1, above), p. 8 and n. 5 (drawing attention to its omission from the dictionaries).

Sir Henry Spelman, *De non temerandis Ecclesijs. A Tract Of the Rights and Respect due vnto Churches . . . The second Edition, enlarged with an Appendix* (London: J. Beale, 1616; STC 23067.8), has the first recorded use of *middle ages* in the language. In the appendix he deals with Psalm 83, and (p. 177) 'namely the 12 *verse*, touching the *taking of the houses of God in possession*, (which indeed is the *center* of the Psalm: what interpretation soeuer it receiueth)'. In the controversial exposition of the psalm and especially of v. 12, many exegetes of all periods are, he tells us (p. 194), on his side of the argument: 'But thus the eldest and newest expositors are wholly for mee, many also (& of the best of them) of the middle ages, none that I know against me.'

Donne's second sermon on Timothy 1: 15 was preached in 1621 (not in 1618, the date of the first of his two sermons on Timothy 1: 15). In it he used 'of the middle age' with reference to Scholastic controversy. It was not printed till the edition of the sermons of 1661; cf. G. R. Potter and E. M. Simpson (eds), *The Sermons of John Donne*, i (Berkeley and Los Angeles, 1953), p. 303, Sermon 9, ll. 80–3 (for the date see p. 142, n. 56).

5   V. E. Löscher, *Die Historie der Mittlern Zeiten, Als Ein Licht Aus der Finsternüß* (Leipzig, 1725). In a good survey (pp. 5–6), Löscher says that the *Studium Historicum medii ævi* has three agreeable daughters: the study of diplomas, the study of coins and the study of seals.

they may even be unable to distinguish the languages in which they are written; thus (in a context which nowhere identifies who the 'most of us' of the following quotation are):[6]

> The literary culture of the early middle ages, except for some German folk poetry such as *Beowulf* (which was probably written down by churchmen anyway), was conditioned by the traditions and needs of the church. Perhaps the chief reason why the literature of the early middle ages is so distant from the interests and outlook of most of us is that it is church literature. Most of us would be no more interested in the writings of present-day bishops and abbots than in the writings of their medieval predecessors.

2. The Dark Ages: *a period of spiritual, intellectual, or political night*

Before the term *the Dark Ages* had been applied to literature, it had been used to characterise more generally the darkness of what seemed to be a long period of intellectual night of an age lost in the most consummate ignorance. The term *the Dark Ages* was applied first to spiritual darkness, and secondly to intellectual darkness. For the notion of spiritual darkness, the state in which pagans, Jews, and heretics dwell, we can go back to St Bernard of Clairvaux, among others; he has a paragraph on the theme:[7]

> Habet mundus iste noctes suas, et non paucas. Quid dico, quia noctes habet mundus, cum pene ipse totus sit nox, et totus semper versetur in tenebris? Nox est iudaica perfidia, nox ignorantia paganorum, nox haeretica pravitas, nox etiam catholicorum carnalis, animalisve conversatio. Annon nox, ubi non percipiuntur ea quae sunt Spiritus Dei?

> [This world has its nights, and not a few of them. What do I say? That the world has nights, when it is itself almost all night, and is always wholly involved in the darkness of night. Jewish faithlessness is a night; the ignorance of the heathen is a night; heretical perverseness is a night; the carnal and animal intercourse of Catholics even is a night. Is it not a night when those things which are of the Spirit of God are not understood?]

Later, writers of the Reformation attach darkness to the Roman Catholic

---

[6] N. F. Cantor, *Medieval History: The Life and Death of a Civilization* (2nd edn; New York and London, 1969), pp. 76–7. N. F. Cantor's writings, both this book and his *Inventing the Middle Ages* (see Section 9 below) were drawn to my attention by Professor Nigel Palmer (St Edmund Hall, Oxford), who, however, did not express agreement (or disagreement) with the views contained in them.

[7] Quoted by Varga, *Schlagwort*, p. 7, from St Bernard of Clairvaux, *Opera* (Venice, 1726), ii. p. 356, *In Cantica*, sermo lxxv, 10; cf. J. Mabillon (ed.), *Sancti Bernardi . . . I. Genuina Sancti Doctoris Opera* (Paris, 1667), col. 1533. The quotation is from the modern standard edition: J. Leclercq, C. H. Talbot, H. M. Rochais and C. Mohrmann (eds), *S. Bernardi Opera*, ii (Rome, 1958), p. 253.

period before the light of the Reformation.[8] English controversialists to take this line include John Milton, who puts the case in a vigorous sentence near the beginning of *Of Reformation*:[9]

> But to dwell no longer in characterizing the *Depravities* of the *Church*, and how they sprung, and how they tooke increase; when I recall to mind at last, after so many darke Ages, wherein the huge overshadowing traine of *Error* had almost swept all the Starres out of the Firmament of the *Church*; how the bright and blissfull *Reformation* (by Divine Power) strook through the black and settled Night of *Ignorance* and *Antichristian Tyranny*, me thinks a soveraigne and reviving joy must needs rush into the bosome of him that reads or heares; and the sweet Odour of the returning *Gospell* imbath his Soule with the fragrancy of Heaven.

Ten years later, in his Latin *Pro Populo Anglicano Defensio*, chapter 8, Milton describes the Middle Ages as an era of political darkness, and uses an expression comparable with *the Dark Ages*; after quoting Cicero on how the power of judicature (*judicandi potestas*) proceeds from the people, he addresses his adversary, Salmasius:[10]

> Vides Parlamentorum veram originem, illis Saxonicis archivis longè vetustiorem. Dum in hac luce veritatis & sapientiæ versari licebit, frustra nobis obscuriorum ætatum tenebras offundere conaris. Quod non eò dici à me quisquam existimet, quasi ego de authoritate & prudentiâ majorum nostrorum detrahi quicquam velim.

> [You see the true beginning of parliaments, more ancient by far than those Saxon records. So long as it may be granted that we dwell in this light of truth and wisdom it is in vain that you try to overwhelm us with the gloom of darker ages. Let no one think that I say this as if I would want anything to be taken away from the authority and wisdom of our ancestors.]

Another ten years later, in a vague reference to an ill-defined 'Dark Antiquity', the historian James Heath writes in his elegy on Thomas Fuller:[11]

> But know Illustrious Soul that we do see
> Those higher Reasons which transported thee
> From the black Art of Dark *Antiquity*
> To th' Speculation of *Eternity*.

---

8 Here Varga, *Schlagwort*, pp. 94–5, quotes Calvin among others.
9 J. Milton, *Of Reformation Touching Church-Discipline in England* (London, 1641), pp. 5–6. Cf. *Complete Prose Works of John Milton*, i (New Haven and London, 1953), p. 524; *The Works of John Milton*, iii/1 (New York, 1931), pp. 4–5. For further quotations from Milton tending in the same direction, see Section 7 below.
10 J. Milton, *Pro Populo Anglicano Defensio* (London, 1651), p. 153; cf. *The Works of John Milton*, vii (New York, 1932), pp. 425–7.
11 James Heath, *An Elegie upon D͞r Tho. Fuller That most Incomparable Writer, Who Deceased* August *the 15ᵗʰ· M.DC.LXI* (London, 1661).

Continental Protestant fervour colours the very title of a book by an early eighteenth-century historian of the Middle Ages, which reads in translation:[12] 'History of the whorish Roman regiment of Theodora and Marozia in which the events of the tenth century and the intrigues of the See of Rome are fully set out, together with an introduction, long called for, to the *Historia Medii Aevi*, several new geographical and genealogical tables, and a number of historical evidences against the Papacy.'

3. *An age of unreasonable religious beliefs: understanding is light, ignorance is darkness; windows to understanding; the light of reason*

In the same year, 1651, as Milton's *Pro Populo Anglicano Defensio*, the theme is taken up by Thomas Hobbes in *Leviathan*, part 4, 'Of the King-dome of Darknesse'; what he says accords with John Locke's view of unreasonable religious beliefs in *An Essay on Human Understanding*. It is to be inferred from their views that the period now called *the Middle Ages* was a period of darkness.[13] The first and longest chapter (chapter 44) of the fourth part of *Leviathan* is 'Of Spirituall Darknesse from MISINTERPRE-TATION of Scripture'. Hobbes says in that chapter:[14] 'The Darkest part of the Kingdom of Satan, is that which is without the Church of God; that is to say, amongst them that beleeve not in Jesus Christ.' In chapter 46, 'Of DARKNESSE from VAIN PHILOSOPHY and FABULOUS TRADITIONS', Hobbes asserts the primacy of Reasoning in dispelling darkness, which is the result of 'not Knowledge, but Faith'.[15] Other than in the heading, and therefore by implication throughout – but by implication only – the image of light and darkness is not used in the brief historical sketch of

---

[12] V. E. Löscher, Historie *Des Römischen Huren-Regiments der* Theodoræ *und* Maroziæ, *in welcher Die Begebenheiten des zehenden* Seculi *und* Intriguen *des Römischen Stuhls ausgeführet werden / nebst einer längst verlangten Einleitung zur* Histor. Medii Aevi, *verschiedenen neuen* Geographischen *und* Genealogischen *Tabellen / und einer Anzahl* Historischer *Beweißthümer wieder das Pabstthum* (Leipzig, 1705). Theodora and her daughter Marozia (as well as, to a lesser extent, Theodora the Younger) are, especially according to Liudprand of Cremona (*c.* 920–972), *Antapodosis* (Book II ch. 48, and Book III chs 18 and 43–6), in the forefront of Roman and particularly papal immorality from Pope Sergius III to Pope John XI; they were the very whores of whom Liudprand uses the invective *scortum impudens* (II. 18 and III. 49), as a result of whose involvement in the papal governance of the time it has been termed a 'pornocracy'; see J. Becker (ed.), *Die Werke Liudprands von Cremona (Liudprandi Opera)*, Scriptores rerum Germanicarum in usum scholarum, 41 (Hanover and Leipzig, 1915; repr. Munich, 1993).

[13] Cf. Varga, *Schlagwort*, pp. 101–3.

[14] Thomas Hobbes, *Leviathan, or The Matter, Forme, & Power of a Common-Wealth Ecclesiasticall and Civill* (London, 1651), p. 334; cf. the modern edition (with an introductory essay by W. G. Pogson Smith), *Hobbes's Leviathan* (Oxford, 1909), p. 473.

[15] *Leviathan* (1651), p. 367; cf. 1909 edn, p. 518.

Philosophy which this chapter contains; Philosophy of the Middle Ages is traced in an adumbration which ends in a general condemnation of 'Gregory the Pope, and S. Bernard' and 'our Beda', included among 'the most sincere men, without great knowledge of naturall causes (such as the Fathers were)', for relying on 'vain reports' of miracles in this world and of the state of those who have entered the next world.[16] In this Hobbes shows himself centrally out of sympathy with the spirit of the Middle Ages, and his antipathy is much reinforced by his analysis of the darkness for which, in his opinion, medieval Rome stood in temporal and spiritual governance, religion and philosophy.

That understanding equals light and that ignorance equals darkness are widespread equations that strongly influence how the application of the word *dark* to the Middle Ages is perceived. Locke uses the image of darkness well, connecting it with the image of windows through which knowledge can pass into the closet of understanding:[17]

> I pretend not to teach, but to enquire; and therefore cannot but confess here again, That external and internal Sensation, are the only passages I can find of knowledge to the Understanding. These alone, as far as I can discover, are the Windows by which light is let into this *dark Room*. For, methinks, the *Understanding* is not much unlike a Closet wholly shut from light, with only some little openings left, to let in external visible resemblances, or *Ideas* of things without; which would they but stay there, and lie

---

16 *Leviathan* (1651), p. 379; cf. 1909 edn, p. 536.
17 I have used (and quote from) John Locke, *An Essay concerning Human Understanding*, ed. P. H. Nidditch (Oxford, 1975), comparing it with the first edition, J. Locke, *An Essay Concerning Humane Understanding* (London, 1690), and, where that does not give a reading, comparing Nidditch with later editions, especially the fourth edition (London, 1700), as indicated in Nidditch's apparatus. The title of the work has the spelling *Humane*; the spelling *Human* was first used, after Locke's death in 1704, in the 6th edn (London, 1710). For the orthographic and semantic development of *human* and *humane*, see *OED*, s.vv. See also E. J. Dobson, *English Pronunciation 1500–1700* (2nd edn, Oxford, 1968), ii. pp. 447–8, § 2, who demonstrates that the matter is phonologically more complicated than the brief statements in *OED* suggest. The semantic distinction in Present English emerges clearly from Samuel Johnson, *A Dictionary of the English Language* (London, 1755), s.vv.; earlier in the century, Nathaniel Bailey has a change in orthography, but he does not distinguish the senses by using spellings as Johnson does: *An Universal Etymological English Dictionary* (London, 1721) has only one spelling: 'HUMANE, . . . belonging to Mankind: Also affable, courteous, gentle, mild.' In this spelling and definition are in line with such slightly earlier dictionaries as (the anonymous) *Glossographia Anglicana Nova: Or, A Dictionary Interpreting Such Hard Words of whatever Language, as are at present used in the English Tongue* (London, 1707): '*Humane*, (Lat.) belonging to Mankind; also Courteous, Affable.' Bailey's *The Dictionarium Britannicum: Or a more Compleat Universal Etymological English Dictionary Than any Extant* (London, 1730) has only one spelling: 'HUMAN . . . of or pertaining to Mankind or the Nature of Man; also affable, courteous, mild, gentle.'
The first quotation is from *An Essay concerning Human Understanding*, II, xi, § 17; 1690 edn, p. 72; Nidditch, pp. 162–3.

so orderly as to be found upon occasion, it would very much resemble the Understanding of a Man, in reference to all Objects of sight, and the *Ideas* of them.[18]

In the chapter 'Of Enthusiasm', first published in the edition of 1700 as the nineteenth chapter of Book IV, striking use is made of the imagery of light and darkness:[19]

> Light, true Light in the Mind is, or can be nothing else but the Evidence of the Truth of any Proposition; and, if it be not a self-evident Proposition, all the Light it has, or can have, is from the clearness and validity of those Proofs, upon which it is received. To talk of any other light in the Understanding is to put our selves in the dark, or in the power of the Prince of Darkness, and by our own consent, to give ourselves up to Delusion to believe a Lie.[20]

The image of light is important in the late seventeenth and early eighteenth century. Locke uses the phrase *the light of reason*:[21]

> But since GOD in giving us the light of *Reason* has not thereby tied up his own Hands from affording us, when he thinks fit, the light of *Revelation* in any of those Matters, wherein our natural Faculties are able to give a probable Determination, *Revelation*, where God has been pleased to give it, *must carry it, against the probable Conjectures of Reason.*

Light and darkness in the philosophers' writings are inessential, no more than convenient imagery: light mainly for knowledge, reason, and understanding; darkness mainly to characterise lack of knowledge, lack of

---

[18] *knowledge to*: Editions before the fourth (1700) have no comma; the fourth edition has 'Knowledge, to'; it reads 'to let in external visible Resemblances, or *Ideas* of things without: would the Pictures coming into such a dark Room but stay there'. *Objects of sight*: Only the first edition (1690) has the misprint 'Objects of sights'.

[19] The new chapter xix is at pp. 422–8 in the 4th edn (1700), with consequent renumbering of the former chapter xix, which becomes chapter xx (at pp. 431 and 433 the running titles fail to change the number from xix to xx).
The quotation is from *Essay*, IV, xix, § 13; 4th edn, p. 427; Nidditch, p. 703. This chapter, 'Of Enthusiasm', makes frequent use of the image of light; thus IV, xix, § 5 (4th edn, p. 423; Nidditch, p. 699): 'GOD . . . cannot be denied to be able to enlighten the Understanding by a Ray darted into the Mind immediately from the Fountain of Light.' Such imagery is not uncommon elsewhere in the *Essay*; at IV, ii, § 1 (1st edn (1690), p. 264; Nidditch, p. 531), Locke uses the image of a kind of knowledge at once perceived as truth: 'This part of Knowledge is irresistible, and like bright Sun-shine, forces it-self immediately to be perceived.'

[20] The 1st edn (1690) has the misprint 'orc anbe'. The first three editions have the comma 'and, if it be not'; it is omitted in the 4th edn (1700).

[21] *Essay*, IV, xviii, § 8 (first in the 4th edn, 1700, p. 420; Nidditch, p. 694). Bishop Berkeley also makes use of the phrase *the light of reason*; cf. G. Berkeley, *A Treatise Concerning the Principles of Human Knowledge* (Dublin, 1710), pp. 116–17, § LXXII: 'If we follow the Light of Reason, we shall from the constant uniform Method of our Sensations collect the Goodness and Wisdom of the *Spirit* who excites them in our Minds.'

reason, lack of understanding. Outside Philosophy, in History, for example, or in Literary History, the application of the image of darkness to the period which we call the Middle Ages is to be seen in contrast to the light of reason, or, in early applications, in contrast to the light of revelation.

4. *Oliver Goldsmith on* the obscure ages

The term *the Dark Ages* was used in the late eighteenth century in contrast with the Enlightenment, now perhaps a German if not exclusively a post-Kantian view of the History of Ideas.[22] Earlier in the eighteenth century than Kant we have Oliver Goldsmith's and David Hume's widely differing accounts of the intellectual darkness of the Middle Ages which followed, inevitably as it seemed, the decline and fall of Rome.

Oliver Goldsmith exercised his ready pen on *the obscure ages* or *this age of obscurity*,[23] with reference to Europe in general (without mention of England in particular): in 1759 Robert Dodsley published Goldsmith's *Present State of Polite Learning*. The second chapter has the title 'A view of the obscure ages', and in it sweeping generalisations fail to conceal a paucity of facts, and of such facts as there are, some are wrong – but then, what else is obscurity? – as is sufficiently shown by the following quotations, the first from the beginning of the chapter, the second from near the end:[24]

> WHATEVER the skill of any country may be in the sciences, it is from its excellence in polite learning alone, it must expect a character from posterity. The poet and the historian, are they who diffuse a lustre upon the age, and the philosopher scarce acquires any applause, unless his character be introduced to the vulgar by their mediation.

[22] Cf. E. G. Stanley, 'The Use in English of the Word *Aufklärung*', *Notes and Queries*, 204 (1959), pp. 328–31; and see I. Kant, *Vermischte Schriften* (Halle, 1799), ii, 'Beantwortung der Frage: Was ist Aufklärung?', pp. 687–700. Cf. E. Cassirer, H. Cohen, A. Büchenau, O. Buek, A. Görland and B. Kellermann (eds), *Immanuel Kants Werke*, iv (Berlin, 1913), Schriften von 1783–1788, pp. 167–76, 538–9.

[23] Cf. W. P. Ker on this work of Goldsmith's, p. 65 below. *OED* s.v. *obscure*, has 'A. adj. †c. *fig.* Intellectually dark; unenlightened. *Obs.*', and reinforcing the sense of obsoleteness expressed by 'obs.', *OED* gives only two quotations for this sense, both from sixteenth-century writers; it has nothing s.v. *obscurity* for the sense in which Goldsmith uses the word.

[24] O. Goldsmith, *An Enquiry into the Present State of Polite Learning in Europe* (London, 1759), pp. 31–2, 38–9; 2nd edn (London, 1774), pp. 25–6, 32–3; orig. publ. without the author's name, which first appeared on the title-page of the second edition; cf. A. Friedman (ed.), *Collected Works of Oliver Goldsmith* (Oxford, 1966), i. pp. 269–70, 272. The second edition has the following variants: *learning alone, it must*: learning alone, that it must; *libraries, or at best*: libraries, or, at best; *curiosity, and not of learning, not by*: curiosity, not by; *fashion of the day to consult books, not nature, and to evaporate*: fashion of the day to write dictionaries, commentaries, and compilations, and to evaporate; *publications can, at least*: publications will, at least.

THE obscure ages, which succeeded the decline of the Roman empire, are a striking instance of the truth of this assertion. Whatever period of those ill-fated times we happen to turn to, we shall perceive more skill in the sciences among the professors of them, more abstruse and deeper enquiry into every philosophical subject, and a greater shew of subtilty and close reasoning, than in the most enlightened ages of antiquity. But their writings were mere speculative amusements, and all their researches exhausted upon trifles. Unskilled in the arts of adorning their knowledge, or adapting it to common sense, their voluminous productions rest peacefully in our libraries, or at best, are enquired after from motives of curiosity, and not of learning, not by the scholar, but the virtuoso.

. . .

The ignorance of the age was not owing to a dislike of knowledge, but a false standard of taste was erected, and a wrong direction given to philosophical enquiry. It was the fashion of the day to consult books, not nature, and to evaporate in a folio, the spirit that could scarce have sufficed for an epigram. The most barbarous times had men of learning, if commentators, compilers, polemic divines, and intricate metaphysicians, deserved the title.

I HAVE mentioned but a very inconsiderable number of the writers in this age of obscurity. The multiplicity of their publications can, at least, equal those of any similar period of the most polite antiquity. As, therefore, the writers of those times are almost entirely forgotten, we may infer, that the number of publications alone will never secure any age whatsoever from oblivion.

5. *David Hume on Anglo-Saxon England*

In the Age of Enlightenment, Thomas Paine's *The Age of Reason* (as the slogan-title of his anti-religious tract names his own age),[25] the darkness of the past is felt to be due to endemic ignorance, superstition and error. David Hume, writing here as a historian rather than as a philosopher, says of the Anglo-Saxons, without referring to darkness or light:[26]

WITH regard to the manners of the Anglo-Saxons we can say little, but that they were in general a rude, uncultivated people, ignorant of letters, unskilful in the mechanical arts, untamed to submission under law and government, addicted to intemperance, riot, and disorder. Their best quality was their military courage, which yet was not supported by discipline or conduct. Their want of fidelity to the prince, or to any trust reposed in them, appears strongly in the history of their latter period; and their want of humanity in all their history. Even the Norman historians, notwithstanding the low state of the arts in their own country, speak of them as barbarians, when they mention the invasion made upon them by the duke of Normandy.

[25] T. Paine, *The Age of Reason* (Paris and London, 1794–1795).
[26] See D. Hume, *The History of England from The Invasion of Julius Cæsar to The Accession of Henry VII* (London, 1762), i. p. 163. Cf. Varga, *Schlagwort*, pp. 116–22.

The conquest put the people in a situation of receiving from abroad the rudiments of science and cultivation, and of correcting their rough and licentious manners.

6. *The darkness following Classical Antiquity and preceding the rebirth of learning; and Petrarch on that period*

David Hume followed in the footsteps of Renaissance scholars in regarding as a period of darkness the age following the glorious period of Classical Antiquity and preceding the rebirth of learning through Humanist scholarship. Sir J. E. Sandys gives an excellent account of the decline of Classical learning in the Middle Ages and its renewal in the Renaissance, and Eduard Norden has a masterly survey of eloquence and the styles of its expression in this period of retrogression, thus especially in his summary of three centuries preceding humanist revival:[27]

Das XI.–XIII. Jahrhundert.

Es war die Zeit, in welcher zum Abschluß kam das, was wir mit 'Scholastik' bezeichnen, einem Namen, der vielen noch dasselbe Grauen einflößt wie einst den Humanisten des XIV. und XV. Jh.: zweifellos mit Unrecht, wenn wir uns auf historischen Boden stellen . . ., sicher mit Recht, wenn wir den Standpunkt jener Humanisten einnehmen, die der Ästhetik zuliebe eben mit der historischen Entwicklung gebrochen haben. Denn für die Geschichte des Studiums der klassischen Schriftsteller bedeutet diese Zeit anerkanntermaßen den größten Rückschritt. Die 'artes' waren an den Universitäten, vor allen an der Sorbonne, das wesentlichste Bildungselement, und nicht einmal sie in der reinen, überkommenen Gestalt: die Grammatik wurde 'spekulativ', Donat 'moralisiert', ja schließlich traten an die Stelle der alten Lehrbücher zwei neue: das berühmte, oder besser infolge der Verhöhnung der Humanisten berüchtigte 'Doctrinale' des Alexander von

---

[27] J. E. Sandys, in the final chapter, 'The Survival of the Latin Classics', of the first volume of *A History of Classical Scholarship* (3rd edn, Cambridge, 1921), pp. 617–78; the rebirth of learning at the end of the Middle Ages in the first chapter, 'Introduction: Petrarch and Boccaccio', of the second volume (Cambridge, 1908), pp. 1–16; and the state of Classical learning in England in the fifteenth chapter, 'England from *c.* 1370 to *c.* 1600', of that volume, pp. 219–50.

I quote Eduard Norden, *Die antike Kunstprosa vom VI. Jahrhundert v. Chr. bis in die Zeit der Renaissance* (3rd corrected edn with supplements; Leipzig, 1915–1918), pp. 711–12, omitting Norden's footnotes and his prophecy that future scholars, when viewing Scholasticism historically, will demonstrate that it has been wrongly impugned.

In French, too, and contemporary with Norden, the night of the Middle Ages had long become a widely diffused concept, and given expression by the commonalty, who were presumably not very learned, as G. Kurth shows when [in *Qu'est-ce que le Moyen Âge?*, Questions Historiques (Paris, 1910), p. 5] he adverts to a locution apparently current, 'selon l'espression vulgaire, . . . une nuit de mille ans' ['according to the vulgar expression . . . a night of a thousand years']. See also the brief sketch of how the concept of 'das finstere Mittelalter' fared in the age of Humanism in Varga, *Schlagwort*, pp. 104–12.

Villa Dei (Villedieu in der Normandie) und der 'Grecismus' des Eberhard
von Béthune, in denen das eigentlich mittelalterliche, d. h. antiklassische
Latein als Norm zugrunde gelegt wurde. Gegen diese dunkle, durch die
Universitäten sanktionierte Richtung sind nun von Anfang an Bestrebungen
in durchaus entgegengesetztem Sinn aufgetreten, die wir daher ohne weite-
res berechtigt sind als echte Vorläufer der Renaissance aufzufassen.

[Eleventh to Thirteenth Centuries.

That age saw the culmination of what we call Scholasticism, a name that
even now induces horror in many, as it did formerly in the Humanists of the
fourteenth and fifteenth centuries: no doubt unjustly when it is viewed
historically . . ., assuredly with justice when we adopt the point of view of
the Humanists who, for the sake of Aesthetics, broke with this historical
development; for in terms of the history of the study of Classical authors
this age represented, as was and is recognised, the greatest retrogression.
The 'artes' were the most important educational element in the universities,
especially at the Sorbonne, and not even the 'artes' in the pure, transmitted
form: Grammar became 'speculative', Donatus was 'moralised'; and eventually two new textbooks replaced older ones, the famous – or rather, in
view of the Humanists' mockery of it, the infamous – 'Doctrinale' of
Alexander of Villa Dei (Villedieu in Normandy) and the 'Grecism' of
Ebrardus Bethuniensis, the basis and norm of which was medieval, that is,
anti-Classical, Latinity. From the very beginning, however, there were endeavours, in a spirit opposite to this dark direction sanctioned by the universities, and we are entitled to regard these readily as genuine precursors of
the Renaissance.]

Neither Sandys not Norden uses the term *the Dark Ages* or its German
equivalent, though the direction of some – not all – medieval Latinity is
seen as running counter to Classical and Humanist Latinity in a dark
direction.

One might have expected Petrarch not only to be aware of the darkness
of the age later called *medium aevum*, but also to express that awareness
in terms at least reminiscent of our *the Dark Ages*; but an excellent study
devoted to Petrarch's sense that his age and the post-Classical period
preceding him was a long period of darkness gets no nearer in wording to
our term than is to be found near the end of *Africa*, when Petrarch takes
leave of his book in a passage which includes these lines:[28]

> Michi degere vitam
> Impositum varia rerum turbante procella.
> At tibi fortassis, si – quod mens sperat et optat –
> Es post me victura diu, meliora supersunt
> Secula: non omnes veniet Letheus in annos

[28] T. E. Mommsen, 'Petrarch's Conception of the "Dark Ages" ', *Speculum*, 17 (1942),
pp. 226–42; I owe the reference to *Africa*, IX, ll. 451–7, to Mommsen, pp. 240–1, n. 3. For
the text see N. Festa (ed.), *L'Africa*, Edizione Nazionale delle opere di Francesco Petrarca,
i (Florence, 1926), p. 278.

> Iste sopor! Poterunt discussis forte tenebris
> Ad purum priscumque iubar remeare nepotes.

The lines have been rendered:[29]

> My life is destined to be spent 'midst storms
> and turmoil. But if you, as is my wish
> and ardent hope, shall live on after me,
> a more propitious age will come again:
> this Lethean stupor surely can't endure
> forever. Our posterity, perchance,
> when the dark clouds are lifted, may enjoy
> once more the radiance the ancients knew.

Though he nowhere mentions such terms as *the Middle Ages*, George Puttenham – a writer important in the history of English versification, though not in the history of ideas – condemns barbarisms and monkish inventions in medieval Latin verse, especially Latin rhyming verse, and shows some humanistic awareness of the correctness of the Ancients.[30]

7. *Milton and Hume on an age the lowest-sunk in ignorance and abandoned by the Muses*

Considerably later than Petrarch, when in the eyes of the learned the new age had dawned, dispelling the darkness of the period from the end of Classical Antiquity till that rebirth of humane letters, such views were expressed in Britain too, and with greater force than by Petrarch. Though not in English, Milton was vehement on the subject in the seventh of his *Prolusiones Oratoriae* (an early work, though published late); he went far beyond condemnation of only the spiritual darkness in which monastics laboured and on to a total rejection of the intellectual endeavours of the age:[31]

> Ubi nullæ vigent Artes, ubi omnis exterminatur eruditio, ne ullum quidem
> ibi viri boni vestigium est, grassatur immanitas atque horrida barbaries;
> hujus rei testem appello non civitatem unam, aut provinciam, non gentem,
> sed quartam orbis terrarum partem *Europam*, quâ totâ superioribus aliquot

---

[29] T. G. Bergin and A. S. Wilson, *Petrarch's Africa* (New Haven and London, 1977), p. 239 (Book 9, ll. 635–41).

[30] See G. Puttenham, *The Arte of English Poesie* (London, 1589; STC 20519), sigs Ciiij^vo–Dij^ro; cf. G. D. Wilcock and A. Walker (eds), *The Arte of English Poesie by George Puttenham* (Cambridge, 1936), pp. 12–15.

[31] J. Milton, *Epistolarum Familiarium Liber Unus: Quibus Accesserunt, Ejusdem, jam olim in Collegio Adolescentis, Prolusiones Quædam Oratoriae* (London, 1674), pp. 141–2; cf. *The Works of John Milton*, xii (New York, 1936), pp. 258–60. See also Section 2 above for Milton on the spiritual darkness of the age.

sæculis omnes bonæ Artes interierant, omnes tunc temporis Academias præsides diu Musæ reliquerant; pervaserat omnia, & occupârat cæca inertia, nihil audiebatur in Scholis præter insulsa stupidissimorum Monachorum dogmata, togam scilicet nacta, per vacua rostra & pulpita per squalentes Cathedras jactitavit se prophanum & informe monstrum, Ignorantia. Tum primum lugere Pietas, extingui Religio & pessum ire, adeo ut ex gravi vulnere, sero atque ægre vix in hunc usque diem convaluerit.

[Where no Arts thrive, where all learning is banished, there remains not a single trace of a good man, but monstrousness and savage barbarism rage all round. I call to witness of this fact no one country, province or people, but Europe itself – a fourth part of the world – from the whole of which had perished for not several preceding centuries all the excellent Arts, and the Muses deserted all the universities of that time over which they had presided for a long while. Blind illiteracy had pervaded and lain hold of everything; nothing was heard in the schools but the insipid doctrines of utterly stupid monks, and that profane and deformed monster, Ignorance, put on the gown and practised boasting from our empty platforms and pulpits and from neglected professorial chairs. Then for the first time Piety went into mourning, Religion lost strength and went to ruin, so that it has hardly recovered, late and with difficulty, even to this day, from that grievous wound.]

No wonder that this very passage has been censured harshly by a Milton scholar who rarely criticises his author so fiercely:[32]

Milton argues that if all learning is banished, stark savagery must prevail. And to support his thesis he gives a gross travesty (in the Renaissance-Protestant manner) of the conditions of life in the Middle Ages.

Hume's summary of the Middle Ages is as devastating, and in its climax the image of light plays a crucial role:[33]

THOSE who cast their eye on the general revolutions of society, will find, that, as all the improvements of the human mind had reached nearly to their state of perfection about the age of Augustus, there was a sensible decline from that point or period; and men thenceforth relapsed gradually into ignorance and barbarism. The unlimited extent of the Roman empire, and the consequent despotism of the monarchs, extinguished all emulation, debased the generous spirits of men, and depressed that noble flame, by which all the refined arts must be cherished and enlivened. The military government, which soon succeeded, rendered even the lives and properties

---

[32] In *Milton: Private Correspondence and Academic Exercises*, trans. by P. B. Tillyard, with an introduction and commentary by E. M. W. Tillyard (Cambridge, 1932), p. xxxv. P. B. Tillyard's translation of this passage is at p. 109; and, slightly altered, it is published also in *Complete Prose Works of John Milton*, i (New Haven and London, 1953), pp. 292–3, where the editor, K. A. McEuen, draws attention (p. 293, n. 5) to E. M. W. Tillyard's comment on the paragraph most of which I quote (and translate) here.

[33] D. Hume, *The History of England*, ii (London, 1762), pp. 440–1.

of men insecure and precarious; and proved destructive to those vulgar and more necessary arts of agriculture, manufactures, and commerce; and in the end to the military art, and genius itself, by which alone the immense fabric of the empire could be supported. The irruption of the barbarous nations, which soon followed, overwhelmed all human knowledge, which was already far in its decline; and men sunk every age deeper into ignorance, stupidity, and superstition; till the light of antient science and history, had very nearly suffered a total extinction in all the European nations.

But there is an ultimate point of depression, as well as of exaltation, from which human affairs naturally return in a contrary progress, and beyond which they seldom pass either in their advancement or decline. The period, in which the people of Christendom were the lowest sunk in ignorance, and consequently in disorders of every kind, may justly be fixed at the eleventh century, about the age of William the Conqueror; and from that Æra, the sun of science, beginning to re-ascend, threw out many gleams of light, which preceded the full morning, when letters were revived in the fifteenth century.

8. *William Robertson's use of the term* the Dark Ages

In this total condemnation Hume is well within a tradition long established in writing of the Middle Ages. Hume, when he indulges 'in the Renaissance-Protestant manner', seems not to have used in his *History of England* the actual term *the Dark Ages*. The historian William Robertson does use it, though only rarely; for example, when he seizes on trial by combat as characterising the Dark Ages:[34]

> AMONG all the whimsical and absurd institutions which owe their existence to the weakness of human reason, this [*scil.* trial by combat], which submitted questions that affected the property, the reputation, and the lives of men, to the determination of chance, or of bodily strength and address, appears to be the most extravagant and preposterous. There were circumstances, however, which led the nations of Europe to consider this equivocal mode of deciding any point in contest, as a direct appeal to heaven, and a certain method of discovering its will. As men are unable to comprehend the manner in which the Almighty carries on the government of the universe by equal, fixed, and general laws, they are apt to imagine that in every case which the passions or interest render important in their own eyes, the Supreme Ruler of all ought visibly to display his power, in vindicating innocence and punishing vice. It requires no inconsiderable degree of science and philosophy to correct this popular error. But the sentiments prevalent in Europe during the dark ages, instead of correcting, strengthened it. Religion, for several centuries, consisted chiefly in believing the legendary

---

[34] Cf. Varga, *Schlagwort*, pp. 122–3. See W. Robertson, *The History of the Reign of the Emperor Charles V* (London and Edinburgh, 1769), i. 'A View of the Progress of Society in Europe from the subversion of the Roman Empire, to the beginning of the sixteenth century', section I, 'View of the Progress in Europe, with respect to interior Government, Laws and Manners', p. 51.

history of those saints whose names crowd and disgrace the Romish calendar. The fabulous tales concerning their miracles, had been declared authentic by the bulls of Popes, and the decrees of councils; they made the great subject of the instructions which the clergy offered to the people, and were received by them with implicit credulity and admiration.

Robertson has a side-note level with the beginning of this paragraph, in which he again refers to 'this practice', namely, judicial combat: 'The introduction of this practice favoured by the superstition of the middle ages.' It is clear, therefore, that he equates *the Dark Ages* with *the Middle Ages*. With less terminological exactness than is conveyed by *the Dark Ages*, he characterises 'those ages of darkness' as with short glimpses of light:[35]

> EVEN the Christian religion, though its precepts are delivered, and its institutions are fixed in scripture with a precision which should have exempted them from being misinterpreted or corrupted, degenerated during those ages of darkness into an illiberal superstition. . . . Charlemagne in France, and Alfred the Great in England, endeavoured to dispel this darkness, and gave their subjects a short glimpse of light and knowledge. But the ignorance of the age was too powerful for their efforts and institutions. The darkness returned, and settled over Europe more thick and heavy than formerly.

9. *'The Dark Ages' in historical writings of the twentieth century*

Such notions remained with the historians for a long time; perhaps they remain with some of them still. Sir Charles Oman has a book with the title *The Dark Ages*, the first volume in Arthur Hassall's popular series, Periods of European History. Chapter 25, 'The Darkest Hour – A.D. 855–887', has Oman's characterisation of that darkest third of a century:[36]

> It was the miserable peculiarity of the second half of the ninth century that it saw Christendom, for the first time since the commencement of the Dark Ages, begin to sink back towards primitive chaos and barbarism. After four hundred years of vacillating but permanent progress towards union, strength, and civilisation, it began to relapse, and to fall back into disunion, weakness, and ignorance. The reign of Charles the Great was to be for long years the high-water mark of progress. The succeeding age rapidly sinks away from it, and it is not till the middle of the tenth century that a rise is once more perceptible.

[35] Robertson, *History of Charles V*, i. pp. 19–20.
[36] C. Oman, *The Dark Ages 476–918* (London, 1901), p. 424. The 1901 edition is the fourth; the first edition (London, 1893), like the second and third, has the title *Europe 476–918*.

Quite recently N. F. Cantor wrote of the twilight-world behind the monastery walls, dismissing in a survey of under a dozen pages the age 'between Rome and the Middle Ages' – a period as long almost as that of Eurocentric North America:[37]

> The once-great Roman Empire, its beautiful cities, its capable government and lawcourts, its deeply learned schools and libraries, descended into the twilight of the Dark Ages of the sixth and seventh centuries, in which literate civilization survived only in a handful of ecclesiastical centers, mostly walled Benedictine monasteries.

10. *The earlier Middle Ages in the writings of literary historians: Thomas Warton and William Godwin*

Historians of literature similarly condemn the earlier Middle Ages.The sense that night had overtaken the civilised world after the Fall of Rome, and that night enveloped England in learning and literature, is felt deeply by Thomas Warton writing on Bede in his *History of English Poetry:*[38]

> His knowledge, if we consider his age, was extensive and profound: and it is amazing in so rude a period, and during a life of no considerable length, he should have made so successful a progress, and such rapid improvements, in sciential and philological studies, and have composed so many elaborate treatises on different subjects. It is diverting to see the French critics censuring Bede for credulity: they might as well have accused him of superstition*. . . .
>
> *[Here Warton has a long footnote:] It is true, that Bede has introduced many miracles and visions into his history. Yet some of these are pleasing to the imagination: they are tinctured with the gloom of the cloister, operating on the extravagancies of oriental invention. I will give an instance or two. A monk of Northumberland died, and was brought again to life. In this interval of death, a young man in shining apparel came and led him, without speaking, to a valley of infinite depth, length and breadth: one side was formed by a prodigious sheet of fire, and the opposite side filled with hail and ice. Both sides were filled with souls of departed men; who were for ever in search of rest, alternately shifting their situation to these extremes of heat and cold. The monk supposing this place to be hell, was told by his guide that he was mistaken. The guide then led him, greatly terrified with the spectacle, to a more distant place, where he says, "I saw on a sudden a darkness come on, and every thing was obscured. When I entered this place

---

[37] N. F. Cantor, *Inventing the Middle Ages: The Lives, Works, and Ideas of the Great Medievalists of the Twentieth Century* (Cambridge, 1991), pp. 17–27; quotation at p. 20.

[38] T. Warton, *The History of English Poetry, from the Close of the Eleventh Century to the Commencement of the Eighteenth Century,* i (London, 1774), Dissertation II, sigs (d4ᵛ)–(f1ᵛ).

I could discern no object, on account of encreasing darkness, except the countenance and glittering garments of my conductor . . ."

When he has finished his footnote, and after some not well-informed praise of the learned art of several early Anglo-Saxon Latin writers, Warton continues, sig. (e4ᵛ):

> But a long night of confusion and gross ignorance succeeded. The principal productions of the most eminent monasteries for three centuries, were incredible legends which discovered no marks of invention, unedifying homilies, and trite expositions of the scriptures. Many bishops and abbots began to consider learning as pernicious to true piety, and confounded illiberal ignorance with christian simplicity. . . . In the mean time, from perpetual commotion, the manners of the people had degenerated from that mildness which a short interval of peace and letters had introduced, and the national character had contracted an air of rudeness and ferocity.
>
> England at length, in the beginning of the eleventh century, received from the Normans the rudiments of that cultivation which it has preserved to the present times. The Normans were a people who had acquired ideas of splendor and refinement from their residence in France; and the gallantries of their feudal system introduced new magnificence and elegance among our rough unpolished ancestors . . . That they [the Normans] brought with them the arts, may yet be seen by the castles and churches which they built on a more extensive and stately plan. Literature, in particular, the chief object of our present research, which had long been reduced to the most abject condition, appeared with new lustre in consequence of this important revolution. . . . These and other beneficial effects, arising from this practice of admitting others besides ecclesiastics to the profession of letters, and the education of youth, were imported into England by means of the Norman conquest.

Warton is not a good historian of English literature of the period during which the vernacular, as recorded in the writings of the Anglo-Saxons, was not accessible to him who was ignorant of Old English; and he was not much better at Anglo-Saxon Latin literature, though, of course, he could read what was available. The reasons were mainly ignorance of the intellectual endeavours of the period, but also an inability to free himself from the criteria for judging them as he contemplated an age to which they could not be applied.

It is easy to multiply quotations to illustrate how the civilisation of Anglo-Saxon England was perceived as being in the darkest night. It is less easy to find the term *the Dark Ages* applied to the Anglo-Saxon period, either in connection with the civilisation of the age in general or, more particularly, with reference to its literature, or even in contrast with the literature of the age immediately following *the Dark Ages*, namely that of Chaucer, as, for example, in William Godwin's *Life of Chaucer*:[39]

[39] W. Godwin, *Life of Geoffrey Chaucer, the early English poet: including memoirs of his*

We are extremely apt to put the cheat upon our imaginations by the familiar and indiscriminate use we make of the terms, the dark, and the barbarous ages. These terms are far from being applicable, without material distinctions, to the times in which Chaucer was born. The muddy effervescence which was stirred up in Europe by the continual influx of the barbarians, subsided in a considerable degree in the eleventh century. William the Norman may be considered as having introduced politeness and learning into this island.

Thus, according to Godwin, the age of Chaucer is not to be included in a general condemnation of 'the dark, and the barbarous ages' which preceded him.

Chaucer himself brought a brief period of light to 'our dark Nation', as Sir John Denham says of him:[40]

> Old *Chaucer*, like the morning Star,
> To us discovers day from far,
> His light those Mists and Clouds dissolv'd,
> Which our dark Nation long involv'd;
> But he descending to the shades,
> Darkness again the Age invades.

A later statement gives greater precision to the nature of the light that Chaucer shed, the light of refinement brought to the rude age in which he lived: Mark Akenside wrote an inscription 'For a Statue of Chaucer at Woodstock' and praises him as the poet,[41]

> who, in times
> Dark and untaught, began with charming verse
> To tame the rudeness of his native land.

Akenside begins his inscription, 'Such was old Chaucer', much as Sir John Denham begins with 'Old *Chaucer*', and in the comparable context of the Ancient World writes of 'Old *Homer*':[42] the manner is conventional; the matter, a commonplace.

---

near friend and kinsman, John of Gaunt, Duke of Lancaster: with sketches of the manners, opinions, arts and literature of England in the fourteenth century (London, 1803), p. 13. A footnote refers to Warton's Dissertation II, from which the relevant passage was quoted above.

[40] Sir John Denham, *On Mr. Abraham Cowley His Death, and Burial amongst the Ancient Poets* (London, 1667), ll. 1–6; cf. Sir John Denham, *Poems and Translations, with the Sophy* (London, 1668), p. 89; and T. H. Banks (ed.), *The Poetical Works of Sir John Denham* (2nd edn, Hamden, Conn.: Archon Books, 1969), p. 149.

[41] *The Poems of Mark Akenside, M.D.* (London, 1772), p. 372. First published in R. Dodsley (ed.), *A Collection of Poems in Six Volumes by Several Hands*, vi (London, 1758), p. 31.

[42] See Section 18 below.

11. *S. R. Maitland's* The Dark Ages

Robertson was recognised in the next century as the historian who gave currency to the term *the Dark Ages*. Thus the ecclesiastical historian S. R. Maitland, in a series of essays first published seventy-five years after Robertson wrote the history of Charles V, took the title *The Dark Ages* from Robertson partly in order to show its inapplicability to the age to which Robertson had applied it.[43] Maitland's essays begin with a refutation of some of the items advanced by Robertson in his 'View of the Progress of Society' (prefixed to his *History of Charles V*), chiefly by showing the inferior scholarship of Robertson and those on whom Robertson bases himself, and a little by demonstrating that their factual basis was weak. He does so by allying himself with greater scholars, among modern scholars Jean Mabillon especially, and he quotes *De Re Diplomatica* with good effect. In his essay Maitland says:[44]

> I do not write without *purpose*; and this purpose I wish to be fully understood. It is to furnish some materials towards forming a right judgment of the real state of learning, knowledge, and literature during the dark ages. The *period* which I have more particularly in view is that extending from A.D. 800 to A.D. 1200; and to this period I wish the reader to apply any general statement or remark which I may offer respecting the dark or middle ages.

A little later,[45] he says:

> At the same time I cannot persuade myself to begin the business without begging the reader not to consider me as the advocate of ignorance, superstition, and error – not to suppose that I wish to hold up the dark ages as golden ages – not to think that I undervalue the real improvements which have been made in learning and in science.

---

[43] S. R. Maitland, *The Dark Ages: A Series of Essays Intended to Illustrate the State of Religion and Literature in the Ninth, Tenth, Eleventh, and Twelfth Centuries* (London, 1844); it was edited (with slight change of subtitle) by F. Stokes, and published in the Catholic Standard Library (London, 1889). The essays were originally published between March 1835 and February 1838 in a journal the full title of which is *The British Magazine and Monthly Register of Religious and Ecclesiastical Information, Parochial History, and Documents Respecting the State of the Poor, Progress of Education, &c.*

[44] 'The Dark Ages', No. 1, *The British Magazine*, vii (1835), p. 242. In book form: 1844 edn, p. 5, 1889 edn, p. 25.

[45] *The British Magazine*, viii (1835), p. 243. In book form: 1844 edn, p. 7, 1889 edn, p. 27.

12. *The first of Hesiod's Five Ages: the Golden Age*

It is a source of some amusement in connection with the Hesiodic myth of the Five World-Ages, the fourth of which, *the Heroic Age*, was much favoured, as we shall see, by the medievalists of the present century as a substitute designation for *the Dark Ages*, that Maitland should advert to the first of the Five Ages, the Golden Age. It is a source of greater amusement that an exhibition of the art of late Anglo-Saxon England, mounted in 1984 by the British Museum and the British Library, should have been given the catchpenny title *The Golden Age of Anglo-Saxon Art*,[46] inappropriately so when Hesiod's Golden Age is recalled. In Thomas Cooke's translation, the passage in Hesiod's *Works and Days* reads:[47]

> Soon as the deathless Gods were born, and Man,
> A mortal Race, with Voice endu'd, began,
> The heav'nly Pow'rs from High their Work behold,
> And the first Age they stile an Age of Gold.
> Men spent a Life like Gods in *Saturn*'s Reign,
> Nor felt their Mind a Care, nor Body Pain;
> The fields, as yet untill'd, their Fruits afford,
> And fill a sumptuous, and unenvy'd Board.
> From Labour free they all Delights enjoy,
> Nor could the Ills of Time their Peace destroy;
> In Banquets they delight, remov'd from Care,
> Nor troublesome old Age intruded there.
> They dy, or rather seem to dy, they seem
> From hence transported in a pleasing Dream.
> Thus, crown'd with Happyness their ev'ry Day,
> Serene, and joyful, pass'd their Lives away.

[46] Cf. the exhibition catalogue, J. Backhouse, D. H. Turner and L. Webster (eds), *The Golden Age of Anglo-Saxon Art 966–1066* (London, 1984). The small number of gold and gilt objects exhibited, together with the use of gold in manuscript decoration, may have been thought to justify the use of the word *golden*, but it hardly justifies the Hesiodic term *the Golden Age*, especially since that comes earlier in Hesiodic chronology than *the Heroic Age*.

[47] T. Cooke, *The Works of Hesiod Translated from the GREEK* (London, 1728), i. pp. 78–9, Book I, ll. 150–63. Cooke (and his printers) introduced the following changes in the second edition (London, 1740), pp. 16–17 (as well as reducing the initial capitals of nouns to lower case):

> *endu'd*: endow'd
> *The two lines,* The fields . . . unenvy'd board: *follow* pleasing dream.
> *all Delights enjoy,*: ev'ry sense enjoy;
> *Care,*: care;
> *intruded there.*: intruded there:

Cf. H. G. Evelyn-White (ed. and trans.), *Hesiod*, Loeb Classical Library (London and Cambridge, Mass.: 1954), pp. 10–11, ll. 109–20.

13. *Henry Hallam and W. P. Ker on* the dark ages *of literature*

1837 is the date of the first quotation in *The Oxford English Dictionary* which applies the term *the Dark Ages* centrally, exclusively almost, to literature: s.v. '*dark*, a., 13. c. **dark ages**, a term sometimes applied to the period of the Middle Ages to mark the intellectual darkness characteristic of the time'. *OED* quotes Henry Hallam, whose *Literature of Europe* was an influential work in the nineteenth century:[48]

> Literature was assailed in its downfall by enemies from within as well as from without. A prepossession against secular learning had taken hold of those ecclesiastics who gave the tone to the rest; it was inculcated in the most extravagant degree by Gregory I., the founder, in a great measure, of the papal supremacy, and the chief authority in the dark ages; it is even found in Alcuin, to whom so much is due, and it gave way very gradually in the revival of literature. In some of the monastic foundations, especially in that of Isidore, though himself a man of considerable learning, the perusal of heathen authors was prohibited.

And a little later:[49]

> The tenth century used to be reckoned by mediæval historians the darkest part of this intellectual night. It was the iron age, which they vie with one another in describing as lost in the most consummate ignorance. This, however, is much rather applicable to Italy and England, than to France and Germany. The former were both in a deplorable state of barbarism.

Reaching a climax:[50]

> It is the most striking circumstance in the literary annals of the dark ages, that they seem to us still more deficient in native, than in acquired ability. The mere ignorance of letters has sometimes been a little exaggerated, and admits of certain qualifications; but a tameness and mediocrity, a servile habit of merely compiling from others runs through the writers of these

---

[48] The relevant fascicule of *The New English Dictionary* (as *OED* was then still called) came out in 1894. R. W. Burchfield (ed.), *A Supplement to The Oxford English Dictionary*, i (Oxford, 1972), adds: '**dark ages** (often with capital initials), also (*a*) often restricted to the early period of the Middle Ages, between the time of the fall of Rome and the appearance of vernacular written documents.' The period defined as (*a*) presumably refers to the usage of archaeologists (other than when dealing with the Mediterranean area) and to historians of literatures north of the Alps writing of vernacular compositions which are, by definition, the products of their speculation, and earlier than the writings of early vernacular authors. H. Hallam, *Introduction to the Literature of Europe, in the fifteenth, sixteenth, and seventeenth centuries*, i (London, 1837), pp. 5–6.

[49] Ibid., p. 10.

[50] Ibid., p. 11.

centuries. It is not only that much was lost, but that there was nothing to compensate for it; nothing of original genius in the province of imagination.

It is all a matter of perception; to turn inside out Locke's 'Windows by which light is let into this *dark Room*' of our understanding, the would-be understander looks in as if to enter it from the outside; and if he could enter he might well say, with the young man in Bede's vision recalled by Warton, 'When I entered this place I could discern no object, on account of encreasing darkness.' Hallam calls the early Middle Ages *the Dark Ages*, and he views them without sympathy for what he finds, from out-side. For several vernacular literatures, including that of Anglo-Saxon England, Hallam lacks the necessary linguistic knowledge, and so all appears dark within.

W. P. Ker wrote well on medieval literature. A book of his appeared in George Saintsbury's series, Periods of European Literature, a series paral-lel with Hassall's Periods of European History in which Oman's *The Dark Ages* had appeared. Ker's book had the same title; in his introductory first chapter he discusses the term *the Dark Ages*:[51]

> The Dark Ages and the Middle Ages – or the Middle Age – used to be the same; two names for the same period. But they have come to be distin-guished, and the Dark Ages are now no more than the first part of the Middle Age, while the term mediæval is often restricted to the later centu-ries, about 1100 to 1500, the age of chivalry, the time between the first Crusade and the Renaissance. This was not the old view, and it does not agree with the proper meaning of the name. The Middle Age, however lax the interpretation might be, distinctly meant at first the time between an-cient and modern civilisation. . . .
> Goldsmith[52] does not recognise what has now come to be the commonplace arrangement among most historians, separating the Dark Ages from the "Mediæval Period properly so called," which is really improperly so called, by a rather violent wresting of the term "mediæval." The old division was much more logical, a consistent and definite refusal to see anything worth the attention of a scholar in the period between the fifth and the fifteenth century. All was "Gothic," all was "Dark"; "dans la cloaque des siècles caligineux et dans la sentine des nations apedeftes,"[53] as it is

---

[51] W. P. Ker, *The Dark Ages* (Edinburgh and London, 1904), pp. 1–3.

[52] Cf. Section 4 above.

[53] Chapelain, by using the word *apedeftes*, recalls the Rabelaisian name for an uncivilised people. Rabelais (or perhaps pseudo-Rabelais, but its authenticity is irrelevant, since any mid-seventeenth-century reader would regard it as by Rabelais) has the *Isle des Apedeftes* as chapter 16 of *Le Cinquième Livre*, version *L'isle Sonante*; see P. Jourda (ed.), *Rabelais œuvres complètes* (Paris, 1962), ii. pp. 333–40; cf. S. Rawles and M. A. Screech (eds), *A New Rabelais Bibliography* (Geneva, 1987), p. 273. The word is derived, as many com-mentators have said, from Greek ἀπαίδευτος 'uneducated'; see W. v. Wartburg (ed.), *Französisches Etymologisches Wörterbuch*, xxv/2, fascicule 135 (Bâle, 1970), p. 1, s.v.

expressed with unusual levity by the poet Chapelain, in his honourable defence of Lancelot and the old romances.

The 1728 edition of Jean Chapelain's *De la lecture des vieux romans* italicises *dans la cloaque des siècles caligineux, & dans la sentine des Nations apedestes* ['In the cesspool of the murky centuries and in the sink of the uneducated peoples']. Presumably, it is italicised because these words are ascribed in the work to 'Mamurra', and characterise his ferocity of expression with the Rabelaisian echo, *apedestes* (better, *apedeftes*). The quality of Mamurra's utterance may have led Ker to select the quotation, because he, as perhaps also Chapelain, delighted in the obvious overstatement of a philistine view with which he, like Chapelain, disagreed.

14. *A parabole by Goethe on poetry – applied to the Dark Ages*

W. P. Ker rejected the darkness of the Middle Ages because to him that period was light when seen from within. One is reminded of one of Goethe's poems: it is on Poetry, which he likens to stained-glass windows:[54]

> Gedichte sind bemahlte Fensterscheiben!
> Sieht man vom Markt in die Kirche hinein
> Da ist alles dunkel und düster;
> Und so sieht's auch der Herr Philister:
> Der mag denn wohl verdrießlich seyn
> Und lebenslang verdrießlich bleiben.
>
> Kommt aber nur einmal herein!
> Begrüßt die heilige Capelle;
> Da ist's auf einmal farbig helle,
> Geschicht' und Zierrath glänzt in Schnelle,
> Bedeutend wirkt ein edler Schein;
> Dieß wird euch Kindern Gottes taugen,
> Erbaut euch und ergötzt die Augen!

---

apaideutos. The spelling with 'f' reflects the pronunciation of v in Byzantine and later Greek; cf. L. Sainéan, *La langue de Rabelais* (Paris, 1923), ii. p. 41. Ker is quoting Chapelain's *De la lecture des vieux romans* from the edition by A. Feillet (Paris, 1870), p. 17; he has an explanatory note (p. 47, n. 53) to explain *apedeftes*. The table of contents of the earlier edition calls the work *Dialogue sur la lecture des vieux Romans*, in P. N. Desmolets's *Continuation des mémoires de litterature et d'histoire*, vi/1 (Paris, 1728), p. 312, and has *apedestes* with long 's' for Feillet's 'f'. Presumably, *apedestes* is the reading of the manuscript, Bibliothèque de l'Arsenal Recueil Contrart tome VIII; it is the form of the word in A. C. Hunter's edition of Jean Chapelain's *Opuscules critiques*, Société des Textes Français Modernes (Paris, 1936), p. 223, the spellings of which have generally been modernised. The manuscript is somewhat later than the date of the text, which is 1646 (see Hunter, *Opuscules*, p. 205).

[54] [J. W. v.] *Goethe's Werke*, Vollständige Ausgabe letzter Hand, iii (Stuttgart and Tübingen, 1828), p. 179; the poem comes as the first of the section headed 'Parabolisch' in his collected verse.

It may be freely translated:

> Poems are stained-glass windows which, when seen
> By looking in from the great square outside,
> Through gloom and dark reveal of light no sign.
> That is the vision of the philistine
> Who may in lifelong sullenness abide
> Because of it, morose of mind and mien.
>
> But come inside, and from within survey
> The sacred house with reverent, joyful cheer.
> The colours now at once shine bright and clear,
> And history and ornament appear,
> Significant and noble their display.
> Children of God, that is a goodly sight;
> Be edified, and give your eyes delight!

The variety of subjects and the ornate skill with which that variety was expressed in the early Middle Ages by English writers of prose and verse make theirs a rich literature, monastic, of course, and therefore usually devout and moral. The verse has been diligently studied with ever-increasing density of attention, and the prose works of the Anglo-Saxons have also had their share of sound scholarship, likewise with increasing density; but relatively more is written on verse than on prose. Because the direction of Old English literature is so different from ours about a thousand years later, we may be led into understandings widely different from what the Anglo-Saxons might have thought of their own work, if we can sufficiently follow them in their endeavours without falling into the trap of identifying our understanding of a distant literature with what we presume to be their understanding of their own literature.

15. *R. W. Chambers on 'The Alleged Decadence of Anglo-Saxon Prose and Anglo-Saxon Civilization'*

One of the most sensitive and learned critics of the literature of the English Middle Ages and the Renaissance was R. W. Chambers earlier this century. His account 'On the Continuity of English Prose from Alfred to More and his School'[55] is now, I think justly, dismissed as presenting a continuity of vernacular prose unbroken by the coming of the Normans, contrary to the available evidence; but he was right in the favourable impression of the variety of vernacular prose from Alfred to the middle of the twelfth century, which he discussed in the fifth section of the work,

---

[55] Part of his introduction to E. V. Hitchcock and R. W. Chambers (eds), *Nicholas Harpsfield's Life of Sir Thomas More*, Early English Text Society, orig. ser., 191 (1932), pp. xlv–clxxiv. The quotation is from pp. lxxvi–lxxvii.

with the title 'The Alleged Decadence of Anglo-Saxon Prose and Anglo-Saxon Civilization', repeated as 'Alleged Anglo-Saxon decadence', the wording of the side-note at the top of each page of the section:

> It is the *variety* of Anglo-Saxon prose which is so remarkable. To the translations made in Alfred's day, and to the Laws, Charters and Wills, we have to add the Gospel Translations, Monastic Rules, Saints' Lives, Oriental legends both religious and secular, Dialogues, rudimentary Scientific, Medical and Astronomical works, Herbals, Lapidaries, even the Novel, in the story of *Apollonius of Tyre*.

16. *Anglo-Saxon verse, the notion of the Germanic Heroic Age; Hesiod's Fourth Age, the Age of Heroes*

R. W. Chambers wrote appreciatively to show that 'later' in Anglo-Saxon literature need not mean 'worse'. Attractively to Anglo-Saxonists, the Anglo-Saxon England of Hallam's 'darkest part of this intellectual night' stands at the centre of Chambers's praise of the variety and excellence of Old English prose. How far is such praise applicable also to verse? The question involves both the dating of the extant poems, a tricky task for most of them, and the judging of their literary quality by standards of later ages.

Connected with these problems is the introduction of the notion of the Dark Ages more favourably styled *the Heroic Age*. That appears to be generally thought of as relevant to Anglo-Saxon civilisation. In the handling of some writers on Anglo-Saxon England, its civilisation and extant literature are all but submerged under the weight of emphasis on recollections of *the Germanic Heroic Age*, the term used by Anglo-Saxonists in preference to *the Germanic Dark Ages*, and sometimes regarded as if it were some kind of near-factual, historical concept appertaining to the period of the westward migration of Germanic peoples, the *Völkerwanderung*, perhaps even to be seen as a parallel to the incursions of warlike Greeks from the north of Greece southwards in Classical Antiquity.

The concept, *the Heroic Age*, goes back to Ancient Greece. As we have seen, Hesiod in his *Works and Days* gives the Five World-Ages: one of them was the Golden Age.[56] The fourth age, after gold, silver and iron, is that of the generation of heroes: warriors and founders of nations. Richmond Lattimore renders the passage (ll. 156–73) thus, retaining the mystery in which Hesiod shrouded this age which preceded his own:[57]

[56] Cf. Loeb edition (see n. 47 above), pp. 12–15.
[57] R. Lattimore (translator), *Hesiod* (Ann Arbor, Mich., 1959; repr. 1978), pp. 37–9. At line 160 Lattimore records a significant variant in translation: 'followed by the great age of Heroes'. See the Loeb edn, pp. 12–15, ll. 156–73 (and ll. 169, 169*a*, *b*). Cf. Thomas

Now when the earth had gathered over this generation
also, Zeus, son of Kronos, created yet another
fourth generation on the fertile earth,
    and these were better and nobler,
the wonderful generation of hero-men, who are also
160   called half-gods, the generation before our own
    on this vast earth.
But of these too, evil war and terrible carnage
took some; some by seven-gated Thebes
    in the land of Kadmos
as they fought together over the flocks of Oidipous;
    others
war had taken in ships over the great gulf
    of the sea,
165   where they also fought for the sake
    of lovely-haired Helen.
There, for these, the end of death was misted
    about them.
But on others Zeus, son of Kronos, settled a living
    and a country
of their own, apart from human kind,
    at the end of the world.
And there they had their dwelling place,
    and hearts free of sorrow
in the islands of the blessed
    by the deep-swirling stream of the ocean,
prospering heroes, on whom in every year
    three times over

Cooke's less mysterious and briefer translation, *The Works of Hesiod* (London, 1728), i.
pp. 82–3, Book I, ll. 210–25:

> To these a fourth, a better, Race, succeeds,
> Of godlike Heros, fam'd for martial Deeds;
> Them Demigods, at first, their matchless Worth
> Proclaim aloud all, thro the boundless Earth.
> These, horrid Wars, their Love of Arms, destroy;
> Some at the Gates of *Thebes*, and some at *Troy*.
> These for the Brothers fell, detested Strife!
> For Beauty those, the lovely *Greecian* Wife.
> To these does *Jove* a second Life ordain,
> Some happy Soil far in the distant Main,
> Where live the Hero-shades in rich Repast,
> Remote from Mortals of a vulgar Cast.
> There in the Islands of the Bless'd they find,
> Where *Saturn* reigns, an endless Calm of Mind;
> And there the choicest Fruits adorn the Fields,
> And thrice the fertile Year a Harvest yields.

The second edition of Cooke's translation (London, 1740, pp. 23–5, Book I, ll. 218–33)
has abandoned the capitalisation of the initial letters of common nouns, and there are minor
changes in punctuation at the end of lines: 'destroy,', 'wife!', 'cast.'.

the fruitful grainland bestows its sweet yield.
These live
far from the immortals, and Kronos
is king among them.
For Zeus, father of gods and mortals,
set him free from his bondage,
although the position and the glory still belong
to the young gods.

17. *Richard Hurd on 'the* heroic *and* gothic *manners'*

The concept of *the Heroic Age,* or, earlier, *the heroic ages,*[58] had in England a wide application. (Bishop) Richard Hurd invoked the spirit of *the heroic ages* when he pointed to eight 'circumstances of agreement between the *heroic* and *gothic* manners', that is, between the manners of the Ancients (including, perhaps, those of the ancient peoples of Germania) and the manners of the men and women as seen in the romances of the later Middle Ages, or 'in the feudal times', as he called the period. The first circumstance was the preoccupation with battles: 'the same particularity of description in the account of battles, wounds, deaths in the Greek poet [Homer, especially in the *Iliad*], as in the gothic romancers'. The fifth circumstance was connected with bastardy. Hurd noted the sympathetic narrative treatment shown in the Heroic or Feudal Ages when bastardy was involved in a romance:[59]

---

[58] In early use *the heroic ages* (plural) is, of course, a single, continuous period, like *the Middle Ages* (plural) in current use. It does not refer to a series of separate ages, periods the literature of each of which might be characterised (by a literary critic surveying them all) as 'heroic' in spirit. Such a modern use of the plural is exemplified by A. Wolf, who uses – misuses, as it seems to me – the English phrase *heroic ages* in italics within his German article, 'Die Verschriftlichung von europäischen Heldensagen', in H. Beck (ed.), *Heldensage und Heldendichtung im Germanischen*, Ergänzungsbände zum Reallexikon der Germanischen Altertumskunde, 2 (Berlin, 1988), pp. 306–7, calling them *heroic ages*, he refers to distinct periods within the literary history (a) of the Anglo-Saxons, and (b) of the several related Germanic peoples, from the Heroic Age of the Germanic Period of Migrations, via the heroic ages of *Beowulf* and of *The Battle of Maldon*, to the heroic age when Icelanders wrote prose sagas.

[59] R. Hurd, *Letters on Chivalry and Romance* (London, 1762), pp. 27 and 35 (Letter IV); repr. in H. Trowbridge (ed.), *The Augustan Reprint Society,* 101–2 (Los Angeles, 1963); cf. E. J. Morley (ed.), Hurd's *Letters on Chivalry and Romance* (London, 1911), pp. 95 and 101. Hurd himself had read the old romances, though he thinks such reading is not something to boast about to the anonymous reader whom he is addressing, p. 24: 'You ask me, where I learned the several particulars, . . . and I acknowledge the omission in not acquainting you that my information was taken from it's proper Source, the *old Romances.* Not that I shall make a merit with you in having perused these barbarous volumes my self.' He goes on to praise and acknowledge his debt to Jean Baptiste de la Curne de Sainte-Palaye, 'Mémoires sur l'ancienne Chevalerie, Considérée comme un établissement politique & militaire', *Mémoires de Littérature tirés des registres de l'Académie Royale des*

Their manners, in another respect, were the same. "Bastardy was in credit with both." They were extremely watchful over the chastity of their own women; but such as they could seize upon in the enemy's quarter, were lawful prize. Or, if at any time they transgressed in this sort at home, the heroic ages were complaisant enough to cover the fault by an ingenious fiction. The offspring was reputed divine.

Nay, so far did they carry their indulgence to this commerce, that their greatest heroes were the fruit of Goddesses approached by mortals; just as we hear of the doughtiest knights being born of Fairies.

18. *The Greek Heroic Age*

So relatively popular a work as Dionysius Lardner's The Cabinet Cyclopædia had 'the Heroic Age' in a substantial *History of Greece* by (Bishop) Connop Thirlwall, with a whole chapter on 'The Heroes and their Age':[60]

We have already described the general character of this period, as one in which a warlike race spread from the north over the south of Greece, and founded new dynasties in a number of little states; . . . every where a class of nobles entirely given to martial pursuits, and the principal owners of the land – whose station and character cannot perhaps be better illustrated than when compared to that of the chivalrous barons of the middle ages – became prominent above the mass of the people, which they held in various degrees of subjection. The history of the heroic age is the history of the most celebrated persons belonging to this class, who, in the language of poetry, are called *heroes*. The term *hero* is of doubtful origin, though it was clearly a title of honour.[61] . . . The history of their age is filled with their

Inscriptions et Belles-Lettres, 1744–1746, xx (Paris, 1753), pp. 597–846, reprinted with an index as *Mémoires sur l'ancienne Chevalerie; Considérée comme un établissement politique & militaire* (2 vols, Paris, 1759). Hurd's quotations appear all to be taken from this work, and translated; but I have not been able to find the French original for 'Bastardy was in credit with both.'

[60] C. Thirlwall, *A History of Greece*, i (London, 1835), ch. 5, pp. 123–4. The present study is concerned with the Germanic Heroic Age, and makes no attempt to trace the application in English of *heroic* to Ancient Greece, whether based on Hesiod or more vaguely. An early use, in a work which ranges widely and has England, not Greece, at its centre, is John Selden's *Titles of Honor* (London, 1614). The first chapter traces the origin of kingship back to a mythical age, and Selden writes near the beginning (p. 2):

> Thus came first Cities to be gouerned by Kings, as now whole Nations are. And in the Heroique times (before the *Olympiads*, when most of the Grecian fables are supposed) such, as shewed themselues first publique benefactors to the Multitude, either by inuention of Arts, Martiall prowesse, encreasing of Traffique, bettering or enlarging the Countrie, or such like, were (saith *Aristotle*) by seuerall Nations, constituted Kings ouer them, and, by generall consent, left lines of hereditarie succession.

[61] The etymology of ἥρως appears to be obscure; see H. Frisk (ed.), *Griechisches etymologisches Wörterbuch*, i (Heidelberg, 1960), s.v., where the etymological sense

wars, expeditions, and adventures, and this is the great mine from which the materials of Greek poetry were almost entirely drawn.

The application of the Hesiodic concept of the Heroic Age to the subject-matter of Greek verse, especially Homer's epics, may have been standard when Thirlwall wrote. The very neatness of Hesiod's mention made suspect the Theban and Trojan allusions at a time, later in the nineteenth century, when disintegrationists were more active; thus F. A. Paley:[62] 'It is not indeed improbable that the whole passage 161–9 was added by the rhapsodists in consequence of the celebrity of the Thebaid and the Iliad, which were alike attributed to Homer.' Whatever the rhapsodists may have done in ancient or late classical times is irrelevant to the development of the Hesiodic Heroic Age as a concept applicable to Germanic verse of the early Middle Ages, and irrelevant, therefore, to the use of the term *the Heroic Age* for the period which Germanic scholars, including Anglo-Saxonists, did not like to call *the Dark Ages*.

Homer himself, in terms of the Five Ages, must have lived after the Heroic Age, in a darker, more sinful age; but somehow that has always been felt to be at variance with his standing. It seemed so, as early as the second half of the seventeenth century, to Sir John Denham, who found it difficult to think of Homer, 'who taught the world to see', as typical of the dark age in which he lived; thus 'The Progress of Learning' (ll. 57–68):[63]

> Here some digression I must make t'accuse
> Thee my forgetful, and ingrateful Muse:
> Could'st thou from *Greece* to *Latium* take thy flight,
> And not to thy great Ancestor do Right?
> I can no more believe Old *Homer* blind
> Then those, who say the Sun hath never shin'd;
> The age wherin he liv'd, was dark, but he
> Could not want sight, who taught the world to see:

'protector' and its supposed etymological affinity to Latin *servare* 'maintain' and Avestic *haurvaiti* 'protect' are stated but not substantiated; this etymology is rejected more firmly by P. Chantraine (ed.), *Dictionnaire étymologique de la langue grecque*, i (Paris, 1968), s.v. That in usage ἥρως is a title of honour, or *politesse* even, is beyond doubt. See also M. L. West (ed.), *Hesiod Works and Days* (Oxford, 1978), p. 190 (commentary on line 159) and especially pp. 370–3 (Excursus I. 3).

[62] F. A. Paley (ed.), *The Epics of Hesiod with an English Commentary* (London, 1883), p. 27. West (see the preceding note), pp. 191–2 (commentary on line 162), does not so much as hint at the possibility that the allusions to Thebes and Troy may not be authentic, or even that they were once thought to be interpolated.

[63] Sir John Denham, *Poems and Translations, with the Sophy* (London, 1668), pp. 175–6 [176 misprinted 166]; and T. H. Banks (ed.), *The Poetical Works of Sir John Denham* (2nd edn, Hamden, Conn.: Archon Books, 1969), p. 114. Cf. section 10 above for Denham on Chaucer.

They who *Minerva* from *Joves* head derive,
Might make Old *Homers* Skull the Muses Hive;
And from his Brain, that *Helicon* distil,
Whose Racy Liquor did his off-spring fill.

19. *H. M. Chadwick*

Ever since Homer has been read in the Middle Ages, and especially in the
Renaissance, he and the Heroic Age have been enveloped in a myth of
loving wonder which goes back partly to Hesiod. As we have seen,
Bishop Thirlwall identified in Anglo-Saxon England a parallel to the
Heroic Age of Greece; and so did Hector Munro Chadwick, whose distinguished work on the language of the earliest recorded English is all but
forgotten,[64] and whose comparativist speculations on the literatures of
Ancient Greece and Anglo-Saxon England, in detail often founded on
careful analysis of the means of expression of Greek epic and Anglo-
Saxon poetry treated as if epic, used to be accepted by many Anglo-
Saxonists, and may still be admired by historians seeking ready answers
from those learned in the early modern vernacular languages to the many
insoluble questions posed by the source material extant in these languages.[65] In a work of his, *The Heroic Age*,[66] the basis of his views is
ultimately as firm as, but no firmer than, the Hesiodic myth of the Five
World-Ages.

However mythical its basis, the appellation *the Heroic Age* for the
period otherwise called *the Dark Ages* is pleasing to innocent Anglo-
Saxonists, who see themselves under attack from academic colleagues
dealing with periods of English literature that can be understood by them
and their students without the essential and frequent resort to grammars
and dictionaries of the language in which it is written. Chadwick was not
the first to seek and find a parallel to the Greece of the Heroic Age in the
myths of Europe further north (including Anglo-Saxon England, and
Scandinavia including Iceland) of a period much later than that of Troy as
celebrated by Homer. George Grote, in his *History of Greece*, which still
had an important place in the scholarship of Chadwick's youth, devoted a
chapter to 'The Grecian Mythical Vein compared with that of Modern

---

64 H. M. Chadwick, 'Studies in Old English', *Transactions of the Cambridge Philological Society*, 4 (1894–9: Cambridge, 1899), pp. 85–265.

65 Cf., for example, N. F. Cantor, *Medieval History* (see n. 4 above), p. 109: 'With the exception of Chadwick's pioneering work, published half a century ago, scholars have yet done little to illuminate early Germanic life through application of this comparative method of studying social attitudes.'

66 H. M. Chadwick, *The Heroic Age*, The Cambridge Archaeological and Ethnological Series (Cambridge, 1912). On Hesiod and parallels in Germanic verse to his *Works and Days* and *Theogony*, see esp. pp. 229–34.

Europe'.[67] Bishop Thirlwall, as we have seen,[68] compared the Greek Heroic Age with an Age of Chivalry later than Anglo-Saxon England but still very much medieval; in that he followed in the footsteps of Bishop Hurd.

Important to Chadwick was the fact that the heroes and, seemingly, historical events of Germanic antiquity, that is, of 'The Heroic Age of the Teutonic Peoples' (as he called his important second chapter) were not confined to the ancient poetry, the 'heroic poems' of any one of the Germanic peoples, but were a shared heritage. A later historian, Lucien Musset, is more cautious on the relationship of the Germanic peoples; in many cases, after they had migrated to new homes their heritage was shared through contacts in historical times rather than through a common origin:[69]

> Depuis la découverte de la tombe royale de Sutton-Hoo, dont les analogies nordiques sont évidentes, nul ne peut douter qu'il n'y ait eu, même après la fin de la migration anglo-saxonne, des contacts entre Angleterre et Scandinavie. L'histoire littéraire apporte un autre argument de poids : l'épopée anglaise du *Beowulf*, dont le sujet est essentiellement danois, prouve que le public insulaire conservait un intérêt soutenu pour les affaires de Scandinavie.

> [Since the discovery of the royal burial of Sutton Hoo, of which the Scandinavian affinities are obvious, no one can doubt that there existed, even after the end of the Anglo-Saxon Settlement, contacts between England and Scandinavia. Literary history brings to bear another weighty argument: the English epic of *Beowulf*, the subject matter of which is essentially Danish, proves that the audience in their island homes preserved a sustained interest for Scandinavian affairs.]

The alliterative verse-form in which the ancient poets celebrated in several languages the heroes of Germanic antiquity was certainly a shared heritage too, as Chadwick sets out in his chapter 5, 'The Poetry and Minstrelsy of Early Times'. In that chapter he distinguishes court-poetry from folk-poetry. The poetry of the former shows a familiarity with courtly etiquette; no person of humble rank is named in these courtly poems; they are free from coarseness, and, in short, have little in common with the 'minstrelsy of some kind . . . cultivated even by peasants in Caedmon's time'.[70]

---

[67] G. Grote, *A History of Greece*, i (London, 1846), ch. 17, pp. 613–48.
[68] See section 18, above.
[69] L. Musset, *Les invasions: Le second assaut contre l'Europe chrétienne* (Paris, 1965), p. 47. The contacts between England and Scandinavia may have occurred at different times, and much depends on how late *Beowulf* is dated for any interpretation of the Scandinavian material in the poem. Cf. several of the articles in C. Chase (ed.), *The Dating of Beowulf* (Toronto, 1981).
[70] Chadwick, *Heroic Age*, p. 83.

20. *Heroes and heroines in ancient poetry; the witness of Tacitus*

I do not know if many Germanic scholars, many Anglo-Saxonists who form a large group among them, still believe any, a little, a great deal, or all of Chadwick's mythical Heroic Age. The denial that the Heroic Age is a reality must not be stretched into a denial that there is such a thing as heroic poetry, or that the subject matter of, for example, *Beowulf* is of the kind that goes into heroic poetry: it is about aristocratic heroes and fights with supernatural and superhuman beings, including a dragon, as well as, incidentally, with tribal warfare. In *Beowulf* tribal warfare is seen as the occupation of princely heroes, rather than in national terms of the conquest of territory or the subjugation of a hostile people; except that, at the end of the poem, an unnamed messenger expresses his fear that, with Beowulf dead, his people will suffer subjugation. The personalisation of national and supranational events is not confined to heroic verse; it used to be one form of History, told as the story of great men and, less often, of great women such as Cleopatra and Agrippina Major in Antiquity, Æthelflæd Lady of the Mercians and Ælfgifu daughter of Richard I of Normandy (Emma the queen) in the Middle Ages, and Queen Elizabeth and Mary Queen of Scots in early Modern Times.

History in verse leads to long poems; long poems can be written about figures whose historicity is doubtful, like Beowulf. Long poems or a succession of related short poems carry the remembrance of past events. Two short references to Germanic song in Tacitus are often quoted as supporting each other in evidence known to him at the very end of the first century AD:[71] 'Celebrant carminibus antiquis, quod unum apud illos memoriae et annalium genus est, Tuistonem deum terra editum' [They (the Germani) celebrate in ancient songs, which are with them the only kind of record and annals, the god Tuisto descended from the earth]. And secondly, writing of Arminius, prince of the Cherusci (*c.*18 BC to AD 16), he says:

> Liberator haud dubie Germaniae et qui non primordia populi Romani, sicut alii reges ducesque, sed florentissimum imperium lacessierit, proeliis ambiguus, bello non victus, septem et triginta annos vitae, duodecim potentiae explevit, caniturque adhuc barbaras apud gentis, Graecorum annalibus ignotus, qui sua tantum mirantur, Romanis haud perinde celebris, dum vetera extollimus recentium incuriosi.

---

[71] *Germania*, 3, and *Annales*, II, 88. Cf. M. Hutton and E. H. Warmington (eds and translators), *Germania*, Loeb Classical Library, Tacitus, i (Cambridge, Mass., and London, revised edn 1970), pp. 130–1; *The Annals*, Loeb, Tacitus, ii (London and Cambridge, Mass., 1931, and repr.), pp. 518–19. See also J. G. C. Anderson (ed.), *Cornelii Taciti de origine et situ Germanorum* (Oxford, 1938), *Germania*, II, 3, and Notes, pp. 39–40; the note on II, 3 refers to *Annales*, II, 88.

[The liberator of Germania, without doubt, and a man who challenged the Roman nation – not in its nonage, as other kings and leaders had done, but in the fullest bloom of its sovereignty – inconclusive in battles, undefeated in war, he completed thirty-seven years of life, twelve of power, and is still the subject of song among the barbarian tribes, though he is unknown to Greek historical records which only admire their own things, and he is not especially famed among the Romans, while we, negligent of recent events, magnify a distant past.]

The statement in *Germania* is in a mythological context, of the earth-born Tuisto and his son Mannus; but the words about the ancient Germanic songs concern their function as history among these illiterate tribes. The statement about Arminius, celebrated in song some eighty years after his death, is directly historical. It comes at the very end of the second book of the *Annales*, and, as often in Tacitus, is designed to teach the Romans that their ways are not necessarily to be admired: he may not be saying that the songs of the barbarians, what we call Germanic heroic poetry, are a glorious manifestation of genius, but rather that the Germanic people, though lacking literacy, and therefore the literary refinement of the Greek and Roman historians, make up for it in their own crude way. Germanic scholars have made the most of both these statements: whatever Tacitus' intention may have been with regard to his Roman readers, he makes it clear that the Germanic tribes known to him had heroic poetry. We know none of this early poetry. Sir Maurice Bowra sums it up well:[72]

> The beginnings of nearly all heroic poetry are lost for us in a remote and unrecorded past. In most cases the earliest examples come from societies where it is already well established and has found its own character. Its first known appearance among the Germanic people is in the region east of the Rhine at the beginning of the Christian era. Writing his *Germania* in A.D. 98 Tacitus says that the Germans celebrate their gods "in ancient songs, which are the only kinds of records and annals which they possess" [a footnote refers to *Germania*, 3]. This proves at least that the Germans had songs which took the place of records and may have resembled the lays of the gods in the *Elder Edda*. But that they were not confined to the gods is clear from Tacitus' next statement that such songs told of the origin of the Germanic tribes. Nor were these their only subjects. For elsewhere, speaking of Arminius, prince of the Cherusci, Tacitus says "he is still sung among barbarian peoples" [a footnote refers to *Annals*, II, 88], that is, Germans. There can be no doubt that in the first century A.D. the Germans had songs both about the mythical past and about recent heroes like Arminius, who was born about 18 B.C. and died in A.D. 16. Before this we know nothing, but it is clear that in Germany heroic poetry was a well-established art at the beginning of the first century, though it may even then have had a long past behind it.

[72] C. M. Bowra, *Heroic Poetry* (London, 1952), p. 372.

21. *Heroic poetry and the mythical Heroic Age*

The term *heroic poetry* seems still acceptable for verse about heroes other than verse romances. I doubt, however, if it should be firmly attached to *the Heroic Age* of a people or of a group of peoples. Whereas heroic verse is a reality to be seen in manuscripts or in printed editions, *the Heroic Age* is a myth. A later work, written jointly by Hector Munro Chadwick and his wife, Nora Kershaw Chadwick, marshals more information about early literature, especially heroic poetry.[73] Their range of learning is formidable, and, though some of the details, about which a particular reader may have fuller information, raise doubts, such doubts rarely combine to shake the edifice they have erected or the foundations under it, the myth of a Heroic Age; and Bowra felt himself able to build on it for his *Heroic Poetry*, in which he ranges even more widely. Heroic poetry is not my subject: 'a remote and unrecorded past', perhaps 'a long past', is my subject. Does heroic poetry prerequire a Heroic Age? I think not: it prerequires only the myth of a Heroic Age. Was the age of Germanic tribes about which Tacitus wrote the Germanic Heroic Age? If it were, that would mean that the Germanic Heroic Age is earlier by far than the earliest of the great figures mentioned in the heroic poetry we have, for, as H. M. Chadwick says,[74] 'tradition has not preserved the name of a single hero earlier than the fourth century who can be regarded as historical with any degree of probability'.

These are dark thoughts about the period which follow the age to which Tacitus and Arminius belonged. Modern dark thoughts, philosophical, historical or philistine, do not turn the period in England between Roman Antiquity and the Norman Conquest, that is, the early Middle Ages, into a Dark Age, even if it is neither a Golden nor a Heroic Age.[75]

---

[73] H. M. and N. K. Chadwick, *The Growth of Literature* (3 vols, Cambridge, 1932, 1936 and 1940).

[74] H. M. Chadwick, *The Origin of the English Nation* (Cambridge, 1924), p. 284.

[75] J. H. Colin Leach (Pembroke College, Oxford) was kind enough to correct and improve my translations of the Latin passages for me. What errors and infelicities remain in them and elsewhere in this paper are mine.

Medieval Mirrors and Later *Vanitas* Paintings

FLORENCE BOURGNE

There has been a steady flow of publications dealing with mirrors during the last hundred years, despite each author's claim that his work amounted to a definitive study. I will thus refrain from so heedless a statement. However, I should like to stress that most studies deal either with mirrors in literature as such – one should cite Herbert Grabes's *Mutable Glass*[1] here – or with mirrors only in art. My modest aim in this paper is to show that, despite this traditional segregation, mirrors in sixteenth- and seven-teenth-century art are the outcome of medieval *specula*, both literary and depicted, and that the reason for this is to be found in the very nature of those medieval mirrors. As far as the Middle Ages are concerned, I will base my argument on the Wilton Diptych,[2] Troilus's ascent to heaven at the end of *Troilus and Criseyde*[3] and especially Guillaume de Deguilleville's *Pilgrimages* and some of their 'off-shoots'. The later paintings which I will use are (in chronological order) mostly by Joos van Cleve (1484–1540), Jacob de Gheyn II (1565–1629), Pieter Claesz (1597–1661) and Pieter Gerritsz Roestraten (1627–98).

I intend to revisit some of the conclusions which are traditionally drawn about the *vanitas* paintings produced by these painters as well as others. The catalogue to the exhibition of seventeenth-century vanities held in Caen in 1990 contains an article by the art critic Ingvar Bergström entitled '*Homo bulla*. La boule transparente dans la peinture hollandaise à la fin du XVIe siècle et au XVIIe siècle'.[4] In this article, Bergström shows that the glass and soap bubbles to be found in paintings of that period are intended as symbols of man's frailty. That the artist should represent

---

[1] H. Grabes, *The Mutable Glass: Mirror Imagery in Titles and Texts of the Middle Ages and English Renaissance* (Cambridge University Press, 1982: translation of *Speculum, Mirror and Looking-Glass*, 1973).
[2] Anonymous, *c.* 1395(?). London: National Gallery.
[3] I will use as standard quotation text the *Riverside Chaucer* (London and New York: Oxford University Press, 1988).
[4] I. Bergström, '*Homo bulla*. La boule transparente dans la peinture hollandaise à la fin du XVIe siècle et au XVIIe siècle', in *Les Vanités dans la Peinture au XVIIe Siècle* (Caen: Musée des Beaux-Arts, 1990), pp. 49–54.

himself in reflection using a glass ball as a convex mirror proves, according to Bergström, that painters, by setting themselves within this fragile and mutable framework, paid lip- or brush-service to the humility *topos*.

Bergström cites several paintings to support this view, in particular a very curious *Hanging glass-ball with reflection*.[5] In this painting, Pieter Roestraten represented a model of a sphere with his own image in it, which he probably re-used in other works.[6] Bergström also reminds us of the analogy already established by Percy Schramm between the orb or *Reichsapfel* and these more brittle globes.[7] This is probably why, in the Louvre *Salvator Mundi* by Joos van Cleve, we find an incongruous window boldly reflecting in the orb held by Christ.[8] Images reflected in glass balls, orbs and mirrors were thus incorporated into the '*vanitas* stylesheet',[9] to the extent that some of them were used as frames for whole paintings, as in the *Hay-cart Allegory* by Gillis van Mostaert's workshop.[10]

Victor Stoichita draws a striking parallel between maps and mirrors in seventeenth-century paintings.[11] These insertions of authorised representations of reality help to establish the validity of the work of art. Moreover, the reflected image of the painter corresponds to the emergence of the painter as *persona*, as illustrated by Pieter Claesz's *Vanitas* painting.[12] I shall not explore any further the implications of these viewpoints, but I find that none of these actually explains whence this predilection for mirrors and reflections originated. That it has a link with the emergence of the 'mirror of the mind' of Jacobean plays is beyond dispute, but this only raises further questions.

We must nevertheless retain the idea that when it came to *vanitas* paintings, mirrors were actually equated with glass balls and orbs in terms of both function and representation. Not only do they both reflect images, they are sometimes difficult to tell apart. This may be due to the emergence of the notion of 'looking-glass', that is, a mirror made of glass and not merely of metal. This notion was favoured by Elizabethan and seven-

---

5   Germany, private collection. Printed in *Les Vanités*, p. 53.

6   Cf. I. Bergström, '*Homo bulla*', p. 53.

7   P. E. Schramm, *Sphaira, Globus, Reichsapfel. Wanderung und Wandlung eines Herrschaftszeichens von Caesar bis zu Elisabeth II. Ein Betragzum 'Nachleben' der Antike* (Stuttgart: Hiersemann, 1958).

8   Joos van Cleve (1484–1540), *Le Christ bénissant* (Paris: Musée du Louvre, no. RF 187).

9   Cf. e.g. Pieter van Roestraten (*c*. 1630–1698), *Vanitas*, last seen at the Robert Noortman Gallery (London) in 1978. Printed in *Les Vanités*, p. 50.

10   Gillis van Mostaert's workshop, *La Charrette de Foin, allégorie* (Paris: Musée du Louvre, no. MNR 399).

11   V. Stoichita, *L'Instauration du tableau* (Paris: Méridiens Klinsieck, 1993), pp. 190–215.

12   Cf. ibid., pp. 243–4, analysis and print of Pieter Claesz, *Vanitas*, *c*. 1630 (Nuremberg: Germanisches Nationalmuseum).

teenth-century pamphlet writers – a fashion which was enhanced by the craze surrounding real looking-glasses.[13] This assimilation developed to such an extent that the three notions of *vanitas*, mirror and glass ball became almost equivalent. Very interestingly, a *Vanitas* by Jacob de Gheyn II was taken up again by Pieter Roestraten, and the immaterial bubble at the top of the niche was replaced, as it were, by a glass ball-cum-artist reflection.[14]

It is my belief that this ultimate artistic development was heralded in medieval art and literature long before puritanical tracts entitled *Looking-Glass for Magistrates* were printed. To demonstrate this point, I will examine first a passage from Deguilleville's *Pèlerinage de vie humaine* and the illustrations it generated, and then a very minute detail in the Wilton Diptych, which I think holds the key to this whole painting.

The *Pèlerinage de vie humaine* begins with a very striking image, that of the heavenly Jerusalem reflected in a huge mirror:

> Si comme j'estoïe en mon lit
> Avis m'ert com je dormoie
> Que je pelerins estoie
> Qui d'aler estoie excite
> En Jherusalem la cite.
> En un mirour ce me sembloit,
> Qui sanz mesure grans estoit,
> Celle cite aparceue
> Avoie de loing et veue (. . .)
>
> Or vous ai dit assez briefment
> De la belle cite comment
> U beau mirour je l'apercu.
>
> [As I was in my bed I dreamt in my sleep that I was a pilgrim who had been goaded into going to the city of Jerusalem. In a mirror, it seemed to me, which was huge without measure, this city I had glimpsed at from afar and seen. (. . .) I have said rather briefly how I glimpsed at this beautiful city in a mirror.][15]

One cannot help noticing the insistence on the size of the vision itself, supposedly filling the dreamer's sky. This image is so potent that in the 1420s, when Jean Gallopes adapted the second *Pèlerinage*, that of the soul, for the Duke of Bedford, he actually made use of this image in his prologue. He introduces the mirror *topos* by quoting from Psalm 117:

---

[13] Cf. H. Grabes's listing of works in the appendix to *The Mutable Glass*, and his analysis of this phenomenon.

[14] The two paintings are Jacob de Gheyn II, *Vanitas* (1603). New York: The Metropolitan Museum. Printed in *Les Vanités*, p. 50, and Pieter Gerritsz Roestraten (1627–1698), *Vanité* (Paris: private collection), catalogue number O.53 in *Les Vanités*, pp. 336–8.

[15] Guillaume de Deguilleville, *Pèlerinage de vie humaine*, ed. J. J. Stürzinger (London: Roxburghe Club, 1893), ll. 34–42 and 203–5.

ce dit lumble prophete dauid / ou .c. et xviie seaulme / de son saultier / Anima mea in manibus meis semper / et legem tuam non sum oblitus / je nay dist il pas oublie ta loy / mais me suis mire ou miroir de verite par lequel eue cognoissance de ma fragilite / et de la dignite de mon ame et du pelerinaige que elle a afaire / et pour ce je la tiens entre mez mains affin quelle ne se fourvoie.

[This says the humble prophet David in the 117th psalm in his Psalter: *I always carry my soul in my hands and I have not forgotten thy law.* I have not forgotten thy law he says, indeed I looked at myself in the mirror of truth, by which I gained knowledge of my frailty, of the dignity of my soul and of the pilgrimage it must accomplish. For this, I carry it in my hands so that it does not stray.][16]

We find here all the constitutive elements of what I will call corrective or 'exemplary *vanitas*': a mirror in which the beholder will see his defects (mark the use of *fragilite*) because he is confronted with the holy truth, and a patronising tone similar to that found in preaching.

This 'exemplary *vanitas*' must be set out against the notion which complements it, which I would call 'negative *vanitas*', a second, darker trend which does not aim at reforming by use of *exemplum*, but presents the viewer or reader with the sorry state of things. These highly critical and at best satirical developments were not very often found under the title *Speculum* in medieval times; the term was used to designate works belonging to the other, more positive trend.[17] As for the darker satirical current, it runs uneventfully from Antiquity to Renaissance. I have chosen not to explore it, because I feel it is more straightforward and calls for fewer explanations. Let us instead examine once more our definition of 'exemplary *vanitas*'.

Its constitutive elements were already present in the first pilgrimage, the *Pèlerinage de vie humaine*. Guillaume de Deguilleville, the author of the work, first invokes Saint Paul's teachings before explaining that he wishes to tell his vision to any audience, rich or poor, kings or pilgrims, sitting or standing.[18] The illuminators did not misread him: he is pictured as a preacher in most manuscripts of the work. In MS Douce 300 two separate illuminations show Guillaume preaching and asleep.[19]

However close in intention Guillaume seems to later *vanitas* paintings, we seem here to be missing a fairly important element: the glass ball. The mirror we are being offered by Deguilleville is by no means likened to a

---

[16] No edition exists yet of this text. I quoted from MS Douce 305, Bodleian Library, Oxford. This passage is on fol. 1v and the translation is mine.

[17] Cf. in particular R. Bradley, 'Backgrounds of the Title Speculum in Medieval Literature', *Speculum*, 29 (1954), pp. 100–15, and 'The Speculum Image in Medieval Mystical Writers', in *The Medieval Mystical Tradition in England* (Cambridge: D.S. Brewer, 1984), pp. 9–27.

[18] Guillaume de Deguilleville, *Pèlerinage de vie humaine*, ll. 1–30.

[19] Oxford, Bodleian Library, MS Douce 300, fol. 1r.

globe. Is the transparent glaze from Joos van Cleve's orb an addition which could not occur before oil-painting? Of course not. By looking at the Wilton Diptych, we shall discover yet another characteristic of these medieval mirrors.

This painting is usually dated to the end of the fourteenth century, without further precision. It pictures Richard II in front of three patron saints on the left panel, kneeling and praying to a heavenly assembly on the right panel, consisting of the Virgin and Child and eleven angels, one of them holding the Resurrection banner. Let us consider the little orb at the top of this banner. Its size (1 cm wide) and medium (tarnished silver-leaf background) make it a fairly obscure detail. But infra-red reflecto-grams such as the one published in the recent exhibition catalogue indisputably show that this miniature globe contains a castle on a little island surrounded by the sea.[20] No doubt this earthly reference in a relig-ious, even heavenly context may be an allusion to an owner or commis-sioner. Chaucer uses a strikingly similar technique at the end of the *Book of the Duchess*, where the lines 'A long castel with walles white, Be Seynt Johan, on a ryche hil'[21] refer to John of Gaunt, his Richmond property and his late wife, Blanche. I think, however, that the depiction of the castle in the orb has deeper significance.

The image of this small island clearly goes back to the *Dream of Scipio*, a passage from Cicero's *Republic* widely known in the Middle Ages thanks to Macrobius' commentary.[22] This text proved a major source of inspiration in the late Middle Ages. Both Dante and Boccacio drew on it, in the *Divine Comedy*[23] and the *Teseida*[24] respectively. I deem it highly significant that Chaucer did not use this passage when adapting the *Te-seida* into what was to become the Knight's Tale, yet used it at the end of *Troilus and Criseyde*.[25] At the end of this 'tragedy', Troilus retraces the steps of Scipio to heaven:

> And whan that he was slayn in this manere,
> His lighte goost ful blisfully is went
> Up to the holughnesse of the eighthe spere,

[20] Cf. D. Gordon, *The Wilton Diptych, Making and Meaning* (London: National Gallery Publications, 1993), p. 57.

[21] Chaucer, *The Book of the Duchess*, ll. 1319–20.

[22] Cf. the introduction to *Macrobius' Commentary on the Dream of Scipio*, ed. and trans. by W. H. Stahl (New York: Columbia University Press, 1952).

[23] One single parallel among many: in *Paradise*, xxii. ll. 134–5, Dante pities the vile appearance (*vil sembiante*) of the earth viewed from the heavens, exactly as the dreamer in Cicero's version of the vision (iii. l. 16). In fact the whole passage ll. 133–53 is influenced by the *Somnium Scipionis*, chapters III–VI.

[24] Cf. the textual notes to the Knight's Tale in *The Riverside Chaucer*.

[25] On this point, cf. the textual notes to the ending of *Troilus and Criseyde* in *The Riverside Chaucer*, and the commentary provided by Barry Windeatt in his edition, *Troilus and Criseyde* (London: Longman, 1984).

Inconvers letyng everich element;
And ther he saugh with ful avysement
The erratik sterres, herkenyng armonye
With sownes ful of hevenissh melodie.

And down from thennes faste he gan avyse
This litel spot of erthe that with the se
Embraced is, and fully gan despise
This wrecched world, and held al vanite
To respect of the pleyn felicite
That is in hevene above; and at the laste,
Ther he was slayn his lokyng down he caste,

And in hymself he lough right at the wo
Of hem that wepten for his deth so faste,
And dampned al oure werk that foloweth so
The blynde lust, the which that may nat laste,
And sholden al oure herte on heven caste;
And forth he wente, shortly for to telle,
Ther as Mercurye sorted hym to dwelle.[26]

A sign of the celebrity of this image is the fact that Guillaume de Deguilleville himself made use of it towards the end of the *Pèlerinage de l'âme*:

Ainsi com je regardoie,
Et que moult m'i delitoie
Mon ange plus haut memena
Et sus le ciel haut me monstra
Une eau qui l'environnoit
Tout entour et forment couroit. (. . .)

Clerement par mi vèoie
Quanqu'avant vèu avoie.
Terre et enfer dedens enclos
Ne me sembloient pas plus gros
Què vne boule petite
Au regard du circuite
Du ciel qui dess[o]us moi estoit
Et estre de cristal sembloit.

[And so as I was looking and taking great pleasure in it, my (guardian) angel led me higher and above the sky showed me water circling it and rushing around it. . . . I saw clearly what I had seen before. Earth and hell, enclosed in it, did not seem any larger than a tiny ball when compared to the diameter of the sky which was below me and seemed made of crystal.][27]

[26] *Troilus and Criseyde*, v. ll. 1806–27.
[27] Guillaume de Deguilleville, *Pèlerinage de l'âme*, ed. by J. J. Stürzinger (London: Roxburghe Club, 1895), ll. 8935–40 and 8945–52.

The image of the 'litel spot of erthe that with the se Embraced is' is exactly the one included in the orb, and the size of the emblem is, I think, very much in keeping with the painter's intention. The Wilton Diptych is a vision of heaven, with saints and angels. The minute earthly globe is there to remind the viewer of the essential difference in scale between heaven and our sublunary world. Thanks to the privileged medium of painting, we are offered a glimpse of the heavenly bliss awaiting the king.

There are several material justifications for assimilating the little orb to a mirror. At first sight it reminds us of the crystal beads, very often of Roman origin, which were re-used in medieval jewel-making to adorn spears and sceptres. This assimilation of the orb to an *intaille* would be an exact parallel of the literary re-using of 'pagan' material.[28] But however tempting, this hypothesis must be discarded because of a technical development which took place from the twelfth century onwards.[29] After a somewhat long period, during which mirrors had been mere polished metal plates, the technique of glass mirror-making was rediscovered. In Roman times the manufacturing of such mirrors had been so disappointing that Saint Paul, in his First Epistle to the Corinthians, expatiated at length on those 'dark mirrors' which only yielded very poor reflections.[30] Corinth being the main centre of mirror-production, no doubt his listeners had first-hand knowledge of those dim images. But at the end of the Middle Ages glass mirrors were produced again by coating the inside of a glass ball with molten metal. This detail accounts for the convex shape of the mirrors of the time. Moreover, there appeared in Germany a range of very small convex mirrors, which pilgrims held towards shrines and holy objects. The reflection of these religious items instantly transformed the mirrors into highly priced relics. The orb was very probably inspired by the existence of these 'bulls' eyes', as they were called.

Let us summarise these conclusions. On the one hand, Guillaume in the *Pèlerinage de vie humaine* explains that the mirror containing Jerusalem is 'without measure'. On the other hand, the earth seen from heaven fits into a minute mirror. This seems to point to some transparent medium, separating heaven and earth and acting as a magnifying glass in one direction only. The only parallel I can think of without dabbling in optics would be that of the goldfish staring out of its tank at the enormous shapes beyond the glass wall. The interest in optics was such at the time that learned viewers of the two types of representations must have been conscious of the optical image implied by them. The 'two mirrors' we

---

28 Cf. St Augustine's justification of this 'strategy' in his famous interpretation of the use by the Hebrew of the Egyptians' gold: *De doctrina christiana*, ii. 1. 40.
29 In addition to the details provided by H. Grabes, I used technical information drawn from B. Goldberg, *The Mirror and Man* (Charlottesville, Va.: University Press of Virginia, 1985), and especially from ch. 6: 'Ancient and Medieval Europe: The Material Mirror'.
30 I Corinthians 13: 12.

thought we were discovering in the *Pilgrimage* and in the Wilton Diptych are in fact one transparent glass ball.

We thus find ourselves before a medieval tradition which unites both preaching elements and ambiguous, glass-ball-like mirrors. It seems, therefore, that the basic elements of 'exemplary *vanitas*' already existed towards the close of the Middle Ages. Does this mean that sixteenth-and seventeenth-century *vanitas* paintings grew and developed from those late medieval roots? To find out, we must examine the future fate of Guillaume de Deguilleville's writings. In a 1946 article, Edmond Faral ticked off librarians for confusing in their descriptions an enormous number of early printed books containing the monk's dream visions in various versions and combinations.[31] Rosemond Tuve, in *Allegorical Imagery*, devoted a whole chapter to describing the production of manuscripts of the *Pilgrimage* well into the seventeenth century.[32] I have chosen a few manuscripts which I think stand out as significant landmarks in the evolution of Deguilleville's works.

MS 1130 from Bibliothèque Sainte-Geneviève is a straightforward version of the *Pèlerinage de vie humaine*, and its first page contains a combined image of Guillaume dreaming and preaching, with a huge mirror separating the two compartments in the picture.[33] The preaching scene is structured in the same way as the famous *Troilus* frontispiece,[34] with quite a good rendering of depth. The *Pilgrimages* subsequently underwent a series of transpositions into prose, and even translations, of which a few examples can readily be given. Bodley Douce 305 is a copy of Jean Galopes's prose version of the second *Pilgrimage*, the *Pilgrimage of the Soul*. No preaching scene is to be found on the initial folios, but instead a standard presentation illustration, which introduces the *prologue du composeur en prose*. The mirror is missing from the dreaming scene pictured below on the same page, because in the *Pèlerinage de l'âme* there is no initial allusion to the heavenly Jerusalem.

Not content with producing a French prose version of this pilgrimage of the soul, between 1422 and 1431 Galopes went on to produce a Latin version of the same text for the same patron, the Duke of Bedford. The original copy is now Lambeth Palace MS 326. There we find yet another presentation illumination, followed by a picture of the monk writing, and a third image of the monk asleep.[35] The 'Jerusalem mirror' is missing

[31] E. Faral, 'Guillaume de Digulleville, Jean Galloppes et Pierre Virgin', *Etudes romanes dédiées à Mario Roques par ses amis, collègues et élèves de France* (Paris: Champion, 1946), pp. 89–102.
[32] R. Tuve, *Allegorical Imagery* (Princeton: Princeton University Press, 1966), ch. 3, pp. 139–218.
[33] Paris, Bibliothèque Sainte-Geneviève, MS 1130, fol. 1r.
[34] Cambridge, Corpus Christi College, MS 61, fol. 1v.
[35] I was unable to consult this manuscript, and resorted to the catalogue established by M. R. James: *A Descriptive Catalogue of the Manuscripts in the Library of Lambeth Palace:*

once more, in keeping with the content of the text. Another family of manuscripts is that which issued from a much later prose version, composed in 1464 for Jeanne de Laval, second wife to the roi René. In these, the initial illumination is a presentation one. The clumsy quality of the text did not prevent this version from being a favourite: an Arsenal manuscript of it (MS 2319) contains an *ex-libris* by a *maistre vinaigrier*, who promises to lavish wine on the person who returns the manuscript to him if it gets lost – a promise made in 1553.[36]

The most interesting witness I have come across when trying to assess the fate of Deguilleville's work is Arsenal MS 507. It is a fairly big volume, copied near Brussels by Brother Antonius Gheens and containing several treatises by Bonaventure, fourteen *quaestiones* by Richard of St Victor, and a complete Latin translation of Deguilleville's three pilgrimages.[37] The prologue attributes the work to Jean Galopes, and is an almost literal translation of the prologue Jean Galopes composed for his French prose version. Yet the version of the Soul pilgrimage does not fit in with the *incipit* and *explicit* given for the Lambeth Palace manuscript. It is an altogether different translation, possibly descended from the one by a Lubertus Hautschild, a Bruges abbot who died in 1417.[38]

It would actually serve my purpose if the translation were a new one, made especially for this compilation, since this could prove that Deguilleville, along with other writers of the same kind, was appreciated in this Flemish-speaking area. We know that a Dutch translation of the *Pèlerinage de vie humaine* was published in 1486 under the title *De boeck vanden pelghrym*. This edition has clear didactic intentions, as the prefatorial remark indicates:

> Dit is dat boeck vanden pelgrim welck boeck / nuttich ende proffitelick is allen kersten menschen / te leren den wech welcken wech men sculdich is te / ghaen of te laten. die haer pelgrimagie doen moe/ten in deser warelt tot den ewighen leuen.

The Medieval Manuscripts (Cambridge: Cambridge University Press, 1932). The manuscript appears under its shelf-mark (326).

36 Paris, Bibliothèque de l'Arsenal, MS 2319, fol. 152v: 'Ce present Liure appertient a pierre De marestz / Maistre vinaigrier et bourgois paris de mourant / A Paris au coin de la Rue michel le conte – / Pres la Rue Gairnier sainct ladre est pour / Enseigne au coin de la Rue limage saincte anne / Quy le trouuera sy le Rapporte et on luy / Donnera sy bon vin quil sen tiendra pour content / Temoing mon saigne manuel Cy mis fact / Le troisieme Iour de feburier lan mil cinq / Cens cinquante Trois.'

37 Paris, Bibliothèque de l'Arsenal, MS 507. The contents of the manuscript (the first four treatises are actually printed) are listed on fol. Bv in a 16th-century hand.

38 Cf. L. Delisle, 'Notice sur un livre d'astrologie de Jean, duc de Berri', *Bulletin du Bibliophile*, 63 (1896), pp. 105–16 and J. Weale, 'Notice sur la fondation de l'abbaye de l'Eeckhout et sur les abbés qui l'ont gouvernée', *La Flandre, revue des monuments, d'histoire et d'antiquités*, 3 (1869–70), pp. 274–382. Unfortunately, Weale did not condescend to explain whence he drew the certitude that Lubertus was the author of such a translation.

[This is the book of the pilgrim, which book is useful and profitable to all Christians, so that they learn the way, which way they ought to follow or to avoid, those who must do their pilgrimage in this world, towards eternal life.][39]

And, lo and behold, this little paragraph on fol. 1r is followed by a full-page print of a mirror floating in the air and containing the city of Jerusalem.

But let us examine the iconography of the 1504 manuscript, MS Arsenal 507. A programme of illustration for it was initiated but never completed, and only a dozen coloured drawings survive. The first drawing, placed at the head of the prologue to the translation, depicts the monk asleep in an enormous and empty room.[40] Nowhere is the city of Jerusalem shown. Yet the illustration precedes the *Pèlerinage de vie humaine*, and we are justified in expecting a mirror. This is all the more frustrating as the text itself has been handled and modified according to the guidelines of 'exemplary *vanitas*'. The closing prayer of the *Pèlerinage de l'âme*, which seems to have been kept to a minimum by Jean Galopes in his Latin translation, is here more to the point than in the French prose version:

> Pour le songe que jay songie ouquel il comme je croy na point de menchonge / ne chose vaine escripte / Advis mest que sans plus attendre / doy donner congie a la loie du monde.

> [Because of this dream which I have dreamt, in which I think there is no lie, nor anything written amiss, I think that, without delay, I must dismiss the law of the (earthly) world.][41]

> Hoc sompnium quod vidi non est presertim inutile visum aut inane. sed potius doceor / abitere omnem seculi vanitatem

> [This dream which I saw is precisely neither seen in vain nor empty (of signification). On the contrary, I am taught (by it) to avoid all worldly vanity.][42]

As we come into the sixteenth century the concept of *vanitas* has entered the text; but its original medium, the mirror, has disappeared from the illuminator's programme. After a period of elaboration which led to juxtaposed images of preaching and dreaming of mirrors, this carefully elaborated equilibrium collapsed. Except when manuscripts or illustrated books were still produced, painting deserted its former textual com-

---

[39] This version has not, to my knowledge, been reprinted since the 15th century. I quote from Printed Book Douce 46, Bodleian Library, Oxford, fol. 1r.
[40] Paris, Bibliothèque de l'Arsenal, MS 507, fol. 117r.
[41] Oxford, Bodleian Library, MS Douce 305, fol. 80v.
[42] Paris, Bibliothèque de l'Arsenal, MS 507, fol. 228v.

panions. The exhibition title *Quand la peinture était dans les livres*[43] is in itself an explanation for the apparent dislocation of the text-cum-illustration compound. As Victor Stoichita shows, the sixteenth and seventeenth centuries are the age of *l'instauration du tableau*. The mirror made this development possible, but progressively drowned in the growing *vanitas* iconography. This may explain why medieval mirrors were clearly isolated and self-sufficient (whether as works of art or literature), whereas in sixteenth- and seventeenth-century *vanitas* paintings they are almost lost in overcrowded still-lives. Pictures become more and more autonomous, the oil medium allows for more and more translucent orbs and spheres, and the fecund mirror of the Middle Ages is now one element within a fully exhaustive and theoretical treatment of vanity.

---

[43] Cf. the catalogue for this exhibition held in Paris in 1993–4: F. Avril and N. Reynaud, *Les Manuscrits à peintures en France, 1440–1520* (Paris: Flammarion, 1993).

The Old Wives' Tale and Dryden

RENATE HAAS

The old wives' tale or, in older terminology, old wives' fable is one of the ancient popular genres in which the Middle Ages continued earlier traditions, to which the period made its own contributions, and which have also lived on into modern times. It has, however, not been established as a clearly defined form. On the other hand, the term has been used too often to be neglected, for throughout the ages it has been employed to disqualify female imagination and creativity. Thus, closer inspection may allow us some glimpses of lost female traditions; and, in the case of Dryden, it lets us see a part of his understanding of fable that has been completely ignored, and attain a fuller understanding of what he did in his famous adaptation of Chaucer's old wives' fable.

English *fable* derives from Latin *fabula*, which in turn derives from *fari* – 'to speak'. Both words have had a great variety of meanings, but since pagan and Christian antiquity the negative senses of *fabula/fable*, namely 'idle talk', 'idle or foolish tale', have been specifically associated with women. The pagan usage can be documented, for example, by Cicero and Horace, and the most famous of the various instances in the Vulgate version of the Bible is St Paul's admonition in his Letter to Timothy (1: 4, 7) to shun *ineptas et aniles fabulas*, 'silly and old-womanish tales'.[1] These negative collocations later passed into the vernaculars, where they also became proverbial.

According to the *Oxford English Dictionary*, 'old wives' fable' is by now archaic; not so, however, 'old wives' tale'. Similarly, in my native German, the loan translation *Altweibermärchen* is still in use and explained by *Ammenmärchen* in the latest *Große Duden*.[2] *Ammenmärchen* is

---

[1] *De natura deorum* iii. 12 and *Saturae* II. vi. 77. (Horace's irony may be slight, but the verb *garrire* shows that it is there. The old wives' fable Horace's rural neighbour 'chatteringly tells' is the one about the country mouse and the city mouse, which has lived on into our days.) See *Thesaurus linguae Latinae* s.v. *anilis, anicularis, fabula* and *fabella*. Various examples are quoted and discussed by Sarah Disbrow in 'The Wife of Bath's Old Wives' Tale', *Studies in the Age of Chaucer*, 8 (1986), pp. 61–7.
[2] *Duden. Das große Wörterbuch der deutschen Sprache*, eds Günther Drosdowski *et al.*, i (Mannheim, ²1993), p. 157.

an old loan-translation of another disparaging collocation quite common in Latin, *fabulae nutricularum*, 'nurses' tales', and although there have been various idealisations of childhood since Romanticism, *Ammenmärchen* has not been upgraded accordingly.

The distinctive quality of the old wives' fable is evidently taken to derive from its non-male teller, an old woman. But as we know that under patriarchy old age is seen to set in rather early in women – much earlier, at any rate, than in men – 'old wives' may well include any mature woman. These women appear to have focused on female experience or, at least, areas of less interest to male arbiters; and they have taken a female, or even feminist, standpoint – unless the male demarcations and defamations have been nothing but empty clichés. Of the various aspects of the literary-critical terms *fabula/fable*, it is their close association with orality and fictionality which has lent itself particularly to devaluation. For in our book culture, orality has been ranked as secondary; and, since Plato, imagination and fictionality have been looked upon with suspicion by thinkers and authorities, the female imagination incomparably more so than the male.

Although relatively few old wives' tales have come down to us, we do have information about the circumstances under which they were produced before the modern media arrived. While the *fabulae nutricularum* were primarily aimed at very young children, the old wives' tales in general may have had various audiences, both all-female and mixed, in contexts of work (such as spinning and weaving) and entertainment, for instance during the long winter evenings. Boccaccio, for one, mentions such possible purposes of old wives' tales as *aut terrorem incutere parvulis, aut oblectare puellulas, aut senes ludere, aut saltem fortune vires ostendere* ('to scare the little ones, divert the girls, amuse the old, or at least show the power of fortune').[3] As far as form and content are concerned, all kinds of popular narrative seem to have been available to old wives for their tales – fairy-tales, ghost stories, animal fables and so on – because in everyday practice their tales will not have been categorically separated from the tales told by men or children.

As Sarah Disbrow has recently shown, in Christian contexts, the categorical separation of *fabulae aniles* (in the meaning both of 'idle talk' and 'idle tales') very much served the purpose of excluding women from authority and its corollary preaching.[4] What Disbrow does not point out, although it is evident from her documentation, is that the defamation of female imagination through this concept was just as emphatic in the work of authors who paved the way for modern secular literature, such as Boccaccio. In his *Genealogia deorum gentilium* XIV, the first post-

[3] *Genealogia deorum gentilium*, XIV.x, ed. V. Romano, ii (Bari, 1951), p. 711.
[4] 'Old Wives' Tale', pp. 61–9.

classical formal defence of poetry, Boccaccio arrogantly labels the *vetulae/ aniculae* (note the condescending diminutions) as *delirantes*.[5]

Most of the earlier old wives' tales that have come down to us were either recorded by men or, even, composed by them. This, naturally, was a mixed blessing. On the one hand, it permitted at least some examples of the genre to pass on into literary tradition and survive; on the other, the male collectors and authors may have manipulated and falsified them to a greater or lesser extent.

The most famous old wives' tale of the English Middle Ages is, of course, Chaucer's *Wife of Bath's Tale*, and some of the recent harsh feminist criticism of it has to do with this problem of male transmission.[6] A look at the plot will therefore give us a first impression of the degree to which the Wife of Bath's fairy-tale is a genuine old wives' fable, particularly if we compare with those fairy-tales through which most of us were socialised, and which Kramarae and Treichler's *Feminist Dictionary* calls 'fairy-tales unfair to women'.[7] First, there is the basic element of a young man going out into the world to prove himself – an element that has been fundamental not only to many fairy-tales but to all kinds of narratives about male protagonists in our Western oral and literary tradition. The reasons for such an adventure (or quest) have been varied, one of them being a major or minor mistake the protagonist has committed at home. The difficulties he has to overcome in his adventure, or the tasks he has to perform, are also open to great variation. In old myths or folk traditions they may take the form of a riddle to be solved, in order, for example, to save one's life, as with Oedipus and the riddle of the Sphinx.

Now, in the *Wife of Bath's Tale*,[8] both the initial mistake and the riddle have a very special character. The young protagonist, a knight from King Arthur's court, rapes a girl whom he happens to meet on his way; and his

---

5   *Genealogia deorum gentilium*, XIV.ix–x, pp. 707 and 711. By making the old wives' tale the product of madness, Boccaccio tries to establish it as the only kind of *fabula* which is completely devoid of truth. But he soon contradicts himself to some degree: see the positive effect of such a tale on Carithes (Charis) in Apuleius's *Golden Ass* and the messages and intentions of old wives with their tales as quoted above. (The story Apuleius lets the old woman tell, retelling it himself in full detail, is that of Cupid and Psyche, which many readers have thought the most fascinating part of the work.) Note that Boccaccio does not include men in their prime among the audiences of old women.

6   See e.g. Arlyn Diamond, 'Chaucer's Women and Women's Chaucer', in Arlyn Diamond and Lee R. Edwards (eds), *The Authority of Experience: Essays in Feminist Criticism* (Amherst, 1977), pp. 72–3, and Sheila Delany, *Medieval Literary Politics: Shapes of Ideology* (Manchester, 1990), pp. 125–9.

7   Cheris Kramarae/Paula A. Treichler, *Amazons, Bluestockings and Crones: A Feminist Dictionary* (London, 1992), p. 149. For the view that since the last century the fairy-tales of certain sections of Western societies have developed an excessive emphasis on a limiting female socialisation, see also Linda Dégh, 'Frauenmärchen', in *Enzyklopädie des Märchens*, Kurt Ranke *et al.* (eds), v (Berlin, 1987), col. 216.

8   All my quotations are from *The Riverside Chaucer*, ed. Larry D. Benson (Boston, 1987).

punishment is closely linked to his crime. The riddle he must solve is what women most desire. The answer, *sovereynetee*, is the opposite to what women suffer when raped. Furthermore, the story does not end with the knight simply repeating the right answer, which he has been told by a crone after one year's vain searching. When the Queen has set him free, he ends up being held captive again and is punished for his rape in like manner; for in his desperation he rashly promised the old hag to fulfil whatever she would ask of him, and so he is now forced to marry her, which almost amounts to his being raped. During their first night, his education is energetically continued by his bride. Finally, when she allows him to choose between having her old and faithful or beautiful with the risk of infidelity, he completely resigns himself to her superior judgement. For this acceptance of her *sovereynetee* he is not only rewarded with a beautiful and good wife, but one who is also prepared to give up her very *sovereynetee* so that the story can end in the utopia of mutual bliss. All this means that here the male adventure plot is balanced by elements dominated by strong female characters. The male protagonist's tribulations are inflicted by women with a clear purpose, and they effect his education in the ways of tender love. *Fayerye* and magic play an important role, especially in bringing about the utopian ending, as if only a fairy – a woman with more-than-natural power – was able to surmount the usual obstacles to such happiness.

Understandably, many Chaucerians have felt that this is quite a good old wives' fable and, even in its particular inconsistencies, appropriate to its rambling teller. The latter is, however, a moot point, because it raises the question of how satirically the Wife is seen, taking into account the Lollard background of women's preaching in Chaucer's age. One may furthermore doubt that the education presented is enough to change a rapist into a more or less ideal lover.[9] Two things are nevertheless important, both here and in comparison with other European literatures: firstly, for once we have a literary old wives' tale quite positively seen, with a preponderance of female views, complexity and artistry, and told by an old wife of exceptional intellectual calibre and humanity; and secondly, Chaucer provided a model for including old wives' tales in similar English story collections.[10]

It was an adaptation of Chaucer's old wives' fable itself which Dryden integrated into his *Fables Ancient and Modern* (published in March 1700). Yet what research has so far completely ignored is the whole

---

[9] In relation to the Wife, the rape has traditionally been seen as part of her social realism and criticism, but, as Josseline Bidard pointed out in the discussion, it can also be viewed as originating in the Wife's strong sexual drives: a mini-rape-fantasy, attributed to a female character by its male author.

[10] E.g. *The Cobler of Caunterburie*, see Helen Cooper, 'The Shape-Shiftings of the Wife of Bath, 1395–1670', in Ruth Morse and Barry Windeatt (eds), *Chaucer Traditions: Studies in Honour of Derek Brewer* (Cambridge, 1990), p. 173.

'old-wives', context, that is, the role of women writers in Dryden's day and the use of old wives' fables under these circumstances.[11] And not only high literature has to be taken into account, but the popular traditions as well. Moreover, we must also look across the Channel, because decisive influences came from France.

In the course of the seventeenth century French women had already attained quite an important position in literature, that is, not only in the less-esteemed or best-selling genres, but also in the most prestigious ones. In 1701, for instance, the Prix de Poésie of the Academie Française itself was awarded to a woman, Catherine Durand.[12] Less prestigious, but enormously influential literary activities were taking place in the female *salons*, where forms of oral tradition, not least female tradition, were used for sophisticated entertainment and literary production, in both of which the ladies explored and criticised gender roles. Riddles, fables and above all fairy-tales were told.[13] Fairy-tales were all the rage, and the vogue was clearly dominated by women, although most of us today only remember the name of a man, Charles Perrault, who at the time preferred to be ambiguous about the authorship of his own fairy-tales.[14] When the products of this fashion were finally gathered together about eighty years later they extended to forty-one volumes.

What facilitated the fairy-tale vogue in the elegant circles where it started was the fact that, in contrast to earlier epochs, the living conditions of children had become clearly separated from the adult world and a corresponding concept of childhood as something separate had developed (as Philippe Ariès has shown).[15] Accordingly, the fairy-tale had clearly become established as children's literature, which in turn allowed sophisticated authors to play with the genre's childish naïveté in adult contexts. The frontispiece of the first edition of Perrault's tales, for instance, showed a plaque captioned *Contes de ma mère l'Oye*, and underneath an

---

11 Even e.g. Judith Sloman, who has tried to illuminate the diverse facets of Dryden's concept of fable: *Dryden: The Poetics of Translation* (Toronto, 1985), pp. 157–73.

12 Nancy Cotton, *Women Playwrights in England, c. 1361–1750* (Lewisburg, Pa., 1980), p. 109.

13 See e.g. Renate Baader, 'Die verlorene weibliche Aufklärung – Die französische Salonkultur des 17. Jahrhunderts und ihre Autorinnen', in Hiltrud Gnüg and Renate Möhrmann (eds), *Frauen Literatur Geschichte. Schreibende Frauen vom Mittelalter bis zur Gegenwart* (Stuttgart, 1985), pp. 58–82, which summarises her detailed study, *Dames de lettres. Autorinnen des preziösen, hocharistokratischen und 'modernen' Salons (1649–1698): Mlle de Scudéry – Mlle de Montpensier – Mme d'Aulnoy* (Stuttgart, 1986).

14 Eds Humphrey Carpenter and Mari Prichard, *The Oxford Companion to Children's Literature* (Oxford, 1984), pp. 178 and 403; and Zohar Shavit, 'The Concept of Childhood and Children's Folktales: Test Case – "Little Red Riding Hood" ', in Alan Dundes (ed.), *Little Red Riding Hood: A Casebook* (Madison, 1989), pp. 130–58, esp. pp. 138–40.

15 *L'enfant et la vie familiale sous l'ancien régime* (Paris, 1960); Shavit, 'Concept of Childhood', pp. 131–6.

old woman, who, while spinning, enthralled children with her narratives; but his speciality was actually the *double entendre*.[16] The female writers, however, seem to have used the new status of the fairy-tale for rather different purposes. Renate Baader has, for instance, pointed out that Madame d'Aulnoy, the most famous of these women, used the fairy-tale to show how suitors, sometimes in the shape of animals, learn to understand the feelings of a young woman, and gradually win her love through performing impossible tasks and through the magic gifts of fairies.[17]

The vogue culminated in the 1690s, particularly the last years of the decade, and according to the *Oxford Companion to Children's Literature* (p. 178), the fairy-tales began to appear in England almost as soon as they were published in France. This is particularly true for Madame d'Aulnoy's work: she was the first to publish a fairy-tale, in 1690, and by 1691 the tale had already appeared anonymously in English. She also initiated the publication of collections of fairy-tales both for France and England. Her *Contes des fées* of 1697 appeared two years later as *Tales of the Fairys* (*sic*), so helping to establish the term 'fairy-tale'. It was not until 1707 that fairy-tales by a male author reached England in translation – and then only under d'Aulnoy's name.[18] By 1709 at the latest the fashion had also reached the younger generation in England, as we can see from Steele's account in the *Tatler* of his godson's sister. Little Betty, he said, dealt chiefly in fairies and sprites for her reading matter, and sometimes on a winter night would terrify the maids with her accounts until they were afraid to go to bed.[19]

In 1699, when d'Aulnoy's *Tales of the Fairys* were published, Dryden was working on his *Fables*. In view of this his ironic reference in the Preface to another famous French authoress, Mademoiselle de Scudéry, no longer appears so fortuitous, particularly if we remember the high esteem in which the *Sapho nouvelle* was held by women writers of the 1690s.[20] Dryden says he has heard that de Scudéry, 'who is as old as *Sibyl*, and inspir'd like her by the same God of Poetry', is also translating Chaucer. Tellingly enough, his informant was a lady of his acquaintance, who kept 'a kind of Correspondence with some Authors of the Fair Sex in

---

[16] See *Oxford Companion to Children's Literature*, p. 128 (rpt. of the frontispiece) and Shavit, 'Concept of Childhood', pp. 141–4.

[17] 'Verlorene weibliche Aufklärung', pp. 81–2. See also Nancy and Melvin Palmer, 'The French *Conte de fée* in England', *Studies in Short Fiction*, 11 (1974), pp. 35–44. As these fairy-tales were very elaborate and long, they were quite close to romances and other fashionable amatory fiction, and the first example d'Aulnoy published was indeed slipped into such a longer work.

[18] Palmer, 'The French *Conte de fée*', pp. 35–9. A translation of Perrault's collection was only published in 1729.

[19] *Oxford Companion to Children's Literature*, p. 179. Steele suggests a gender-specific division of interests. His godson favoured stories about male fighters.

[20] Baader, 'Aufklärung', p. 68.

France'.[21] The contacts with French women, and notably with women writers, were very important to English women in their struggle against prejudice, which after the Restoration had once more gained weight;[22] for the greater advances in France could be used as arguments for their cause. In the late 1690s the fight seems to have reached a critical phase. Even in the public sphere of drama women had made considerable inroads. In a single year, from December 1695 to 1696, no less than five new plays by female writers had been staged in London. This had heated up the discussion and led to harsh, unfair attacks on the 'petticoat authors'. A burlesque of one of the plays of 1695–6, Delarivière Manley's *The Royal Mischief*, entitled *The Female Wits*, exposed Manley and the other women playwrights to public ridicule. Its venomous satire seems to have silenced Manley for ten years. But then, in 1706, she returned anonymously with a feminist play, *Almyna*, which she had based on a fairy-story from the recently translated *Arabian Nights*.[23]

Finally, in considering the popular traditions which formed the context for Dryden's reworking of Chaucer's old wives' fable we should not neglect the characteristics which the Wife of Bath had acquired in balladry. To some extent she had become the stock-figure of the Wanton Wife of Bath, as the titles of broadside variants featuring 'wanton' instead of 'old' or 'new' suggest. From the content of the ballad and its publication history, however, another trait of hers emerges as well: her Chaucerian talent for interpreting the Bible her own way and refuting self-righteous orthodoxy. The authorities must have thought this deeply subversive, because the ballad's first seventy years of existence – from 1600 to 1670 – are recorded only in terms of a series of attempts to suppress it.[24] And their reasons are amply illustrated by the role women preachers played during the Civil War, by Hobby's finding that well over half the texts published by women between 1649 and 1688 were prophecies[25] and by the numerous later copies and variants of the ballad.

When we turn to Dryden's handling of Chaucer's old wife and her tale, two features are most striking. The first is that Dryden evidently recognised the parallels between the 'old wives', use of the fairy-tale in the *Wife of Bath's Tale* and contemporary female practice, and that this led him to intensify the elements of faery and magic within the tale. These seemingly nostalgic emphases of the neo-classicist, his 'medievalising' of his medieval model, have greatly puzzled experts. Without considering the female

[21] *The Poems of John Dryden*, ed. J. Kinsley, iv (Oxford, 1958), p. 1459. All quotations are from this edition.

[22] See Elaine Hobby, *Virtue of Necessity: English Women's Writing, 1649–1688* (London, 1988), *passim*, e.g. pp. 85–8.

[23] Constance Clark, *Three Augustan Women Playwrights* (New York, 1986), pp. 1–33 and 171; Cotton, *Women Playwrights*, pp. 81–109.

[24] Cooper, 'Shape-Shiftings', pp. 180–2.

[25] *Virtue*, pp. 26ff.

context for the tale they have not been able to see Dryden's reasons. The impression that such procedures already come quite close to those of the Romantics, of course, provides no explanation.[26] The second striking thing is that Dryden does not 'translate' the *Wife of Bath's Prologue*, and thus greatly reduces the lively presence of the Wife. In the Preface he gives reasons for this – which does not, however, preclude self-contradictions. For, on the one hand, he names the broad-speaking, gap-toothed Wife of Bath as evidence of Chaucer's comprehensiveness, emulating God's plenty; while on the other he repeatedly rejects her *Prologue* as too licentious.[27]

> If I had desir'd more to please than to instruct, the *Reve*, the *Miller*, the *Shipman*, the *Merchant*, the *Sumner*, and, above all, the *Wife of Bathe*, in the Prologue to her Tale, would have procur'd me as many Friends and Readers, as there are *Beaux* and Ladies of Pleasure in the Town. But I will no more offend against Good Manners: I am sensible as I ought to be of the Scandal I have given by my loose Writings; and make what Reparation I am able, by this Publick Acknowlegdment. (pp. 1455–6)

Dryden was yielding to Collier's accusations and the recent trend towards respectability. But while he still defended Chaucer's and his own attacks on depraved clergy (pp. 1453 and 1461ff.), he found the Wife of Bath objectionable and singled her *Prologue* out as the most scandalous piece in Chaucer. He may have done so half-heartedly and to some degree under the impression of her popular image. However, as he was a respected writer, and the first to give a detailed and careful criticism of Chaucer, the assessment carried with it great weight.

Ambivalent as Dryden was about Chaucer's Wife of Bath, he seems to have been no less so about contemporary 'old wives' and their activities. Apart from the ironic reference to de Scudéry he does not mention any female writers in the Preface, but associates the tastes of female readers (not only of the 'Ladies of Pleasure in the Town') with levity and 'Sweetmeats', in contrast to the 'solid Meat' which real – male – connoisseurs appreciate.[28] He concludes the Preface with Horace's conclusion of *Satire* I. i. 10, distancing himself from his attackers as nothing but noisy teachers of pupils in petticoats.[29] The allusions with which Dryden enriches Chaucer's tale are also equivocal. On the one hand, they accentuate female standpoints: for instance, to the divergent answers the young knight receives in his search for the solution, Dryden adds:

---

[26] E.g. Earl Miner, 'Chaucer in Dryden's *Fables*', in Howard Anderson and John Shea (eds), *Studies in Criticism and Aesthetics, 1600–1800* (Minneapolis, 1967), pp. 58–72, esp. p. 62.

[27] *Poems of John Dryden*, pp. 1455–6 and 1460.

[28] Ibid., pp. 1445 and 1452.

[29] Loeb's translation of *discipularum*, which retains Horace's possible homosexual innuendo.

> One thought the Sexes prime Felicity
> Was from the Bonds of Wedlock to be free:
> Their Pleasure, Hours, and Actions all their own,
> And uncontroll'd to give Account to none.   (ll. 135ff.)

Here we have the emancipatory ideals of seventeenth-century women in their most radical form: rejection of marriage, which some recommended in view of all its legal and social constraints.[30] This quotation is followed by a rejection of stupid husbands – another addition of Dryden's, quite typical of his time and of emancipated women. Their wish to cultivate their minds, think for themselves and establish female wisdom beside the male one sustains not only much of the plot, but is repeatedly given direct expression by Dryden. For instance, when the hag substantiates her claim:

> 'Twas I who taught
> The Knight this Answer, and inspir'd his Thought.
> None but a Woman could a Man direct
> To tell us Women, what we most affect.   (ll. 295ff.)

Similarly, King Midas lets his wife into his secret as he thinks her 'passing prudent; and a parlous Wit' (l. 168) – motivations absent in the original. There is, however, a pun contained in 'a parlous Wit', which may strike us as ambivalent: *parlous* ('exceedingly clever') also evokes the genitive of parlour (*salon*). And the ambivalence is heightened by the statement with which Dryden makes the Wife introduce the Midas example:

> But that's a Fable; for our Sex is frail,
> Inventing rather than not tell a Tale.   (ll. 153ff.)

So we have the old cliché of women's idle talk and idle tales again, in the midst of the positively viewed old wives' fable.

Recently scholars, notably A. C. Spearing, have drawn attention to numerous further instances where Dryden undermines the *Wife of Bath's Tale*.[31] These largely derive from his inclination towards satire and innuendo, which may remind us of Perrault's similar tendencies and which contradicts the intentions he himself states in the Preface.

Thus, Dryden's old wives' fable has been a rather mixed blessing to women and their emancipatory endeavours, and is substantially more

---

[30] For France see Baader, 'Aufklärung', pp. 79–80, and for Britain see Aphra Behn, *passim*, and Margaret Cavendish's 'The Discreet Virgin' and 'Ambition Preferred Before Love' (Hobby, *Virtue of Necessity*, p. 91).

[31] 'Rewriting Romance: Chaucer's and Dryden's *Wife of Bath's Tale*', in Morse and Windeatt (eds), *Chaucer Traditions*, pp. 238–48. This includes an acute analysis of Dryden's dubious attempts at excusing the initial rape. His 'humorous' complicity should also be seen against the first upsurge of home-grown pornography, which had come in the wake of the Restoration. Hobby, *Virtue of Necessity*, pp. 86–7.

negative than Chaucer's. Dryden used the old wives' fairy-tale, which owed its current appeal not least to its emancipatory potential, merely to toy with it; to parade his talent and wit; to prove his comprehensive reading through allusions to the great authors between Chaucer and himself; and so, ultimately, to secure himself a place in the great literary tradition.[32] And he succeeded. It was his *Fables* which were his most widely read work in the eighteenth century and which established him as something of a classic. In the second half of the century his *Wife of Bath's Tale* became the basis for various Continental translations and adaptations,[33] so that both he and Chaucer gained full entrance into European and 'world' literature. In this reception his separation of the tale from its old-wife teller had even severer consequences, because on the Continent there was no parallel popular tradition through which the figure of the Wife of Bath would be familiar. Thus, after the loss of the female focus, the male authors were able to toy freely with the tale's central riddle.

To my knowledge, only very recently has the *Wife of Bath's Tale* been rewritten into a true old wives' tale. This version is very simple, in a contemporary popular style. Like the Continental versions under the immediate impact of Dryden, it focuses on the central question. It does away completely with the rape, and also with the knight's education, and may be said to belong to world literature in as much as its author is an Indian woman who taught at universities in India and Canada and now lives in Devon. But perhaps, despite its simplicity, it may also become world literature in the sense that it forms part of the new literary tradition which is fair to women. This might give us occasion to discuss further the relationship between, and relative values of, traditional male high literature and female popular traditions. And we might also ponder the question of whether the special interest of not a few modern revivers of medieval works has really been one of teaching women to take a narrow role – one that, at best, is representative of only a small section of the medieval spectrum. But for lack of space I will limit myself to presenting just this

---

[32] See also Spearing, 'Rewriting Romance', pp. 243–4; David Bywaters, 'The Problem of Dryden's *Fables*', *Eighteenth-Century Studies*, 26 (1992), pp. 29–55, esp. pp. 30–2; and Cedric D. Reverand, *Dryden's Final Poetic Mode: The Fables* (Philadelphia, 1988). Concerning chauvinism in Dryden's earlier use of de Scudéry and other French authors, see David B. Kramer, 'Onely Victory in Him: The Imperial Dryden', in Earl Miner and Jennifer Brady (eds), *Literary Transmission and Authority: Dryden and Other Writers* (Cambridge, 1993), pp. 55–78.

[33] The 1757 translation into French, the first French version of a full Chaucerian tale, and a second translation into French in 1764, Voltaire's *Ce qui plaît aux dames* (1763), Favart and Duni's *La Fée Urgèle ou Ce qui plaît aux dames* (1765); Schiebeler and Hiller's *Lisuart und Dariolette oder Die Frage und die Antwort* (1766–7) and J. F. Löwen's *Das Rätsel oder Was dem Frauenzimmer am meisten gefällt* (1766). Concerning the French versions, see Alfred C. Hunter, 'Le "Conte de la femme de Bath" en français au XVIIIe siècle', *Revue de littérature comparée*, 9 (1929), pp. 117–40.

version. It is by Suniti Namjoshi and is taken from her *Feminist Fables*, published in 1981:[34]

> But suppose that Queen Guinevere's Court had said to Arthur, 'If it pleases you, Your Majesty, "what women most want" is a woman's question, and it would be more fitting to send off a woman to find the right answer'. And suppose Arthur had agreed, then what would have happened? Imagine the scene. Queen Guinevere is on the throne. She looks at her ladies and asks for volunteers. A few step forward, but their husbands object, their fathers object, their children are too young, they are too young, and besides it's most improper. The Queen gives up. Arthur is sorry, but he had expected as much. He summons his knights and they throng about him. He has a hard time deciding which one to choose. He picks one at random. And after a year the knight comes back with the loathly damsel and a suitable answer. The answer's a good one and the men laugh. Then they settle down to a good dinner. Nothing is changed, no one is hurt, and even the knight's satisfied because the loathly damsel is changed overnight to a beautiful woman. Chivalry flowers. They are all of them gallant, and have shown some concern for the Woman Question.

---

[34] Virago Press (1994), p. 20; we are grateful to Virago Press for permission to quote this passage.

Modernising the Medieval:
Eighteenth-Century Translations of Chaucer

DEREK BREWER

Chaucer is unique in the history of English and European literature in that, medieval as he is, his work has been continuously read, commented on, imitated and eventually translated and/or modernised ever since it first appeared over six centuries ago.

The variety of views and attitudes expressed in that long period may at first sight seem to illustrate the notion that there is no absolute truth in our perceptions of art or even life: that all is so conditioned by circumstance that everything is relative. That would be wrong. The work commented on is always recognisably and relatedly the same in every age, even where perceptions are provably wrong. There are culture-transcendent truths, and texts. But of course the inter-subjective nature of all art creates genuine differences of perception, and in some cases a different age may reveal a previously unperceived or little-valued aspect of the original. It will, however, be the general argument of this paper that a changed response, especially in the translation of a text, may well tell us more about the period of the translation or the personality of the translator than it does about the original. Only an unusual genius, like Dryden, may create a genuinely fresh emphasis or perception.

In the history of the reception of Chaucer the eighteenth century is of special interest. It sees the beginning of modern criticism, the modern idea of a national literature, modern textual criticism, and modern incomprehension of Chaucer's language. The basis of study of the period may be found in Spurgeon, Brewer and Bowden (see References).

Up to the seventeenth century the chief response to Chaucer was appreciation of his elaborate rhetorical style and nobility of sentiment, though in the sixteenth century come modifications. His language is praised as being, in Spenser's words, a 'well of English undefiled' (Brewer, 1978, i. p. 114), but it was becoming increasingly difficult. His comedy begins to be praised, but the key text was still *Troilus and Criseyde*.

Critics still regarded his times as, in Sidney's words, 'misty and barbarous'. Although there was a sort of medieval revival even in Elizabethan times, as with Spenser's consciously archaic style and vaguely Arthurian theme, medieval authors were not read with any feeling for historical difference.

It will be seen that Dryden offers a most interesting example of the transition from a reading of Chaucer which shares and responds unaffectedly to his general outlook, values and style (for example in his attitude to chivalry, to love and so on) to one which is both unconsciously and consciously more 'modern'. Dryden accepts much without question, as earlier readers had done, but he also introduces new notes, interest in individual characterisation and so forth.

The new responses to Chaucer are revealed in several ways: by editorial work on original texts, by commentary and in translation. Editorial work and commentary have received some attention from modern scholarship. The subject-matter of the present essay is the investigation of a selection of translations from Dryden onwards in brief critical detail. It will, however, be well first to recall the underpinning existence of the texts and the progress of textual scholarship.

In the seventeenth century there were two complete Chaucer editions, of 1602 and 1687: these were essentially reprints, slightly modified, of Speght's 1598 edition. There were also two insignificant partial translations, one into English, one into Latin (as being more permanent a language), of *Troilus and Criseyde* (Brewer, 1978, i. pp. 13, 149–51).

Editing Chaucer in the eighteenth century saw a change. There was only one complete edition of the whole *Works* by Urry (1721), and after his premature death by the two Thomases (Brewer, 1978, i. pp. 21, 36). Although much condemned, and up to a point rightly so, 'Urry' took a new line. It went back, or claimed to go back, to manuscripts, and was the first to print the *Retractation*, which would ultimately be of great, though problematical, importance to our general understanding of Chaucer. Like the earlier editions, it included a number of apocryphal texts. The editors also rightly recognised that Chaucer's verses scan. In consequence they mended them, rather on the model of Dryden, but with little regard to philological science or manuscript accuracy, as a consequence of which the edition was savaged by the brilliant and scholarly Tyrwhitt in his edition of *The Canterbury Tales* of 1775. The real advance and merit of the perceptions of the Urry–Thomas text have consequently never received their due, and the edition has been condemned, except by the present writer, ever since. Give a dog a bad name and hang him. The edition also has a substantial Introduction by Dart, giving, it is true, the fanciful life of Chaucer initiated by Speght, but trying also to take further Speght's view of Chaucer as a 'classic', and his attempt to place Chaucer in his cultural setting, which again, as an attempt, is thoroughly praiseworthy (Brewer, 1978, i. pp. 36, 208–12). A partial, more scholarly edition by Morell (1737), which got no further than *The Knight's Tale*, followed 'Urry', illustrating the developing concern with historically accurate texts almost unknown in earlier centuries (Brewer, 1978, i. pp. 37, 193–7). Tyrwhitt's edition of *The Canterbury Tales* (1775) marks the beginning of true scholarly editing. It also confirms the switch of interest, notable since Dryden's *Fables*, from *Troilus and Criseyde* to *The Canterbury Tales* as Chaucer's greatest and most interesting achievement (Brewer, 1978, i. pp. 36–7).

Though Samuel Johnson is grudging and inaccurate in his references to Chaucer, and makes the commonplace remark about the barbarous age in which he lived, he recognises his status as a classic. Chaucer is included as the first English poet in the publisher John Bell's *The Poets of Great Britain from Chaucer to Churchill* (1782), comprising 109 volumes in duodecimo in which Chaucer's complete works, *The Canterbury Tales* as edited by Tyrwhitt, and the rest plus apocrypha from 'Urry', occupy the first fourteen volumes. Other booksellers' reprints followed, though the collection to which Johnson contributed the prefatory lives excluded Chaucer. The editing of Chaucer's text received no significant improvement after Tyrwhitt until Skeat's great work of 1894.

From the beginning of the eighteenth century literary interest, as already noted, shifts to the varied poems of *The Canterbury Tales*. Amongst these, while chivalry and pathos are still valued, the comic tales become more emphasised. In general *The Canterbury Tales* are treated as a collection of separate tales, but a partial sense of the collection as a unified whole begins slowly to emerge towards the end of the century.

Chaucer begins to be treated by Dryden as representing the whole English nation, and by the time we come to Thomas Warton in 1774 he is not only a 'man of the world' but a pure native British genius, and a universal one, only hindered by struggling with a barbarous language and a national want of taste (Brewer, 1978, i. pp. 227–30). However, he taught his countrymen how to write English. By the time we reach Godwin (1803) we find him the central figure of English culture in the fourteenth century, and Godwin asserts that the study of our native language and literature is equal to that of Greece and Rome (Brewer, 1978, i. pp. 239–40). Godwin completes the turn away from *Troilus and Criseyde* by his adverse criticism of the poem. Chaucer thus becomes part of the developing sense of English and British national culture, and the displacement of the (especially) Latin literary heritage by one in English.

Although a feeling for the 'Gothic' in literature (as in architecture) – exemplified particularly in Hurd's *Letters of Chivalry and Romance* (1762) – developed in the eighteenth century, flowered with the Romantics and can be seen in Wordsworth, understanding of Chaucer on the whole benefited little from it. The other, contrary tendency, already marked in Dryden, more strongly emphasises naturalistic characterisation and realism, echoing in a minor way the development of the eighteenth-century novel. This tendency in turn encourages the taste for comedy. The eighteenth century's pleasure in comedy perhaps deserves more recognition. Pope achieves true greatness not in epic but in the parody of epic. Parody, satire, farce, down to humble jest-books, flourish, albeit beside the sentimental and the Romantic. Comedy may in general be accompanied by pathos or sentimentality; but with Chaucer it is largely, though not exclusively, associated with indecency. 'Bawdy Chaucer' arrives. This latter association is still dominant today in the popular mind in so far as Chaucer is noticed. In the US 'Chaucerian' language is a metaphor for 'bawdy'.

Before touching on the main body of translations of *The Canterbury Tales* we should note some other pieces. Dryden himself, in his *Fables*, to be more fully discussed below, translated the apocryphal *The Flower and the Leaf.* The poem has some charm, and is heavily indebted to Chaucer. Dryden dresses it up in elaborate eighteenth-century costume, a picture of a fantasised Middle Ages, with some topical comments. In consequence the poem retained its attraction for readers until expelled from the canon. There were two translations of *The Court of Love*, then also taken to be genuine. One was by Arthur Maynwaring, published by Tonson in 1709, as part of a collection entitled *Ovid's Art of Love*, reprinted (with his other works) in 1715, and a dozen more times throughout the eighteenth century. The other was by A. S. Catcott, printed at Oxford. However, both, though good poems, are short exercises in brisk couplets, with little romance and a flippant ending. More significant were the numerous imitations of Chaucer's style, almost all of them facetious and representing what was thought to be characteristic of Chaucer. An outstanding example is Gay's *An Answer to the Sompner's Prologue of Chaucer* (1717), which is coarse and supposedly comical. These reflect the general tone of Chaucerian imitation in the eighteenth century, of which another example is Pope's juvenile essay (not published till 1727), which, being by Pope, is witty enough. Pope himself while still young took hints from Chaucer's *House of Fame* to construct his *Temple of Fame*. This is a rather more serious poem, deserving more attention than it can be given here, but admirably discussed by Geoffrey Tillotson (*Works*, London, 1940, iii. pp. 209–40). From our present point of view the most remarkable thing about it is the radical changes that Pope deliberately and effectively made. In this respect at least it may serve to support the main theme of this paper, the type of changes found in translations or modernisations of *The Canterbury Tales*, which is that changes tell us little about Chaucer, much about the eighteenth century.

The nature of modernisation, or 'translation', of Chaucer in the eighteenth century must begin with Dryden's *Fables*, conveniently if (for periodisation) ambiguously published in the year of his death, 1700. The *Preface*, perhaps the most important single piece of criticism on Chaucer ever written, need not be discussed here. The poems are translations from Homer, Ovid and Boccaccio as well as from Chaucer, so Chaucer is in classic and sophisticated company. Dryden was a man of the seventeenth century and shared (even to extravagance in some of his works, such as the heroic plays) the concepts of honour and love implicit in medieval literary representations of chivalry. For him *The Knight's Tale* is Chaucer's best, a 'noble tale'. He also refrains from translating some of Chaucer's tales on the grounds of their indecency. Nevertheless, he also inaugurates the taste of the eighteenth and later centuries. Both in his *Preface* and in his translations he laid the foundations of understanding and appreciating Chaucer which were built on for the next two and a half centuries, and which, for some, are still almost unchanged today. This is partly because of the degree of true insight he possesses. In this respect Dryden genuinely signals an improvement in perception of what is really in Chaucer's work, which had been less understood, or at least less registered, before. But Dryden is also modern, in that he clinches the realisation of the remoteness and difficulty of Chaucer's language. Hence he 'gives up the words': he must translate. In his *Preface* he lays down a theory of translation at the three levels of close, free and adaptive, or metaphrase, paraphrase and imitation. It is sometimes argued that translation of any kind is an illustration of what is in the original text. More often it will be seen, even with Dryden, that the text becomes a crutch or an excuse, or a passport, for new writing under the guise of old, a paradoxical exemplification of Chaucer's own remark, 'Ther is no newe gyse than it nas old' (*The Knight's Tale*, l. 2125). The theory of translation has been learnedly and subtly discussed, and this is not the place to treat it further. Rather, we should look at details of actual practice in the eighteenth century, starting with a few examples from Dryden and Pope, and continuing with Bowden's valuable collection.

Dryden's translations of Chaucer have also been frequently and valuably discussed. Boitani's study surveys the previous scholarship, as well as including a consideration of *The Two Noble Kinsmen*. He shows how Dryden accepts and develops elements in *The Knight's Tale*, at the same time altering and, from his point of view, 'improving' on Chaucer. As an example, while (unlike many modern critics) he accepts the logic of the final speech of Chaucer's Theseus, Dryden adds to the speech a whole new section, and, 'above all, he subtly modifies some details of the latter part of the tale so as to prepare the ground for a less traumatic ending' (Boitani, p. 195). 'Dryden then appends a moral which has no antecedent in Chaucer' (p. 196). Thus 'the conclusion of Dryden's "fable" becomes a true neo-classical triumph' (p. 196). There is nothing objectionable about such changes. They are part of the traditional retelling of stories such as Chaucer and Shakespeare themselves excelled in. The only point here is that, while it may reflect a response to Chaucer in one sense, it is not itself Chaucer, nor does it bring out anything implicit in Chaucer's poem, but opposes Chaucer's point. It is not 'wrong', unless one argues that it represents a truly Chaucerian element, which obviously it does not. The situation is more complex than that.

It will be worthwhile to examine a few lines of Dryden's to see in detail the kind of change he makes; and where better to begin than at the the opening lines of *Palamon and Arcite*:

> In Days of old, there liv'd, of mighty Fame
> A valiant Prince; and *Theseus* was his Name:
> A Chief, who more in Feats of Arms excell'd
> The Rising nor the setting Sun beheld,
> Of *Athens* he was Lord; much Land he won,
> And added Foreign Countries to his Crown:
> In *Scythia* with the Warrior Queen he strove,
> Whom first by Force he conquer'd, then by Love;
> He brought in Triumph back the beauteous Dame,
> With whom her Sister, fair *Emilia*, came.
> With Honour to his Home let *Theseus* ride,
> With Love to Friend, and Fortune for his Guide,
> And his victorious Army at his Side.
> I pass their warlike Pomp, their proud Array,
> Their Shouts, their Songs, their Welcome on the Way:
> But, were it not too long, I would recite
> The Feats of *Amazons*, the fatal Fight
> Betwixt the hardy Queen, and *Heroe* Knight;
> The Town besieg'd, and how much Blood it cost
> The Female Army, and th'*Athenian* Host;
> The Spousals of *Hippolita* the Queen;
> What Tilts and Turneys at the Feast were seen;
> The Storm at their Return, the Ladies Fear:
> But these, and other Things, I must forbear.

In contrast to Chaucer, Dryden adds some pseudo-medieval glamour. There is more explicit detail, reference to 'tilts and turneys' so as to 'set the scene', and then he omits Chaucer's serious reference to Theseus's chivalry and wisdom. He also adds characteristic eighteenth-century description. He calls Hippolita 'the beauteous Dame', a stilted cliché for which Chaucer gives no excuse. He gives Theseus 'with Honour', 'Love to Friend and Fortune for his Guide', abstractions which are not in Chaucer, and adds specific 'shouts, songs', also not in Chaucer. In Dryden's first 20 lines there are 15 adjectives: Chaucer in his first 20 lines has 8, and moves the story further along. In other words, Chaucer is barer, harder, less abstract (for his word *chivalrye* has fairly concrete meanings), yet is less descriptive, less explanatory. Chaucer's first section of 34 lines has 12 adjectives, for which Dryden has 36 lines with 26 adjectives (or 27 if you include the demonstrative 'This'). Dryden is more explicit, more pictorial. Dryden ends his 36 lines with a cluster of 3 adjectives, 'This ancient story, whether false or true', which adds extra ideas, nudges the reader, undermines our confidence by introducing doubt and adds abstraction. These extras have only slight justification in Chaucer's own apparently simpler style, and they weaken his effects. Dryden achieves his own extravagant, explicit effects based on Chaucer by means which are quite un-Chaucerian. Thus Chaucer writes of the 'red' statue of Mars painted on Theseus's white banner as 'glowing', 'that alle the feeldes glyteren up and down' (l. 977). This itself is a rather extraordinary and puzzling image, and not a very explicit one. Dryden in a sense correctly expands as:

> And all the godhead seemed to glow with fire;
> Even the ground glittered where the standard flew
> And the green grass was dyed to sanguine hue.   (ll. 112–14)

Although and partly because this seems to spell out what Chaucer meant, the effect is different. Dryden has introduced a luridly romantic note, where Chaucer just has 'red' and 'glittered'. Dryden sharply evokes green grass, dyed not simply 'red' but 'sanguine'. The word 'sanguine' introduces new associations, an artificially heightened style. With the same sort of explicitness Dryden enlarges briefly on the horrors of medieval battle unremarked by Chaucer: yet he omits Chaucer's very characteristic line, which implies a whole different mentality to warfare, that Theseus slew Creon 'manly as a knyght' (l. 987). Or again, for Chaucer's 'And swoor his oath as he was trewe knyght' (l. 959) Dryden writes, 'That by the faith which knights to knighthood bore' (l. 100).

Dryden's version is more remote, referring to an ideal he himself does not share; it is more indirect and more abstract. Chaucer's word 'knight' is both concrete and heavily laden with favourable value concepts (for illustration, see Derek Brewer in Boitani and Mann, pp. 238–40). These may not be acceptable today, and it is fascinating to see how Dryden unintentionally weakens them; but there is no doubt that they are what Chaucer meant.

These examples lead to an important generalisation. For Chaucer, such words as 'knyght' and 'manly' are heavily laden with all the complex values of honour and bravery associated with admirable men. Such language is best regarded, in Bernstein's phrase, as a 'restricted code'. Codes of this kind reflect a society of absolute and unquestioned values, closely linked in a collectivist unity, with little individual subjectivity. They have an 'essentialist', stationary, stereotyped view of the world, with little analysis and in which much is taken for granted. Chaucer's society was male-orientated and aggressive, like virtually all traditional agrarian communities. The restricted code with limited vocabulary compresses abstract and concrete in a highly emotional, yet formal style. Statements are made to be accepted at face value; cause and effect are neither explained nor questioned. Such is the restricted code of chivalry in Chaucer. Interestingly enough, however, in other poems – notably his bawdy ones – he can go beyond the seriousness of chivalry in some ways; Chaucer, especially, has a genius for containing contradictory elements in his world-view.

Some of these elements the modern Western world has, often rightly, abandoned. What remains may be more to our general taste. We take the fruit we prefer, and let the chaff be still, as our master Geoffrey advises.

Dryden, with his coloured, expressive adjectives, his explanations of cause and effect, his sympathies and sentiment, his realism, is already well on his way, even in *The Knight's Tale*, to the elaborated code of modern times. This elaborated code requires analysis, representation of cause and effect, rationality, accountability (which implies previous questioning), subjectivity, and ultimately relativism. Being very complex, it also leads to a much higher level of abstraction. These are some of the dominant mental characteristics in post-seventeenth-century modern, or at least post-modern Western societies.

For Dryden the change of basic attitude is still partial and still often implicit, unconscious. He does not consciously query the code of honour and love which underlies *The Knight's Tale*. It is a noble Tale for him, as indeed for almost everybody until a few years ago, and he says it is his favourite among *The Canterbury Tales*. He can still recognise and respond to Chaucer's world and values, yet even he has inevitably moved on. We see from Dryden's own heroic plays of love and honour how artificial such values have become for him, and he cannot avoid imparting some of the same artificiality to his version of *The Knight's Tale*. It is as if Palamon and Arcite wore perruques and Emily wore hoops in her skirts, as they act out their heroic drama.

Yet, this said, we can also perceive a not entirely dissimilar element of high-strung artificial drama in Chaucer's tale itself. To that extent at least, it may be said that Dryden has brought out and displayed something that we might not have been quite so conscious of before. But he does it at the expense of Chaucer's total effect. Chaucer actually says that the story he has put into the Knight's mouth (though he probably composed it before *The Canterbury Tales*) is an old tale; and, as elsewhere, notably at the end of the tale of Griselda, he has his reservations about such high-flown sentiment and behaviour. Even in *The Knight's Tale* itself he does not restrain an occasional flippancy, such as that at the expense of female constancy (l. 2681). But because Chaucer shares the same values as his heroes he can take them for granted, and can afford to express the flippancies to which all noble ideals are inevitably exposed because of the partial ignobility of ordinary human nature. Dryden and eighteenth-century writers generally, while still nominally adhering to such ideals, felt the need to explain, to account for cause and effect, to dress them up. The emerging profound cultural differences came to be slowly realised in part throughout the eighteenth century, but that is part of the stream of commentary. And the cultural similarities, though dwindling, remained until the early twentieth century or even later.

Dryden also modernises by adding sentiment and personal, occasionally inappropriate, feeling, as when Palamon is said to be thinking of his country. Although we can detect traces of national feeling for Englishness in Chaucer and others in the fourteenth century, the sentiment 'for country' is much more characteristic of the eighteenth century. Dryden also adds an aura of the Latin classics as understood in the eighteenth century. Furthermore, he includes additional, though not entirely un-Chaucerian, touches of anti-clericalism and anti-feminism. He sounds a genuinely new and un-Chaucerian social note, where he adds in description of the festivity

> the common crew
> Shut out, the hall admits the better few   (ll. 468–9).

There is a subtle difference here. Dryden was the first great critic to use the word 'low' as both a social and a literary condemnation. Chaucer also, as we know from remarks elsewhere (*The Clerk's Tale*, ll. 995–1001), despises the common herd; but he does not have this kind of class-feeling.

No later moderniser in the eighteenth century took on *The Knight's Tale*, partly because Dryden's version was so good and readily available, and more profoundly, we may suspect, because its ethos became less and less sympathetic. On the other hand, in refraining from translating the bawdy tales because of their indecency, Dryden anticipates the nineteenth rather than either the later eighteenth or the twentieth centuries.

We should now look at Dryden's other translation, that of *The Wife of Bath's Tale*, brilliantly discussed by A. C. Spearing. He remarks that Dryden:

> greatly intensifies the separation of the sexes and commits himself far more explicitly to a male readership and a definition of woman as a deviation from the male norm . . . Dryden's definition of woman is only a special case of his general Augustan habit of assigning individuals firmly to larger and more abstract categories, or indeed of substituting categories for individuals. (Spearing, p. 239)

When it comes to romance, Spearing finds that Dryden's rewriting opposes Chaucer's. Far from sharing Chaucer's scepticism about the fantasies of medieval romance, Dryden in *The Wife of Bath's Tale* reveals:

> that nostalgia for the imaginary that has coloured so much subsequent reading of medieval culture. Dryden follows Chaucer in using the Arthurian opening as peg for satire on the Church and in part he updates Chaucer's topicality . . . (but) . . . is also attracted by what has become archaic in this satire . . . and he further expresses a longing for the pre-rational past not uncommon in the Age of Reason but entirely foreign to Chaucer.
> (Spearing, pp. 242–3)

These examples show the nature of Dryden's changes.

Pope read Chaucer with pleasure all his life. Amongst his many 'imitations' of earlier poets (no anxiety of influence there) one of the earliest was the comic brief imitation of Chaucer already referred to, coarser than anything Chaucer ever wrote. Also when young (about the year 1704) Pope modernised *The Merchant's Tale*, published in Tonsen's *Miscellanies*, 1709, and *The Wife of Bath her Prologue*, published in Steele's *Miscellanies*, 1713 (both ed. Butt, 1963). The modernisation of *The General Prologue* to *The Canterbury Tales* and *The Reeve's Tale*, appeared in 1712 attributed to the actor Betterton but now generally attributed to Pope (Bowden, pp. 3–13).

In general Pope continues Dryden's line, but he is more modern than Dryden. In contrast to Dryden he sets his seal on 'bawdy Chaucer' with the schoolboyish sniggering at sex characteristic of such eighteenth-century writers as Sterne. He has less natural feeling for Chaucer's other characteristics than Dryden, is rather more anti-feminist, is more analytical, generalising and inclined to abbreviate. As an example we may take his translation of *The Reeve's Tale*. This is a fairly close one, which loses nothing of its bawdiness. But Pope does add some sentiment between Allen and the Miller's daughter, and changes the ending so that the Miller's wife persuades the Miller that nothing has happened. Pope probably found this change in Boccaccio's version of the same story. It is told with a touch of typically eighteenth-century antifeminism. Pope's style avoids the syntactically simple but powerful parataxis (that is, the connection of main clauses by 'and') which Chaucer often uses, and nowhere more effectively than in the fight in the bedroom (*The Canterbury Tales*, i. ll. 4292–307). In sixteen lines Chaucer uses the word 'and' twelve times, with the syntactically closely similar 'but' twice. This is again the restricted code, avoiding subordination of clauses, and hence avoiding explanation, cause and effect, analysis and division. As Spearing has noted in relation to Dryden, elegant variation is preferred to simple repetition, which was always avoided in the eighteenth century. Otherwise Pope does not change much. He keeps the general structure, but without the 'ands', so losing some of the sense of breathless speed and the comic climax, which he further dissipates by the un-Chaucerian (though quite medieval) ending.

In addition to what Pope had translated, there were eight versions of various *fabliau*-type tales published between 1712 and 1733, two of them being of *The Reeve's Tale*, two of *The Miller's Tale* and two of *The Shipman's Tale*, and one each of *Friar* and *Summoner*. In the eighteenth century, all told, there were seventeen translations of fabliaux, three of *The Squire's Tale*, two of *The Nun's Priest's Tale*, one of *The Clerk's Tale*, which demonstrates the taste for indecency of the fine gentlemen and ladies of the period.

These translations tell us more about the eighteenth century than about Chaucer. They cannot be taken seriously as considered views of how to read Chaucer, though they do have a rather subtle relationship with what Chaucer was thought to represent. If Chaucer's bawdy poems were not quite the key with which he unlocked his own or eighteenth-century hearts, they nevertheless touched a chord. They serve no argument for the relativism of poetic judgement: they are indeed Chaucer modernised, but also adapted, changed almost out of recognition. They do to Chaucer what Chaucer did to Boccaccio, and what other traditional writers like Shakespeare do to their sources, making them not new, but different. Those eighteenth-century readers who only read these modernisations may have had a different view of Chaucer from ours, but their views were based on at best indirect evidence.

The most extraordinary rendering of Chaucer is the anonymous version of *The Reeve's Tale* published in 1715. It is true that the unknown author claims to have written it thirty years before, so we may be libelling the eighteenth century by attributing this version to it. In tone the rendering has something in common with the writing of Sir John Mennis, the seventeenth-century dirty-minded courtier and rhymester (1591–1671) who was Pepys's colleague, who wrote Chaucerian imitations and who, according to Pepys, doted 'mightily' on Chaucer (Brewer, 1978, i. p. 154).

The Anonymous, in what he calls 'an Exercise upon Chaucer's Reeve's Tale', expands 404 lines to 2602. It is written in octosyllabics in mock-epic style, with much extra classical material (e.g. 543ff.), more superficial characterisation, more satire, more anti-feminism. A long and totally irrelevant dialogue between Allen and John on the nature of translation as well as of university studies is introduced. Equally irrelevant is the disgustingly scatological addition at 2365ff. As sometimes happens in popular comic tales, scatology tends to drive out sex.

A similar work is the translation of *The Shipman's Tale* by Henry Travers, an otherwise unremarkable clergyman, in 1731. As usual, there is more explanation, greater coarseness. An anachronistic social note of contempt for tradesmen is introduced. Sexuality is blurred, and scatology added. The vein of scatological humour is no doubt entirely human; but some societies, centuries and writers indulge it more than others. It is found in fifteenth- and sixteenth-century jest-books, especially German and Dutch ones. Rabelais and Cervantes, but not Shakespeare, indulge in it; so, rather notably, does the eighteenth century, with Pope, Swift, Smollett and to some extent Sterne. The nineteenth century is sternly clean. And so is Chaucer, apart from the rare joke about farting.

The story is not finished yet. I have remarked that Dryden refrained from translating Chaucer's *fabliau*-type tales, and that he quite specifically did not translate *The Wife of Bath's Prologue*, on the grounds that these works were too indecent. Many of the later versions of the bawdy tales, loose in every sense, make up for that. There were, however, other currents as well. In 1741 a hack writer, Samuel Boyse, produced a translation of *The Squire's Tale* which turns the princess Canace into a slightly tetchy eighteenth-century duchess, but at least gives a notion of the romance to be found in Chaucer. (Two very much later translations in 1794 and 1796 similarly transform Canace's relation to her servants, briefly and barely described by Chaucer, when she gets up at dawn.) Fussy detail, extra rationalisation, a touch of domestic comedy are added. Boyse also adds some very un-Chaucerian romantic scenery, as for example in lines 961–70, which begin:

> By Oxus' side, engirt with wood-brow'd hills
> A spacious compass lay the sylvan scene;
> Through which clear-streaming ran two mazy rills
> That fed the soil with ever-living green.

Here are the ideals of the eighteenth-century English landscape garden, as expounded by Repton and Kent.

In 1741 there appeared *The Canterbury Tales of Chaucer, Modernis'd by several Hands*, edited by George Ogle in 3 volumes. It was incomplete, but is perhaps an early hint of a concept of *The Canterbury Tales* as a whole, rather than as a collection of separate tales, for Ogle himself contributed translations of ten Prologues, which of course constitute links, to the *Tales*. The only tale he himself translated was *The Clerk's Tale*, with Prologue and Conclusion, which draws to an end the third volume. *The General Prologue*, and other tales which appear, are drawn from a variety of translators, except that Ogle substitutes his own version of *The General Prologue*, ll. 1–38, following this with Betterton's translation. Bowden assumes that Ogle intended to complete the set of *Canterbury Tales* with other translations, which would have been an advance; but for whatever reason he failed to do so, and died five years after publication. His project was sufficiently popular to be reprinted in Dublin the following year, presumably pirated, with the *Life of Chaucer* from Urry's edition added and wrongly attributed to Urry (2 vols, Dublin: George Faulkner, 1742). As a translator, Bowden notes that Ogle at least doubles the length of Chaucer's text, himself remarking that he added rather than diminished (Bowden, p. 80). *The Prologue to the Clerk of Oxford's Tale* is 82 lines long for Chaucer's 56, yet omits the grim Chaucerian remark that 'alle shul we dye' (iv. p. 38). It expands the flowery description of the countryside to which Chaucer's Clerk refers, only to condemn it as irrelevant, as does Ogle's version, self-contradictorily.

The tone of Ogle's version is well conveyed by the first two lines of the tale itself:

> Down at the foot of Vesulus the cold
> (Thus ancient bards the moral tale unfold) . . .

The second line serves only to distance and trivialise the story. It is followed by 12 lines of eighteenth-century, lush, hyperbolic description of landscape containing 14 adjectives, which render 5 lines by Chaucer containing 7 adjectives – for him an unusually high proportion. Here we learn more about the eighteenth-century picturesque (not unattractive in itself) than about Chaucer's quite different concentration on the 'delitable sighte' of agricultural prosperity.

Ogle wisely makes no attempt to render the rhyme-royal stanza of Chaucer's *Clerk's Tale*, but sticks to the ten-syllable couplet, and an un-Chaucerian, antithetical style. Thus when Griselda is freshly dressed for her wedding, Chaucer remarks

> Of which thise ladyes were not right glad
> To handle hir clothes wherinne she was clad   (iv. ll. 375–6)

Ogle makes of this, from l. 767 on:

> In flock the fair, to dress the rural maid
> On nuptials pleas'd to lend their useful aid:
> Some mov'd by duty; by good nature some:
> Some meditating marriages to come;
> And ruminating some on pleasures past:
> Some curious, and some envious: most, the last.
> But all, on entrance, loud surprise express'd,
> To see the courtly bride so country dress'd.
> For nobly born, and delicately bred,
> Her rude apparel rais'd a gen'ral dread.
> Such linen, never felt! seen garments such!
> So rough! so coarse! they almost swoon to touch.
> Deep principled in vain affected airs,
> Of framing fears, and counterfeiting cares;
> Of feigning woe, where they rejoice at heart;
> And pain dissembling, where they feel no smart

and so on for another 38 lines, to her hair being combed:

> And store they had of adventitious charms
> Rings for the hands, and bracelets for the arms;
> With pearly rows, with golden bands was grac'd
> The rising bosom, and the falling waist;
> And last a crown was plac'd upon her head,
> That prominent with gems a mingled lustre shed.   (ll. 821–7)

These last seven lines of Marie-Antoinette medievalism translate Chaucer's:

> A corowne on hire heed they han ydressed,
> And sette hire ful of nowches grete and smale.
> Of hire array what sholde I make a tale?   (iv. ll. 381–3)

Well might Chaucer ask. Ogle's exuberance makes sixty-five lines of

115

eighteenth-century social comedy out of Chaucer's terse but pregnant five. It can be argued that his expansion does, unlike some, illustrate the rich density, the power of implication and suggestion, that a sympathetic reader with some imagination can find in Chaucer's apparent simplicity and bareness. Chaucer's inner power, which is unlike that of the Romantic poet's evocative associationism, and Chaucer's centrality of comment, combined with his 'essentialism', are paradoxically suggested by a comparison. Yet still, when all this is said, for the very reason of its anachronistic explicitness what we have is very unlike Chaucer's work. Such a judgement is not merely relative to a late-twentieth-century reading. It is a transcultural truth, based on the objective factor of the number of lines, though going beyond such unequivocal simplicity.

Ogle latinises Walter's name to Gualtherus and the Earl of Panyk to Penagius, presumably to add dignity. He adds moralising comments, and, at the end, has the son and daughter of Penagius (who, with his wife, Walter's sister, has fostered Griselda's daughter and son) marry Griselda's children, thus rendering more specific the vaguely mentioned 'fortunate marriages' referred to by Chaucer, and adding another personally sentimentalised touch. Thus what is in origin a folk-tale, with all the power and extravagance of the genre, having already been made perilously realistic by Chaucer, is made yet more realistic, moralistic, sentimental and improbable by Ogle.

It is easy enough to contrast in poetic achievement these well-intentioned but modestly talented enthusiasts with one of the greatest poets in English. We need not deny them some entertainment value in an eighteenth-century fashion. We note the underlying cultural changes. Ogle, in this respect like Dryden, is, when compared with Chaucer, much more descriptive, Romantic in taste, superficially more realistic, more cynical, more patronisingly – or patriarchally – satirical of women. He is interested, though somewhat trivially, in the inner life of characters, their motives, thoughts and feelings. Chaucer is remarkable in his own time for developing such an interest, but expresses it much more rarely, and when he does it is penetratingly brief.

Ogle's work as evidence of reader-response shows a cheerful disregard for many of Chaucer's characteristics. He shows a generally warm response to a tale which is refreshingly different from the continuous repetition of the bawdy tales. Ogle gives Griselda something of her due, even if he indulges in the fashionable eighteenth-century sneers about women, and concludes with a final sneer, not in Chaucer, retracting the praise of Griselda to, of women, 'a few' (1868, cf. iv. l. 938).

Medieval rhetoric was much stronger on amplification than abbreviation, and Chaucer himself was no mean amplifier in *Troilus and Criseyde*. His eighteenth-century modernisers worked, albeit unconsciously, in the same vein, as already illustrated. An even stronger example is offered by one of the other modernisers in Ogle's 1741 volume, Henry Brooke, who modernised *The Man of Law's Tale* and who has a taste for the sentimental rather than the bawdy. Bowden points out that for Chaucer's line 'Allas, Custance, thou hast no champioun' (ii. l. 631), Brooke supplies some 500; he 'has king Alla issue a call for a champion, and has Constantia despair the next day on her funeral pyre until a mysterious black knight appears to slay the false accuser (with God's help) and then lift his helm to reveal ... King Alla, now her husband-to-be' (Bowden, p. 119). This is exactly the kind of medieval romance theme which Chaucer avoids and repudiates, as for example in *Sir Thopas* and his jest about Sir Lancelot (*The Squire's Tale, The Canterbury Tales*, v. 1. 287) – which last, needless to say, finds no place in Samuel Boyse's gushing account.

With other digressions, the 1064 lines of Chaucer's *Man of Law's Tale* are rendered in 1828 lines by Brooke. Romance digression is flavoured with epic simile, classicising touches of style, and abstract for concrete nouns. Thus Chaucer's beginning

> O hateful harm, condicion of poverte
> With thurst, with coold, with hunger so confounded   (ii. ll. 99–100)

is translated:

> Hence Want, ungrateful visitant, adieu!
> Pale empress hence, with all thy meager crew –
> Sour Discontent, and mortified Chagrin,
> Lean hollow Care, and self-corroding Spleen;
> Distress and Woe, sad parents of Despair
> With wringing hands, and ever rueful air

and so forth. *The Prologe of the Mannes Tale of Lawe* has 35 lines, rendered by Brooke in 169 in the same empty, overblown style. Chaucer's sharp apostrophe, with its mixture of abrupt English monosyllables and Latinate complexities, has a poetic power never to be obtained by vapid adornments. The contrast between Chaucer's style and his eighteenth-century translator's is to this extent instructive: it adds to our understanding of Chaucer by showing what his poetry is not. It cannot be claimed that this is how the translators and their contemporaries actually read Chaucer. More likely, the exigencies of rhyme, the attraction of being paid for extra length, the desire to liven old Chaucer up with a modern touch or two, such as descriptions to modern taste, were stronger motives than an unconscious response to Chaucer's text. Maybe they thought that this was how Chaucer ought to have written – that is, like an eighteenth-century rhymester. If so, they were mistaken. Yet, as Bowden shows, these versions were reprinted and thus presumably popular, along with those of Dryden and Pope.

The translations have a cheerful, carefree tone, free from the anxiety of influence or scholarship or much interest in Chaucer's original. Their attitude is summed up by Andrew Jackson, an amusing and original London bookseller who translated the Wife of Bath's portrait in *The General Prologue* and her *Prologue*, and the *Shipman's* and *Manciple's Tales*, in 1750: he had rescued the living from the dead, he says:

> And what was *Sterling Verse* so long ago
> Is here *new-coin'd* to make it *Current* now   (Bowden, p. 151).

The first serious attempt to give a more comprehensive account of Chaucer's 'new-coined Verse', and to include some prose, was made in 1795, when William Lipscomb published eleven prologues and tales, plus *The Squire's Prologue*, having already published *The Pardoner's Prologue and Tale* in 1792 plus the tales in Ogle, that is, almost the whole of *The Canterbury Tales*, by adding a dozen of his own to Ogle's collection of 1741. Although Lipscomb still alters and adapts in eighteenth-century mode, he really seems to be trying to give a general idea of *The Canterbury Tales* as a whole, perhaps inspired by Tyrwhitt's edition. It is quite significant that he translates the whole long, prose, moralising *Tale of Melibeus*, along with Biblical references. But by the same token he omits the *Miller's* and *Reeve's Tales*, though admitting the *Shipman's* (for which inclusion one reviewer blamed him). In this last respect we see a reflection of the continuing debate about the acceptability of Chaucer's indecency, with the bias now moving not to a different view of Chaucer, but to a different taste, and a readiness to reject what it is agreed is actually there.

There seems no case to argue that Lipscomb read Chaucer differently from earlier eighteenth-century writers. He read him in the same way, but instead of approving and expanding on indecency, he disapproved. A different view of Chaucer was to that extent available to ordinary readers who did not read the original, except that the older translations were still around.

A single, anonymous version of *The Miller's Tale* also appeared in 1791, of which apparently only one copy survives. This is preceded by a very sensible and frank discussion of the question of indecency. It is a quite close translation, but the writer says specifically, in words which are very delicately expressed, that he has softened the original thought to 'cloath it in language, the most delicate I could find, to express an event so indelicately singular' (Bowden, p. 169).

Bowden's labours have collected various other renderings, including an anonymous one of 1769, which is quite remarkable and unique in that it shortens a tale, that of *The Nun's Priest of the Cock and Fox* and one which is notably digressive in Chaucer, to a mere 68 lines, by severe surgery which cuts off even the escape of Chanticleer (Bowden, pp. 165–6). Something of Chaucer (referred to as 'sage Chaucer' in the first line) survives in its flippancy, description and dialogue. Because it is so abbreviated, the poem gives a less distorted view of Chaucer than do the expanded versions, with their multiple un-Chaucerian additions; but the view is a mere glimpse.

Wordsworth records of himself that as an undergraduate at Cambridge between 1787 and 1791, at Trumpington in the hawthorn shade he laughed with Chaucer and heard him tell his tales of amorous passion (*The Prelude*, ed. E. De Selincourt, Oxford, 1926; 1805 version, ll. 276–9). The reference must be to *The Reeve's Tale*, whose action takes place in Trumpington, while the plural indicates that he read the other bawdy tales as well. He may well have read them in one of the eighteenth-century versions, for in later life he claimed that he first became acquainted with Chaucer's poems through the set of *Works of the British Poets* published by Anderson in 1795 and left with him by his brother John in September 1800 (*The Poetical Works of William Wordsworth*, ed. E. De Selincourt and Helen Darbyshire, Oxford, 1949, iv. p. 443). On the other hand, he seems to have written this part of *The Prelude* in 1801, and may have projected a current interest back to an earlier period. In December 1801 the Wordsworths read Chaucer with the enthusiasm of discoverers. From 2 to 9 December Dorothy Wordsworth records her reading Chaucer, beginning with *The Manciple's Tale*, and going on to *Palemon and Arcite*, and *The Tale of Constance and the Syrian Monarch* in *The Man of Law's Tale*. They resumed from 22 to 26 December, when Dorothy read aloud *The Miller's Tale*. During these days William translated *The Manciple's Tale, The Prioress's Tale*, the apocryphal *Cuckoo and the Nightingale*, and, though not noted by Dorothy, *Troilus and Criseyde* v. ll. 519–686. The choice of poems to translate reflects the mature Wordsworth's taste for sobriety of sentiment, love in nature, the pathos of suffering. The translations are close and accurate within the constraints of modern verse form, and much less strikingly deviant than earlier versions. Perhaps they are so good because Wordsworth's poetic enthusiasm was only responding to the topics, not moulding them. The other poems read by Dorothy show the admirable range of Chaucer's verse, from serious to comic, which they both enjoyed.

Wordsworth fittingly matches Dryden in poetic greatness to conclude the century Dryden began, though Wordsworth's translations were not published till 1820, and *The Manciple's Tale*, at the request of friends who thought it immoral, was never published. (Wordsworth's comment on the poem, *Works*, 1949, iv. p. 471, is very perceptive.) Both poets share the characteristics of the two centuries that they respectively bridged, pointing both before and behind. The story of Chaucer's reception as a whole in the eighteenth century, as revealed in translation, is that of a more accurate understanding of his text, despite the extravagances of the earlier part of the century. But as true understanding and enjoyment increase, so poetic influence as such decreases. For all Wordsworth's greater accuracy of translation, there seems more than a century's distance between him and Dryden in their response to Chaucer. Paradoxically, the irrelevant gusto even of some of the wilder eighteenth-century versions of the bawdy tales may suggest a more spontaneous response released by reading Chaucer. The translators saw some opportunities he appears to point to, and the translations consequently suggest a more creative poetic influence exerted by his work than is found in the more accurate, cooler reception of the nineteenth century. Maybe it is true that, as Wordsworth says, 'We murder to dissect': an alarming thought for 'scientific' literary criticism. Poets, even penny-a-line versifiers, are at liberty to misinterpret; perhaps, as Harold Bloom some time ago suggested, it is necessary for them to do so.

Works Cited

Bernstein, Basil, *Class, Codes and Control*, i (2nd edn, London, 1974)

Bloom, Harold, *The Anxiety of Influence* (New York, 1973)

Boitani, Piero, 'The Genius to Improve an Invention', in Morse and Windeatt, *Chaucer Traditions*, pp. 185–98

Bowden, Betsy, *Eighteenth-Century Modernisations from* The Canterbury Tales (Cambridge, 1991)

Brewer, Derek, *Chaucer: The Critical Heritage*, i (London, 1978)
———— 'Chaucer's Poetic Style', in *The Cambridge Chaucer Companion*, ed. Piero Boitani and Jill Mann (Cambridge, 1990)

Butt, John (ed.), *The Poems of Alexander Pope* (London, 1963)

Morse, Ruth and Windeatt, Barry (eds), *Chaucer Traditions* (Cambridge, 1990)

Spearing, A. C., 'Rewriting Romance: Chaucer's and Dryden's *Wife of Bath's Tale*', in *ibid.*, pp. 234–49

Spurgeon, Caroline F. E. (ed.), *Five Hundred Years of Chaucer Criticism and Allusion 1357–1900* (3 vols, Cambridge, 1925)

The American Middle Ages:
Eighteenth-Century Saxonist Myth-Making

LAURA KENDRICK

'But America didn't have a Middle Ages! Why should an American, of all people, be a medievalist?' This question was posed to me by my French relatives, who assume that study of the past is not done out of any gratuitous curiosity. Why, indeed, does an American think it perfectly 'natural' to study the Middle Ages? Why are there thousands of medievalists teaching on American campuses (often at least partially built in Gothic revival styles)?[1] In the late eighteenth and nineteenth centuries Europeans discovered their national identities in their medieval histories, but how can Americans do the same? Not only is American history not supposed to 'start' until after the European Middle Ages were ending, but it is supposed to begin in opposition to them. As the historical *doxa* goes, the 'New World' provided for its European settlers an escape from the 'Old World' still burdened by the remnants of its medieval past and feudal institutions.

But what does it mean to 'have' a Middle Ages? Lynn White argued, in a 1965 essay, that 'a blind spot in the study of the history of the United States is failure to recognize our detailed and massive continuity with the European Middle Ages' even to the point that 'today the United States is closer to the Middle Ages than is Europe'.[2] Because many of the everyday tools and technologies of the American frontier, from log cabins to covered wagons, barbed wire and whisky were inventions of the Middle Ages, White considered that the Middle Ages 'lived on' in the West. Although my own field of investigation here is the American historical

---

[1] In its peak year of enrolment, 1978, the Medieval Academy of America, the largest professional organisation for medievalists, counted 3,901 members, almost all resident in the US and Canada. See Luke Wenger, 'The Medieval Academy and Medieval Studies in North America', *Medieval Studies in North America: Past, Present, and Future*, ed. Francis G. Gentry and Christopher Kleinhenz (Kalamazoo, Mich.: Medieval Institute Publications, 1982), p. 25.

[2] Lynn White, 'The Legacy of the Middle Ages in the American Wild West', *Speculum*, 40 (1965), p. 191.

imagination, and not the history of technology, I too have come to the paradoxical-seeming conclusion that America *did* have a Middle Ages, by which I mean not only that Americans developed their own peculiar understandings of the European Middle Ages, but that they imaginatively transplanted the Middle Ages to the American continent. To be sure, the American Middle Ages are a fabrication – just as are, to some extent, all stories of the past, all histories. That the American Middle Ages were invented rather than real is less important, in many respects, than that they were invented at all.

Upon closer inspection, it turns out that some of the most important contributors to a myth of the American Middle Ages are those same Americans whom we remember for their calls for separation from Europe and the European past – men such as Thomas Jefferson, writer of the Declaration of Independence, and Ralph Waldo Emerson, who, in 'The Poet' (1844) and 'The American Scholar' (1841) tried to declare the independence of American letters. Upon the foundations of pre-existing European inventions of the medieval past, many of which they borrowed, these same Americans and many others have constructed a myth of an American Middle Ages in which 'Anglo-Saxons' replayed the period from 300 to 1500 and, in so doing, 'rectified' the errors of European history.

The myth of the American Middle Ages bears a certain resemblance to the myth of America as Eden and of the American of European ancestry as a new Adam, beginning history over again in a fresh 'American' Garden of Paradise.[3] The new beginning is imagined as a return to an idealised past, a time before 'corruption' set in. But, whereas the myth of the American as Adam is fully primitivist and turns the historical 'clock' back to Edenic zero, thereby erasing the presence of the original Indian inhabitants of the Americas, the myth of the American Middle Ages turns the historical 'clock' back only part-way, to reset it in the 'middle', in a period identified as a time of transition and struggle. As opposed to the myth of the American as Adam, the myth of the American as 'Saxon' could take account of conflict between the new inhabitants of America and the original ones, between European immigrants or their descendants and the Indians, between 'Saxons' and 'Americans' (for the latter name was not commonly used to identify anyone other than Indians until well into the nineteenth century).

In the imagination of the myth-makers the globe was a kind of clock, with the ages in the civilisation of man marked around its girth, so that, by moving westward against the direction of the earth's rotation, one moved 'back in time' to a more primitive stage of human history.[4] As Thomas

---

[3] R. W. B. Lewis, in *The American Adam* (Chicago: University of Chicago Press, 1955), discovered this myth prevalent in American literature of the period from 1820 to 1860.

[4] In the sixteenth and seventeenth centuries some fine clocks were made in the form of a

Jefferson put it in a letter to William Ludlow of 6 September 1824, a man travelling eastwards from the Rocky Mountains to the East Coast would see the equivalent of 'a survey, in time, of the progress of man from the infancy of creation to the present day':

> the savages of the Rocky Mountains . . . he would observe in the earliest stage of association living under no law but that of nature, subscribing and covering themselves with the flesh and skins of wild beasts. He would next find those on our frontiers in the pastoral state, raising domestic animals to supply the defects of hunting. Then succeed our own semi-barbarous citizens, the pioneers of the advance of civilization, and so in his progress he would meet the gradual shades of improving man until he would reach his, as yet, most improved state in our seaport towns.[5]

In the so-called 'progress of civilisation westward', the settlements of the American frontier represented a kind of middle state, between contemporary European civilisation to their east and a primitive savagery to their west. On this imaginary time-line the American frontier was imagined as a sort of revival of the early Middle Ages in Britain: just as the legendary Saxons Horsa and Hengist and their followers, beginning in the fifth century, had pushed the supposedly more primitive, 'painted' Picts and the original 'British' from Britain and established democratic institutions that would reach full flower under King Alfred, so the freedom-loving ancestors of these ancient Saxons, a remnant of the old race, migrated to America and drove out the more primitive, 'painted' Indians (the native 'Americans') in order to establish democratic institutions.

The analogies between American Indians and the native inhabitants of Britain prior to the Saxon invasion had been drawn in the literal sense of the term as early as the late sixteenth century, when the Virginia pioneer

celestial globe encircled about its 'equator' by a calibrated calendar ring; such globe-clocks are often depicted in paintings of this period next to clocks with two-dimensional round faces and other instruments for measuring time. Even sundials might take the form of a globe. For example, in an engraving from 1720, a pedestalled sundial-globe has hours marked in Roman numerals about its circumference. This method of spatialising time as the unidirectional progress of a marker around a circle or globe suggests that the past is a *place* left behind. Logically, then, to reverse the direction of movement around the circle or globe is to *go back in time*. The spatial location of the Americas, far to the west of Europe, provided an opportunity for eighteenth-century primitivists to represent what was happening in the present as if it were happening in the past, thereby powerfully conflating cultural with chronological primitivism. Photographs of early timepieces collected in museums and represented in paintings may be found in *The Clockwork Universe: German Clocks and Automata, 1550–1650*, ed. Claus Maurice and Otto Mayr (New York: Neale Watson, 1980), figs 113–16; and Alfred Chapuis, *De horologiis in arte* (Lausanne: Scriptor, 1954), plates 81, 92, 94, 127. On the distinction between cultural and chronological primitivisms, see Arthur O. Lovejoy and George Boas, *Primitivism and Related Ideas in Antiquity* (1935; New York: Octagon, 1965), pp. 1–11.

5 *The Writings of Thomas Jefferson*, ed. Andrew A. Libscomb and Albert Ellery Bergh, 20 vols (Washington, DC: Jefferson Memorial Association, 1903–7), xvi. p. 74.

John White supplemented pictures of naked and tatooed American Indians with pictures of similarly naked and tatooed early Europeans (but without any identifying labels). Illustrators who imitated his models interpreted his tattooed, naked Europeans as early Picts ('painted men') and Britons, and named them so. The primitive condition of the ancient Britons was institutionalised in 1611, in the illustrations accompanying John Speed's *Historie of Great Britanie*, as well as in the title page of his *Theatre*, where the ancient Briton is naked and painted like an Indian, and the Roman, Saxon, Dane and Norman distinguish themselves by their 'baroque plumes and swagger clothes'.[6] The progressive movement of 'democracy and civilisation' westward across the American continent was imagined after the mythical image of Britain's 'democratisation' by the Saxons, who arrived on her coast and gradually pushed the natives westward and northward.

The similarity between native Britons and American Indians was an Enlightenment truism by 1770, when Bishop Percy compared the two in the preface to his translation of Mallet, *Northern Antiquities*: 'The ancient Britons in the time of Caesar painted their bodies, as do the present Cherokees of North America, because it would naturally enough occur to the wild people of every country, that by this practice they might render themselves terrible to their enemies.'[7] The very banality of such a comparison was emphasised by the Scottish historian William Robertson in his *History of America* in 1777:

> In every part of the earth the progress of man hath been nearly the same, and we can trace him in his career from the rude simplicity of savage life, until he attains the industry, the arts, and the elegance of polished society. There is nothing wonderful then in the similitude between the Americans and the barbarous nations of our continent.[8]

The analogies of Enlightenment anthropology made it possible to imagine the settlement of the American continent as a replay of earlier British history, beginning with the conquest of the ancient Britons by the Saxons. Imagined as a temporal borderline between savagery and contemporary civilisation, the mythical American Middle Ages gradually moved westward across the continent.

One of the major inventors of the myth of the American Middle Ages

6 See T. D. Kendrick, *British Antiquity* (London: Methuen, 1950), p. 125 and plates 12–16.
7 Paul Henri Mallet, *Northern Antiquities*, trans. Bishop Thomas Percy, i (London, 1770), p. 8.
8 William Robertson, *The History of America*, i (London, 1777), p. 268. For further seventeenth- and eighteenth-century comparisons between culturally 'primitive' tribes in the New World and historically ancient or early medieval European peoples, see Margaret T. Hodgen, *Early Anthropology in the Sixteenth and Seventeenth Centuries* (Philadelphia: University of Pennsylvania Press, 1964), pp. 343–9.

was Thomas Jefferson, whom we like to remember as an Enlightenment thinker, a man who idealised Reason and Natural Law and granted these greater authority than historical precedent. Yet it was Jefferson who proposed, in August 1776, that the Great Seal of the United States, an emblem of national authority, be engraved with two mythico-historical scenes that he saw as sanctifying and justifying precedents for migration, conquest and the founding of a new nation. On one side of the seal he proposed an engraving of 'the children of Israel in the wilderness, led by a cloud by day and pillar of fire by night', a scene that would provide divine sanction for the new American nation; and on the other side of the seal, in order to provide a secular or legal justification by analogy, he proposed an engraving which he described as follows: 'Hengist and Horsa, the Saxon chiefs from whom we claim the honor of being descended, and whose political principles and form of government we have assumed'.[9] In his *A Summary View of the Rights of British America* (1774), Jefferson had already used the Saxon precedent to argue for the 'natural' right under 'universal law' of a people to leave their native land and set up a free government elsewhere. He had reminded the British that their Saxon ancestors

> had . . ., in like manner, left their native wilds and woods in the North of Europe, had possessed themselves of the island of Britain then less charged with inhabitants, and had established there that system of laws which has so long been the glory and protection of that country . . . Nor was ever any claim of superiority or dependance asserted over them by that mother country from which they had migrated: and were such a claim made it is believed his majesty's subjects in Great Britain have too firm a feeling of the rights derived to them from their ancestors to bow down the sovereignty of their state before such visionary pretensions. And it is thought that no circumstance has occurred to distinguish materially the British from the Saxon emigration.[10]

Jefferson took the Saxon myth very seriously, not only as a historical precedent for American Independence, but also, due to the high value he

[9] *The Papers of Thomas Jefferson*, ed. Julian P. Boyd, i (Princeton: Princeton University Press, 1950), pp. 494–5. This information comes from a letter John Adams wrote to his wife on 14 August 1776. The proposal Jefferson officially recorded as his own was merely a slightly different *mise-en-scène* of Franklin's original proposal for one side of the seal: Moses calling down God's wrath on Pharaoh in the act of pursuing the Israelites across the Red Sea. Jefferson apparently abandoned the 'children of Israel in the wilderness' for the greater political impact of Franklin's proposed image, which was to be accompanied by the motto 'Rebellion to tyrants is obedience to God'. Hengist and Horsa were dropped as well – in favour of a less exclusive representation of origins. The artist whom the committee consulted for the other side of the seal, and whose plan they adopted, suggested a coat of arms that was a composite of the emblems of 'the Six principal nations of Europe from whom the Americans have originated'.

[10] *Papers*, pp. 121–2.

placed on Saxon 'democracy', as a moral sanction for the conquest of native populations.[11]

In a letter written at the time of this proposition for the Great Seal, Jefferson reflected upon the Saxon precedent:

> Are we not the better for what we have hitherto abolished of the feudal system? Has not every restitution of the antient Saxon laws had happy effects? Is it not better now that we return at once into that happy system of our ancestors, the wisest and most perfect ever yet devised by the wit of man, as it stood before the 8th century?[12]

The writer of the Declaration of Independence wanted to 'restore' and revitalise, in the new American setting, pre-eighth-century 'Saxon' laws he believed had been corrupted over the course of subsequent British history, beginning with the imposition of feudal law at the Norman Conquest. Toward the end of *A Summary View* Jefferson rejected as inappropriate the application of 'corrupted' post-Conquest British law in America, on the grounds that 'America was not conquered by William the Norman, nor its lands surrendered to him, or any of his successors'.[13] Jefferson was not alone in the belief that America offered a chance to do history right this time by preserving Saxon liberty and democracy.[14]

Quite a few of the men we call 'revolutionary forefathers' would have denied, at least in public, that they were radical innovators and claimed to

---

[11] It is by no means clear that Benjamin Franklin was as ardent a Saxonist as Jefferson. The year before Jefferson's *A Summary View*, Benjamin Franklin exploited the Saxon example in his satirical proclamation of 22 September 1773, 'An Edict by the King of Prussia', wherein the King of Prussia announces his intention to put money in his coffers by taxing and regulating English commerce and manufactures for the sole reason that Hengist and Horsa, the fifth-century colonisers of Britain, had been German subjects: 'WHEREAS it is well known to all the World, that the first German Settlements made in the Island of Britain, were by Colonies of People, Subjects to our renowned Ducal Ancestors, and drawn from *their* Dominions, under the Conduct of Hengist, Horsa, Hella, Uffa, Cerdicus, Ida, and others; and that the said Colonies have flourished'. By calling the long roll of increasingly silly-sounding Saxon conquerors' names, Franklin tends to ridicule the Saxon myth along with any English imperial claims based on such flimsy historical precedents. According to a mightily amused Franklin, British readers of the London newspaper where he published the 'Edict' did not find it preposterous from the outset, but were *'taken in*, till they had got half through it' – that is, way past the 'colonisation' of Britain by Hengist, Horsa and the rest. See *The Papers of Benjamin Franklin*, ed. William B. Willcox, xx (New Haven: Yale University Press, 1976), pp. 415, 438.

[12] 'To Edmund Pendleton,' 13 August 1776, *Papers*, p. 492.

[13] *Papers*, p. 133.

[14] For a brief account of the Saxonism of the revolutionary generation in America, see Reginald Horsman, *Race and Manifest Destiny: The Origins of American Racial Anglo-Saxonism* (Cambridge, Mass.: Harvard University Press, 1981), pp. 15–25; fuller accounts may be found in H. Trevor Colbourn, *The Lamp of Experience: Whig History and the Intellectual Origins of the American Revolution* (Chapel Hill: University of North Carolina Press, 1965) and Bernard Bailyn, *The Ideological Origins of the American Revolution* (Cambridge, Mass.: Harvard University Press, 1967).

be revolutionary only in the etymological sense of this term, which derives from Latin *revolvere* ('to roll back'). In America, they attempted to roll back the historical clock to an earlier time. Richard Bland went only so far in 1766 as to suggest, in his *An Inquiry into the Rights of the British Colonies*, that 'it would be a Work worthy of the best patriotick Spirits in the Nation [England and its colonies] to effectuate an Alteration in this putrid Part of the [English] Constitution . . . by restoring it to its pristine Perfection' or 'original Purity'. As Bland stated in the beginning of the *Inquiry*, the time of this 'original Purity' was when the Saxons conquered and democratised Britain, when 'every Freeholder was a Member of their Wittinagemot, or Parliament', when every landowner had a say in government.[15] George Mason urged his fellows in the Fairfax Independent Company (militia), in April of 1775, to 'cherish the sacred deposit' of Saxon liberty, for America had become 'the only great nursery of freemen now left on the face of the earth'.[16] Rhetoric based on these same assumptions continued on America's shores long after the declaration of the country's independence. For example, in 1790, in a series of lectures on law, the first of which was attended by President Washington and the officers of the Federal Government, James Wilson argued that 'the common law, as now received in America, bears, in its principles, and in many of its more minute particulars, a stronger and a fairer resemblance to the common law as it was improved under the Saxons, than to that law as it was disfigured under the Norman government'.[17] To Wilson, the constitution of the United States 'renewed' the ancient English constitution.

If the Revolutionary forefathers claimed to be reviving and saving early Saxon liberty and democracy for the world, while its corruption continued in England (and it had already been eradicated entirely in Northern European absolutist monarchies, as Robert Molesworth pointed out in his 1694 *Account of Denmark*),[18] yet these American patriots did not invent the Saxon myth out of whole cloth. They merely adapted an already extant myth to American circumstances. Britain had a long history of idealising the 'Saxon' period in order to authorise and sanction real changes by presenting them as restorations, that is, returns to an original, pure state, before corruption set in. It was for the purpose of sanctioning and justifying

[15] Richard Bland, *An Inquiry into the Rights of the British Colonies* (Williamsburgh, 1766), pp. 7, 11–12.

[16] *The Papers of George Mason, 1725–1792*, ed. Robert A. Rutland, i (Chapel Hill: University of North Carolina Press, 1970), p. 231. Mason quotes this phrase from an unnamed 'learned and revered writer' who Rutland suggests 'may have been "Junius", the contemporary Whig partisan who contrasted British corruption with American virtue' (p. 232).

[17] *The Works of James Wilson*, ed. Robert Green McCloskey, i (Cambridge, Mass.: Harvard University Press, 1967), p. 348.

[18] Robert Molesworth, *An Account of Denmark as It Was in the Year 1692* (London, 1694), 'Preface,' b7v–b8v.

the institutional and doctrinal changes involved in the English Reformation that sixteenth-century British antiquarians, such as the Anglican Archbishop Matthew Parker, turned to the investigation of Old English manuscripts, wherein they tended to 'discover' what they themselves projected there: the purity of the 'primitive' Church before its corruption by Roman influence, and the introduction of 'heretical' doctrines such as clerical celibacy, transubstantiation, auricular confession – in short, all those aspects of the Roman Catholic Church to which Protestant reformers objected. Reformers such as John Foxe, in the English version of his *Actes and Monumentes*, published in 1570, and filled with quotations from newly edited Old English manuscripts, argued that the 'true' religion was brought to England during the days of the Primitive Church, and survived there in a pure form until the late-sixth-century arrival of Pope Gregory's Roman Catholic missionaries, who gradually set about displacing it. Old English documents that did not support the Reformers' views were dismissed as corrupt, and 'pure' ones imagined in their place. Foxe argued that, especially in the period immediately following the Norman Conquest, 'papists' had destroyed most of the Old English documents of the primitive English church, while at the same time altering and revising others in 'heretical' (Roman Catholic) ways.[19] The idealisation of a Saxon church that preserved the purity of primitive Christianity was a way of justifying change by disguising it as a return to origins.

In America, the Saxon example was used to justify the complete separation of Church and State (an eventuality that sixteenth-century British antiquarians, such as Archbishop Matthew Parker, would certainly not have condoned). American patriots simply took the Anglican arguments about the corruption of extant documents one step further. According to Jefferson, King Alfred's codification of common law had been corrupted by some pious monkish copyist. In a letter of 5 June 1824 to the radical British Saxonist John Cartwright, Jefferson concluded a long exposition on this fraud:

> and I might go on further to shew, how some of the Anglo-Saxon priests interpolated into the text of Alfred's laws, the 20th, 21st and 23rd chapters of Exodus, and the 15th of the Acts of the Apostles, from the 23rd to the 29th verses. But this would lead my pen and your patience too far. What a conspiracy this, between Church and State! Sing Tantarara, rogues all, rogues all, Sing Tantarara, rogues all![20]

Such clerical forgeries Jefferson believed to be the source of the mistaken

[19] Foxe's theories are discussed in Allen J. Frantzen, *Desire for Origins: New Language, Old English, and Teaching the Tradition* (New Brunswick, NJ: Rutgers University Press, 1990), pp. 39–40.

[20] *Writings*, xvi. pp. 50–1. The readings upon which Jefferson drew for such arguments are detailed by Colbourn, *The Lamp of Experience*, pp. 160–71.

conception that there had ever been an alliance between Church and State in Saxon England. Christianity had no part in the 'ancient Saxon constitution' that Jefferson and other revolutionaries purported to restore, in its original purity, in America.[21]

Whereas sixteenth-century British reformers constructed the myth of a pure proto-Protestant, Saxon church, free of Rome (but not of the Saxon secular government), seventeenth- and eighteenth-century British scholars and politicians, bent on reforming British political institutions in the direction of a more limited monarchy and broader representation, sought historical precedents in the 'Saxon' past once again, but this time in its secular rather than religious institutions. Their strategy for justifying change was to deny that novelty – a new state of affairs – was its aim; instead, they claimed that change was necessary only for the purpose of restoring a prior, better state, in this case the lost and corrupted liberties and democracy that had once belonged to their Saxon ancestors prior to the Norman conquest of England.[22]

The myth of Saxon democracy did not have its beginning in Britain, much less in America. It began in Rome, when Tacitus chose to criticise Roman decadence implicitly by idealising, really rather moderately, the individual virtues and civic institutions of the German tribes, especially their election and limitation of the authority of their kings and their vestment of power to decide important matters in regularly held general assemblies.[23] French Protestant writers of the sixteenth century, such as

---

[21] In this same letter to John Cartwright, which he begins by congratulating Cartwright for his book pointing out the English constitution's 'rightful root, the Anglo-Saxon', Jefferson notes that the American Constitution is *not* the product of erudite legal research, but rather the expression of natural law written in 'our hearts': 'Our Revolution commenced on more favorable ground. It presented us an album on which we were free to write what we pleased. We had no occasion to search into musty records, to hunt up royal parchments, or to investigate the laws and institutions of a semi-barbarous ancestry. We appealed to those of nature, and found them engraved on our hearts' (*Writings*, xvi. pp. 43–4). However, because Jefferson regarded the hearts and natures of the American Constitution's framers as 'Saxon', the 'law of nature' that they discovered in their hearts was ancient Saxon law.

[22] In his chapter entitled 'The Norman Yoke' in *Puritanism and Revolution: Studies in Interpretation of the English Revolution of the Seventeenth Century* (London: Secker and Warburg, 1958), Christopher Hill summarises the seventeenth-century English version of the Saxon myth thus: 'Before 1066 the Anglo-Saxon inhabitants of this country lived as free and equal citizens, governing themselves through representative institutions. The Norman Conquest deprived them of this liberty, and established the tyranny of an alien King and landlords. But the people did not forget the rights they had lost. They fought continuously to recover them, with varying success. Concessions (Magna Carta, for instance) were from time to time extorted from their rulers, and always the tradition of lost Anglo-Saxon freedom was a stimulus to ever more insistent demands upon the successors of the Norman usurpers' (p. 57).

[23] Limitation of kingship is treated briefly in chapter 7 of *Germania*, and public assemblies in chapter 11. On the classical tradition of idealising 'hard primitives', see 'The Noble Savage in Antiquity' in Lovejoy and Boas, *Primitivism and Related Ideas in Antiquity*.

François Hotman in his Latin *Franco-Gallia* (1573), which was translated into English in 1711 by Robert Molesworth, embroidered upon Tacitus' account of the democratic institutions of the Germans. Hotman equated Tacitus' Germans with the Franks, and went on to describe their liberation of Gaul from Roman 'oppression' (an allegory for Roman Catholic oppression) and their supposed investment of supreme power in an annual general council of the nation or 'Parliament of the Three Estates', whose supreme authority he traced through the Capetian dynasty down to Louis XI in 1467.[24] It was not until nearly two centuries later that Montesquieu wrote, in *De l'esprit des lois*, that the government of the Germans as described in Tacitus had evolved into the parliamentary government of Great Britain, 'that beautiful system . . . devised in the woods'[25] – a felicitous phrase that echoes through subsequent Saxonist writing and was especially appreciated by revolutionary American writers, who thought the 'woods' of the New World to be the right place for reviving Saxon democracy.

By the mid-seventeenth century in England, Tacitus' *Germania* was no longer the only account used to puff up the reputation of the Saxons. Antiquarians had discovered medieval documents such as the late-thirteenth-century *Mirror for Justices* and the fourteenth-century *Manner for Holding Parliament*, documents that (out of medieval partisan motives not taken into consideration) idealised or invented Saxon parliamentary customs. English jurists such as Edward Coke argued, on the basis of these documents, that the Norman Conquest had curtailed Anglo-Saxon institutions such as a bi-cameral parliament including representatives from the shires and boroughs.[26] However, it was the exiled Huguenot Paul Rapin de Thoyras's *History of England*, first published in French in 1724 and then in a very widely read English translation by Tindal in 1726, that seems to have done most to establish the reputation of the Saxons in England and America. This *History*, in its English version, advertised as part of its contents 'A Dissertation on the Government, Laws, Customs, Manners, and Language of the Anglo-Saxons, Particularly, the Origin,

---

[24] François Hotman, *Franco-Gallia, or an Account of the Ancient Free State of France and Most Other Parts of Europe, before the Loss of Their Liberties*, trans. Robert Molesworth (London, 1711), p. 72. In 1573, Hotman wrote, ' 'tis not yet a hundred years compleat, since the Liberties of *Francogallia*, and the *Authority* of its *annual General Council*, flourish'd in full vigour and exerted themselves against a king of ripe Years [Louis XI], and great Understanding . . . So that we may easily perceive that our *Commonwealth*, which at first was *founded* and *establish'd* upon the *Principles of Liberty*, maintained itself in the same free and sacred State, (even by Force and Arms) against all the Powers of Tyrants for more than Eleven hundred years' (p. 122).

[25] Montesquieu, *Oeuvres complètes*, ed. Roger Caillois, ii (Paris: Gallimard, 1951), bk. 11, ch. 6, p. 407: 'Si l'on veut lire l'admirable ouvrage de Tacite *sur les moeurs des Germains*, on verra que c'est d'eux que les Anglois ont tiré l'idée de leur gouvernement politique. Ce beau système a été trouvé dans les bois.'

[26] Hill, *Puritanism and Revolution*, pp. 58–67.

Nature, and Privileges of Their Wittena-Gemot, or Parliament: Wherein Are Several Things Absolutely Necessary for the Understanding of the Present Customs and Laws of England'. The main feature of Saxon government, according to Rapin de Thoyras, was its democratic principles:

> the Saxons had no Kings in Germany, when they sent over the first Troops to assist the Britons under the Conduct of Hengist. Their Territories were divided into twelve Provinces, over each of which a Head or Governour was appointed by the Assembly-General of the Nation, wherein the Supreme power was lodg'd. This Assembly was call'd Wittena-gemot, that is to say, the Assembly of the Wise-Men . . .

Once he had conquered Britain, Hengist supposedly took upon himself the sovereign title of King; but this did not, according to Rapin de Thoyras,

> exempt him from all Dependance on the Wittena-gemot in his own State, which in conjunction with him regulated all important Affairs. Moreover, by mutual Consent, there was established a General Assembly of the whole Seven Kingdoms, wherein Matters relating to all in Common were debated. Hence this Form of Government, which consider'd the Seven Kingdoms as united in one Body, was call'd the Heptarchy, that is, the Government of Seven.[27]

It was not only Saxon democracy, but the image of a Saxon federal or confederated government that Americans such as Thomas Jefferson, whose favorite historian was Rapin de Thoyras, claimed to be reviving in America.[28]

In 1771 an anonymous author published in London and Dublin *An Historical Essay on the English Constitution*. This document boldly equated common law – in its pristine, Saxon version – with natural law, that is, with reasoned principles concerning the 'rights of man'. The *Historical Essay* had considerable influence on American patriots. For example, Jefferson owned a copy,[29] and we might detect the *Historical Essay*'s influence on John Dickinson's *A New Essay on the Constitutional Power of Great-Britain over the Colonies in America*, published in Philadelphia in 1774, wherein, bolstered by a citation from Blackstone, he equated the Saxon example of limited monarchy with principles of 'nature' and 'reason':

> That the power of the king was neither unrestrained nor infinite was the constitution of our German ancestors on the continent, and this is not only

---

[27] Paul Rapin de Thoyras, *The History of England*, trans. N. Tindal, ii (Dublin, 1726), p. 138.

[28] On Jefferson's judgement in 1825, 'there is as yet no general history so faithful as Rapin's; and on editions in Jefferson's successive libraries, see Colbourn, *The Lamp of Experience*, pp. 177, 217–21.

[29] Colbourn, *The Lamp of Experience* (p. 218), lists it in Jefferson's collection.

consonant to the principles of nature, of liberty, of reason, and of society, but has always been esteemed an express part of the common law of England, even when prerogative was at the highest.[30]

Even more importantly, the *Historical Essay* was excerpted and packaged for the American colonies by a patriot who called himself Demophilus and advertised the work with the descriptive title *The Genuine Principles of the Ancient Saxon or English Constitution, Carefully Collected from the Best Authorities, with Some Observations, on Their Peculiar Fitness, for the United Colonies in General, and Pennsylvania in Particular.* Demophilus quoted long passages from the *Historical Essay* to the effect that the Saxons made 'the elective power of the people the first principle of the constitution' and thus 'founded their government on the common rights of mankind', developing 'a perfect model of government, where the natural rights of mankind were preserved, in their full exercise, pure and perfect, as far as the nature of society will admit it'. Demophilus' own commentary consisted chiefly of encouraging his compatriots to renew the Saxon governmental model. Immediately under the title pointing out the 'peculiar fitness' of these 'Ancient Saxon' principles to the American situation, he placed on his title page an epigram from Sidney: 'All human Constitutions are subject to Corruption and must perish, unless they are *timely renewed* by reducing them to their first Principles'. Demophilus plugged the Saxon model again in his introduction:

A CONVENTION very soon to sit in PHILADELPHIA; I have thought it my duty to collect some sentiments from a certain very scarce book, entitled an *Historical Essay on the English Constitution*, and publish them, with whatever improving observations our different circumstances may suggest, for the perusal of the gentlemen concerned in the arduous task of framing a constitution.

Later, he was even more explicit:

The Colony [Pennsylvania], having now but one order of freemen in it; and to the honor of Pennsylvania, but very few slaves, it will need but little argument to convince the bulk of an understanding people, that this ancient and justly admired pattern, the old Saxon form of government, will be the best model, that human wisdom, improved by experience, has let them to copy.[31]

Not insignificantly, the American *Declaration of Independence* (with its famous opening argument based on natural rights that are 'inherent and

[30] John Dickinson, *A New Essay on the Constitutional Power of Great-Britain over the Colonies in America* (Philadelphia, 1774), p. 96.
[31] Demophilus, *The Genuine Principles of the Ancient Saxon or English Constitution* (Philadelphia, 1776), pp. 4–6, 17.

inalienable') first appeared in print, published in Philadelphia in 1776, as a sort of appendix to Demophilus' *Genuine Principles*. The Saxon historical precedent – the myth of a primitive Saxon democracy – provided the ballast for revolutionary arguments based on natural rights deduced by reason.

In a fundamental and largely implicit sense, the Enlightenment appeal to universal or 'natural' law in order to oppose unjust historical, or customary, laws was really just a more radical appeal to historical precedent – that is, to a historical precedent theorised rationally, a precedent that was entirely stable and unchanging from the very beginning of time. The law of nature was, in short, imagined as the ultimate historical precedent. Enlightenment thinkers who idealised the life of 'natural' man (man who lived in nature and/or by the 'laws of nature') tended to equate nature with the past, and even to use nature to represent the past in ways that it had not done formerly.[32] According to the age-old conventions of pastoral verse, for example, nature stood in a kind of eternal opposition to culture (civilisation in the sense of the refinements of city or court life); although a natural or 'soft primitive' life was idealised in pastoral verse, usually to criticise city or court life by comparison, it was not presented as an earlier state in the 'progress' of civilisation. Nor did classical primitivists necessarily associate life in nature with the past. The 'hard primitive' Germanic tribes which Tacitus idealised (although far more moderately than those who would quote him) were his contemporaries, and he did not suggest otherwise. For later promoters of the myth of Saxon democracy, however, Tacitus' Germanic tribes lived primitively in nature and in the past, so that the two were easily conflated. It is not surprising, then, that the relatively uncultivated natural setting of the American continent should have given European settlers, as they pushed the frontier westward, the impression that they were moving 'back' in time to an earlier era.

Tacitus' observations, such as that the German tribes had no cities but lived scattered and separated in the groves and meadows, never permitting houses to touch each other, enabled eighteenth-century idealisers of the Saxons, following Montesquieu's example in *De l'esprit des lois*, to present them as simple men living in a state of nature relatively uncorrupted by civilisation. For example, the British poet James Thomson, in his long, widely read poem entitled *Liberty*, published in the 1730s, gave the personified Liberty the following speech recounting the Saxons' conquest of

---

[32] Enlightenment thinkers were by no means the first to associate a state of nature with the earliest stage of human society and, in that sense, with the most distant past. For example, in the 2nd century BC, Varro stated in his *De re rustica* (II. i. 4) that 'the most distant stage was that state of nature in which man lived on those products which the virgin earth brought forth of her own accord' (trans. William D. Hooper, Cambridge, Mass.: Harvard University Press, 1967). The myth of Eden is another example. Nevertheless, it was not until the eighteenth century that a state of nature came to be so closely associated with the past that, for example, a wild landscape in a painting could be used to *signify* the past.

Britain and attributing their love of freedom to nature uncorrupted by the refining, enslaving subtleties of civilisation:

> Then (sad Belief!) from the bleak Coast, that hears
> The *German* Ocean roar, deep-blooming, strong,
> And yellow-hair'd, the blue-ey'd *Saxon* came.
> He came implor'd, but came with other Arm
> Than to protect. For Conquest and Defence
> Suffices the same Arm. With the fierce Race
> Pour'd in a fresh invigorating Stream,
> Blood, where unquell'd a mighty Spirit glow'd.
> . . .
>   Untam'd
> To the refining Subtilties of Slaves,
> They brought an happy Government along;
> Form'd by that *Freedom*, which, with secret Voice,
> Impartial *Nature* teaches all her Sons,
> And which of old thro' the whole *Scythian Mass*
> I strong inspir'd. *Monarchical* their State,
> But prudently *confin'd*, and *mingled* wise
> Of each harmonious Power.[33]

The question of why the German tribes should have preserved their liberty so well when other nations had not was posed by Paul Henri Mallet in his *Histoire de Danemark* (1758), written in French at the Danish court and translated into English in 1770 by Bishop Thomas Percy, who popularised Mallet's work under the title *Northern Antiquities or a Description of the Manners, Customs, Religion and Laws of the Ancient Danes, and Other Northern Nations, Including Those of Our Own Saxon Ancestors.* Mallet's explanation of the Germanic tribes' tenacious hold on liberty stressed, as Montesquieu had done, the influence of their rude natural environment, and their simple life devoid of the unnatural sophistications of civilisation:

> But how came these men to preserve themselves in so great a degree of liberty? This was owing to their climate and manner of life . . . They were free, because they inhabited an uncultivated country, rude forests and mountains; and liberty is the sole treasure of an indigent people . . .[34]

Liberty, Mallet suggested, was best preserved 'in the woods'. Revolutionary patriots in America liked to think so too.

The lack of enervating luxury in the New World was presented by late-eighteenth- and early-nineteenth-century American writers as a condition beneficial to the preservation and even the fulfilment of Saxon

---

[33] James Thomson, *'Liberty', 'The Castle of Indolence', and Other Poems*, ed. James Sambrook (Oxford: Clarendon, 1986) p. 109, vv. 668–97.
[34] Mallet, *Northern Antiquities*, pp. 162–3.

virtues. Jefferson's proposition for the Great Seal of the United States, with the Saxon leaders Hengist and Horsa 'backed' by the divinely sanctioned migration of the tribes of Israel to the Promised Land, suggests that he envisioned the British migration to America as the salvation of democracy by a surviving remnant of Saxondom. Just as Saxon democracy supposedly thrived (better than in continental Europe) in the rude natural conditions of Britain after its transplantation there, so Jefferson and others imagined that Saxon democracy would be 'reinvigorated' by its transplantation from Britain to America, from a corrupting state of advanced civilisation to a more primitive 'natural' state (analogous to that of Britain at the time Horsa and Hengist supposedly conquered it for democracy).

Jefferson even went so far as to urge, with considerable success, the teaching of the ancient Anglo-Saxon language in America's universities.[35] To set the linguistic clock back in this way would, he believed, invigorate the English language as well as promote democracy. Toward the end of his letter to John Cartwright of 1824, Jefferson wrote that students at the new University of Virginia would study 'principles of government . . . founded in the rights of man' and also Anglo-Saxon. Indeed, Jefferson's aim was for students to read about principles of government *in* Anglo-Saxon: 'As the histories and laws left us in that type and dialect, must be the text books of the reading of the learners, they will imbibe with the language their free principles of government.'[36] To enable such osmosis, beginning in 1798 Jefferson drafted his *Essay on the Anglo-Saxon Language*, which he expanded several times before his death in 1826. The version the University of Virginia finally published in 1851 contained Jefferson's brief Anglo-Saxon grammar, as well as a specimen teaching edition of the first twelve chapters of Genesis in Anglo-Saxon.[37]

In his 1818 *Report* to the committee charged with creating the University of Virginia, Jefferson expressed his ambitions for the Anglo-Saxon language and the American nation in no uncertain terms: 'A language already fraught with all the eminent science of our parent country, the future vehicle of whatever we may ourselves achieve, and destined to occupy so much space on the globe, claims distinguished attention in American education.'[38] Indeed, Jefferson argued that the compulsory study of Anglo-Saxon texts in the original would not only inoculate students with a love of Saxon liberty and democracy, but improve their English by a return to the 'pure' source of the language. It was Jefferson's

---

[35] See Stanley R. Hauer's fundamental essay on this topic, 'Thomas Jefferson and the Anglo-Saxon Language', *PMLA*, 98 (1983), pp. 879–98, and, more recently, Frantzen, *Desire for Origins*, pp. 15–19, 203–7.

[36] *Writings*, xvi. p. 51.

[37] *Writings*, xviii. pp. 359–411. The full title of this work is *An Essay towards Facilitating Instruction in the Anglo-Saxon and Modern Dialects of the English Language*.

[38] Roy J. Honeywell, *The Educational Work of Thomas Jefferson* (1931; New York: Russell and Russell, 1964), p. 255.

tendentious belief that Latin scholars, in an effort to make Anglo-Saxon conform to Latin grammar, had complicated and corrupted it by adding such features as grammatical gender and inflections. Jefferson's own grammar, and the more elaborate grammars and dictionaries he called for, would, as he put it, 'liberate' Anglo-Saxon 'from these foreign shackles'; they would 'recruit and renovate the vigor of the English language, too much impaired by the neglect of its ancient constitution and dialects, and would remove, for the student, the principal difficulties of ascending to the source of the English language'. Had Jefferson realised his fondest wishes, the language spoken in America today might be 'liberated' Anglo-Saxon, a radical linguistic innovation in the legitimating guise of return to a mythically pure and perfect medieval origin: the 'ancient constitution' of the English language.[39]

---

[39] *Writings*, xviii. pp. 391–3. By 1850 not only the University of Virginia, but also Randolph-Macon College, the University of Alabama, Amherst College and Harvard offered undergraduate instruction in Anglo-Saxon. During the rest of the century Anglo-Saxon language studies mushroomed in America, and did more to support than to call into question myths of the American Middle Ages, which flourished especially in American literature of the period we call 'Renaissance'.

Coleridge, Scholasticism and German Idealism[1]

RENÉ GALLET

Though there is no lack of studies of Coleridge's debt to German ideal-ism,[2] a full-length examination of his relationship to scholastic philosophy and theology is not easily found. The main reason for this is, of course, that his thought has long been perceived as being primarily dependent on such German idealists as Kant and Schelling. It is still commonly felt that Coleridge's somewhat loose terminology and thinking provide a sufficient explanation for such a strange coupling of authors not easily reconciled, whereas it might be read as suggesting the need for a different or wider interpretative framework, capable of accommodating various aspects of their respective systems.

The absence of studies on the present subject also originates in the feeling that the question simply does not arise. But this assumption needs to be questioned in view of Coleridge's numerous references to scholastic thought, which cannot simply be ignored or evaded. They are found first in the crucial transitional phase of his intellectual development that took him from his early enthusiastic endorsement of Hartley's philosophical and religious outlook[3] to his own mature vision.

Scholastics enter his intellectual horizon no later than February 1801 (*CL* ii. p. 681).[4] Though their works are not yet known to him directly, the demotion of Locke's empiricism to the unoriginal form of a scholastic option has already taken place: 'The Conceptualists who *moderated*

---

[1] This is a simplified version of 'Coleridge, la scolastique et l'idéalisme allemand' (forthcoming).

[2] E.g. G. N. Orsini, *Coleridge and German Idealism* (Carbondale and Edwardsville, Ill.: Southern Illinois University Press, 1969).

[3] On which I have concentrated in the first chapter of *Romantisme et postromantisme de Coleridge à Hardy (nature et surnature)* (Paris: L'Harmattan, 1996).

[4] The following abbreviations will be used: *AR* (*Aids to Reflection*), *BL* (*Biographia Literaria*), *CL* (*The Collected Letters of S. T. Coleridge*, Oxford: Clarendon Press, 1956–71), *M* (*Marginalia*), *NB* (*The Notebooks of S. T. Coleridge* [London: Routledge and Kegan Paul, 1957–]), *PL* (*The Philosophical Lectures* [London: Pilot Press, 1949]), *SM* (*The Statesman's Manual*). All references are to the *Collected Works*, Bollingen Series LXXV, unless otherwise stated.

between these and the Realists coincided with Mr Locke fully and absolutely' (*ibid.*, Coleridge's emphasis). It is interesting here to see Coleridge moving backwards in time to a pre-Lockean context, where Greek philosophers admittedly loom larger than scholastic ones, rather than moving closer to the contemporary, especially German, scene. So when he does turn to German idealism this cannot be viewed simply as a shift that follows the course of time. The seeming retrogression to the scholastic age is part of a widening and deepening of his own reflection, in which some of Kant's and Schelling's notions will ultimately find their places within an intellectual framework of his own.

His first-hand acquaintance with a major scholastic author apparently dates from the summer of 1801, when he went to the Durham Cathedral Library specifically to consult the works of Scotus. The metaphorical sacrifice of Locke that ensues

> I mean to set the poor old Gemman on his feet again, and in order to wake him out of his present Lethargy, I am burning Locke, Hume, and Hobbes under his Nose they stink worse than Feather or Assafetida   (*CL* ii. p. 746)

shows that more than intellectual curiosity is at stake. The episode occurs at a moment of deep personal and spiritual transformation. Coleridge is under the impression that his vocation as a poet has come to an end (*CL* ii. p. 714), and that his vocation as a thinker may be about to begin. The significance of his scholastic readings, then, cannot be ignored, even if they are far from being unique.[5] A letter of December 1803 assures us that for the last two years scholastics had been his main intellectual or spiritual support.

> God bless the old Schoolmen. They have been my best comforts, and most instructive Companions for the last two years. – Could you believe, that I could have come *to this*? (*CL* ii. p. 1020, Coleridge's emphasis)

This is at a time when his knowledge of Kant is limited and often deeply unsatisfying: 'Kant I do not understand' (*M* ii. p. 249); 'But Kant, and all his School, are miserable Reasoners in Psychology and particularly Morals' (*ibid.*, p. 253).

His high regard for scholastic thought hardly shows any sign of having abated in later years. In a marginal note of the mid-1820s his estimate of Scotus could not be more favourable: 'I can think of no other instance of *metaphysical Genius* in an Englishman', though he admits himself to be 'too little conversant with /his/ Volumes' (*M* ii. p. 1136, Coleridge's emphasis). He voices a similar feeling in his *Philosophical Lectures*, where he claims he has read 'a considerable portion of the works of

---

5 See P. Deschamps, *La formation de la pensée de Coleridge (1772–1804)* (Paris: Didier, 1964), pp. 455ff.

Thomas Aquinas and /Duns Scotus/' (*PL* p. 280), adding, 'I should be perplexed to name any books which impressed me with a deeper sense of the power of the human mind.' A much earlier note, possibly belonging to the time when he first read them, shows how strongly he felt about these 'despised' thinkers: 'I pray to God that I may hereafter be enabled to do justice to these despised schoolmen' (*M* ii. p. 13).

However strong it may be, such a feeling still falls short of espousing their views on philosophy or theology. And Coleridge's keen interest in them was by no means unprecedented. They were occasionally referred to or even praised by Hartley, Berkeley and various seventeenth-century Anglican divines, to whom Coleridge turned even before his empiricist convictions had completely failed him (*CL* i. p. 245). Leibniz, who valued scholastic thought (and came to adopt some of its concepts, such as Scotus's *haecceitas* in his *Discours philosophique*), may also have played the part of an intermediary, helping Coleridge to turn the Schoolmen into a positive model after they had fallen into disrepute in original Protestantism and in the philosophy of the Enlightenment (and Coleridge's unitive approach may be reminiscent of Leibniz's own harmonising intellectual style, though on a more modest scale and in a more eclectic manner).

There is ample evidence that scholastic thought became a kind of paradigm for Coleridge in fields ranging from terminology to ontology. He adopted such scholastic terms as *haecceitas* and *omneitas* alongside the more common *natura naturans* and *natura naturata* which Berkeley (in *Siris*) or Spinoza (in his *Short Treatise*, for instance) had acknowledged to be derived from scholastic practice.

The adoption of such terms, however abstruse they may sound, is in keeping with a personal intellectual style favouring fine distinctions, which in turn calls for the 'desynonymisation' of closely related notions. This more or less remotely parallels the scholastic method, which he praises in the *Biographia Literaria* (i. p. 287)[6] before adopting one of Schelling's notions ('potence': its affinities for him with the scholastic notion of *potentialitas*, the opposite of 'act', cannot be excluded). That this is not to be seen merely as a tactical move is proved by a marginal note to the *Reliquiae Baxterianae* where his own initials are inserted into the text and identified with Baxter's first-person assertions:

> no books so suited my disposition as Aquinas, Scotus, Ockam, and their disciples; because I/ΣTX/ thought they narrowly searched after Truth, and brought things out of the darkness of Confusion: for I could never from /ΣTX/ my first studies endure Confusion. (*M* i. p. 286)

---

6 The footnote ('Kant used Scholastic and Latin terms for similar reasons') may be true, but it could also be misleading, since one might be made to feel that Coleridge was following Kant's example in this, whereas the latter's attitude to scholasticism can be more conventionally dismissive 'simple innovation de l'esprit scolastique', 'contre nature': *Critique de la raison pure* (Paris: PUF, 1968), p. 431.

Identical remarks are made in his *Philosophical Lectures* (*PL* p. 317), where the scholastic approach is seen as making for clarity and systematic thinking.

Though he was plainly unable to live up to such standards, the idea of an *opus maximum*, the elusive or unrealistic pursuit of his later years, may be indebted to the model of the medieval *Summae*, at least more clearly than to Kant's separate critiques or Schelling's changing systems. An all-embracing organic construction like St Thomas's *Summa* must have been congenial to him, though there are no signs that he ever intended something like an imitation.

Some important scholastic themes were also close to his own preoccupations. At first he appears to have been interested in their pre- or anti-empiricist positions in the epistemological field, but he was no doubt also led to a fuller assessment of their sometimes divergent metaphysical conceptions. One of his central concerns bears on the relationship between philosophy and religion;[7] and he more than once praises the Schoolmen for not making 'an abhorrent division' (*PL* p. 279) between the two (as Kant, in his view, did). His firmly held position on the subject apparently prompted him to minimise the differences between rival schools. Even Occam is presented as reconciling reason and faith in a way that clearly had a particular appeal to him: 'so beautiful a definition of faith' (*PL* p. 280). One consequence is that scholastic views are seen not only as containing some of Locke's subsequent theses, but also as providing much of the inspiration behind the Reformation: 'I indeed am persuaded that to the scholastic philosophy the Reformation is attributable' (*PL* p. 316). On other occasions, however he prefers to point out the pantheistic threat lurking in some of their systems, and especially Scotus Erigena's, whose excuse may be that he is following the example of 'some of the Mystic Greek Fathers' (*NB* iii. 3516).

It is also worth noting that the transition from a unitarian to a trinitarian conception should have been made possible for him through a 'scholastic inference' (*BL* i. p. 204). Whether the term is to be taken in a strictly historical sense or simply as a mode of reasoning is not quite clear. That the former interpretation is not impossible is shown in *Aids to Reflection*,

---

[7] If Coleridge's assumption is not recognised (and admitted through some form of 'willing suspension of disbelief', since in modern, post-Reformation, times the two modes of thinking are commonly seen as mutually exclusive) it is easy to make havoc of his views, to deconstruct instead of trying to reconstruct them. On this central issue he can be felt to bypass Luther's seeming divorce between faith and reason. He must have been helped in this by the Cambridge Platonists, as well as some 17th-century Anglican divines. But this conciliatory position also conforms substantially to Hartley's approach, whose influence he may never have completely outgrown. Similar views were held by many schoolmen and early Fathers: see E. Gilson, *La philosophie au Moyen-Âge* (Paris: Payot, 1962), p. 18; the special *Communio* issue, xvii, 2–3, 'Sauver la raison' (mars–juin 1992), is also worth consulting.

where the idea of the Trinity is again said to be accessible on merely rational grounds as 'a Theorem in Metaphysics valid in the Schools' (*AR* p. 177), which largely agrees with St Anselm's position.[8]

Coleridge's linking of philosophy and religion, reason and faith, naturally led him to take an interest in the scholastic proofs of God's existence.[9] His preference is for a priori proofs, since a posteriori proofs would, in his eyes, make God dependent on empirical reality, whereas a priori proofs are more compatible with His absoluteness, and ultimately rest on the persistence of His image (reason, in a broad sense) in man.[10] This is the thinking behind Coleridge's high praise of St Anselm's 'metaphysical acuteness' (*PL* p. 277) and of his 'ontological proof',[11] which is recognised as antedating Descartes' own demonstration. Coleridge's divergence from Kant on this subject (though he seems to minimise it, if the tentative text is to be trusted) should be noted along with its momentous corollaries. When he examines the problem again, as in *Aids to Reflection*, where he asserts the dependence of the cosmological (or empirical) proof on the ontological one (*AR* p. 185), his commitment to the latter can hardly be doubted (*AR* pp. 554–5).

But his acceptance of St Anselm's argument is not passive: he seems to have reshaped it, or given it a different emphasis. In St Anselm's approach faith leads to intelligence,[12] whereas Coleridge rather presents reason as a preliminary stage, leaving room for free assent.

To this ontological argument taken from St Anselm, Coleridge adds a conception of God's essence as 'pure act' which is more Thomistic in origin (*AR* p. 555),[13] though he ascribes the notion at least once to

8   E. Gilson, *La philosophie au Moyen-Âge*, p. 242.

9   See J. Barth, *Coleridge and Christian Doctrine* (New York: Fordham University Press, 1987), pp. 96ff., for a fuller examination of the problem.

10   Origen's thought, which is also present behind Hartley's notion of 'universal restoration', must directly as well as indirectly have played a role in his revalution of man's inner nature: see H. Crouzel, *Théologie de l'image chez Origène* (Paris: Aubier, 1956). How such an influence can be reconciled with Coleridge's professed admiration for Luther (whose theology can be felt to be antithetical to that of Origen) probably deserves a full-length study.

11   The validity of the term has sometimes been questioned; see 'L'argument ne relève pas de l'ontologie', in J. L. Marion, *Questions cartésiennes* (Paris: PUF, 1991), p. 258.

12   'Ce que j'ai cru jusqu'ici par ton don, maintenant je le comprends par ta lumière de telle façon que, même si je ne voulais pas croire que tu existes, je n'aurais pas pu ne pas le comprendre.' *Fides quaerens intellectum* (Paris: Vrin, 1964), p. 17.

13   The unmistakable scholastic resonance of the notion, which is centrally reasserted in *BL*, is toned down in the edition of the *Collected Works*. R. Modiano sees the intervention of the Thomistic idea of 'Pure Act' in *CL* iii. p. 4427, anticipating similar statements in *BL*, as an 'obfuscation' of Schellingian sources: *Coleridge and the Concept of Nature* (London and Basingstoke: Macmillan, 1985), p. 192. But the important divergence with Schelling, as well as the patristic echoes of the passage, are apparently overlooked. Contrary to St Thomas's 'Pure Act', Schelling's Absolute, like that of Hegel, initially contains an aspect of deficiency, or *potentialitas*: E. Brito, *Dieu et l'être d'après Thomas d'Aquin et Hegel*

Boethius (*M* i. p. 232). His combination of ideas from partly divergent systems (St Thomas rejected the ontological argument) is probably not as inconsistent as it might seem. Again Coleridge adapts the notion to his more recent perspective and to his own needs. 'Pure act' is thus made more or less synonymous with the idea of *causa sui*, ascribed by him to scholastic thought (*CL* v. p. 134), though it seems to belong to a later age.[14] And the notion is apparently filtered through or combined with more recent categories, especially Fichte's conception of the absolute self as an 'act' or self-positing principle. Coleridge himself points to this influence (*BL* i. pp. 157–8), but other sources, some of them scholastic, may have contributed to his voluntaristic reinterpretation of the notion.[15] When he first adopted it, before studying Fichte, he already read it in this voluntaristic light, contrasting the divine *Actus Purissimus* with his own painful sense of 'mere Passiveness' (*NB* ii. 2078), so that his Hartleian intellectual background, not to mention his psychological disposition, must also have influenced his reception of the scholastic concept. Like St Thomas, however (e.g. *Summa Theologiae*, Ia, q.13, a.11) he ultimately grounds the notion on God's self-revelation in the book of Exodus (Exod. 3: 14), the metaphysical significance of which he is at pains to stress in the notorious twelfth chapter of the *Biographia Literaria* (i. p. 275n).[16]

The remark is often seen as an unwelcome addition to his awkward transcription of Schelling's ideas. But it merely reaffirms a long-held ontological principle which he states in unequivocally scholastic terms at

(Paris: PUF, 1991), p. 34. The resulting ontology would then seem to be diametrically opposed to that of Coleridge. It is somewhat ironic that Schelling should have finally approved of the scholastic notion of God as pure act in a later phase of his thought (X. Tillette, *Schelling: Une philosophie en devenir*, Paris: Vrin, 1992, i. p. 524), thus following Coleridge's example.

[14] J. L. Marion, 'Entre analogie et raison: la *causa sui*', in *Descartes: Objecter et répondre*, eds J. M. Beyssade and J. L. Marion (Paris: PUF, 1994), pp. 308ff.

[15] Mention could be made of Boehme: 'La volonté abyssale – explique Boehme – est le Père éternel', M. Vetö, *Le fondement selon Schelling* (Paris: Beauchesne, 1977), p. 304. But Occam, often recognised to be a determining factor in shaping Luther's outlook, also emphasised the pre-eminence of the will in God: 'il n'y a pas de règle au-dessus de la volonté divine. Cette volonté est elle-même la règle suprême.' C. Boyer, *Calvin et Luther: Accords et différences* (Rome: Università Gregoriana Editrice, 1973), p. 117. But for St Thomas himself 'la volonté de Dieu *est* son être': E. Brito, *Dieu et l'être d'après Thomas d'Aquin et Hegel*, p. 273, Brito's emphasis.

[16] It could also be pointed out that Coleridge's phrasing ('ground of existence'), though not devoid of Schellingian echoes, also belongs to a wider context of thought, since an all but identical phrase is applied to God later in Hopkins's 'The Wreck of the Deutschland' ('Ground of Being', xxxii, 6). One reason for this conjunction may be that, though entirely free of Schelling's influence, Hopkins was also conversant with scholastic thought. And the precedent of Coleridge's admiration for Scotus is usually forgotten in discussions of his enthusiastic discovery of the *Opus Oxoniense* in July 1872. But there is no need to stress the differences between the two poets.

the beginning of chapter 9 (i. p. 143),[17] before he starts borrowing heavily from Schelling. One suggestion could be that his subsequent borrowings on the whole belong to a particular field, that of epistemology or of the subject–object relationship (*principium cognoscendi*, which would correspond to his own notion of the *Logos*), a field in which Coleridge would naturally welcome up-to-date anti-empiricist contributions, and that they tend to be fitted, less than neatly, into an ontological framework[18] (*principium essendi*, linked to his notion of 'act') which remains scholastic in origin.

It may be helpful to remember that Coleridge subscribed to this form of ontology (before May 1804: *NB* ii. 2078) at a time when he was also making his far from uncritical way through Kant's new conceptual territory, and several years before he became acquainted with Schelling's thought. The outcome of this all-important transitional phase, in which he absorbed non-empiricist material coming from various quarters (while keeping empiricist notions like 'fancy' or 'understanding' in a subordinate place) can be observed in the almost paradigmatic 1806 letter to T. Clarkson (*CL* ii. pp. 1195ff.). His vision is already grounded ontologically on the divine '*actus purissimus sine* potentialitate' (Coleridge's emphasis). References to Kant's epistemology appear only later (though Coleridge is not entirely responsible for this) and are part of a perspective that may be described broadly as a form of Christian Platonism that must have coloured his scholastic readings and in which the divine *Actus Purissimus* (or Father) eternally generates the *Logos* (or Son), who in turn generates the inner *Logos* in Man (which it became easy to identify with an un-Kantian version of Kant's 'reason'). A similar type of integration may have been attempted in the *Biographia Literaria*, though his rather crude helping of himself to Schellingian material is what catches one's attention, rather than the (admittedly less than perfect) process of assimilation.[19] However,

---

[17] Scholastic precedents are mentioned in the footnote. But Coleridge's 'definite similarity' with Kant (i. p. 143n.) in the related issue of truth and Being may strike one as somewhat overstated. The three notions of truth, Being and the Supreme Being as *Actus Purissimus* are found in immediate succession and cohere, resulting in a metaphysical vision that can hardly be described as Kantian.

[18] That this seems to conform to Coleridge's approach and to the overall structure of his thought (which can be obscured when one limits oneself to a piecemeal comparison with other authors) is suggested by an 1818 letter: 'and from Philosophy to derive a Scientia Scientarum, and by application of its Principles and Laws a reversed arrangement of the Sciences: namely by *Descent* instead of the hitherto plan by Ascent. 1. Theology. 2. Ethics. 3. Metaphysics' (*CL* iv. p. 864, Coleridge's emphasis).

[19] A detailed examination of the problem cannot be given here. But Coleridge soon became aware of its existence as well as of the difficulty inherent in Schelling's views in this particular phase of the latter's intellectual development, namely the tension which Coleridge perceptively diagnoses between his *Naturphilosophie* and his transcendental idealism (*CL* iv. p. 874: the same remark is made by X. Tillette, 'La relation à la philosophie de la Nature est le bord vulnérable de l'idéalisme transcendental', in *Schelling*, i. p. 195).

his own perspective is more easily perceived if one takes into account the complementary exposition of it in *The Statesman's Manual*, which is free of such obtrusively foreign material (and where the Schoolmen are vindicated again (*SM* p. 103).

This is also where the key notion of 'symbol' is given its full-fledged definition, within the framework of a metaphysics of participation[20] which also underlies St Thomas's *Summa*.[21] It is a conjunction which may have played a part in Coleridge's almost fervent adoption of the idea of God as pure act, which is so unlike Kant's or Schelling's own positions, and on which his whole vision rests. As a result the definition of a symbol, at least in this particular discussion of it, should probably also be seen in its ontological and theological implications (as impure, participative, or finite act) rather than in a merely aesthetic context[22] ('partakes', *SM* p. 30, and 'the same Power in a lower dignity, and therefore a symbol', *SM* p. 72, point to the underlying idea of participation). But whether Coleridge stuck to a genuinely Thomistic view of participation or, as is likely, interpreted it in a more Platonic light,[23] is a technical question that one may be excused for leaving unanswered.

---

[20] J. Barth identifies this precisely: *Coleridge and Christian Doctrine*, pp. 19 *et passim*.

[21] See L. Millet, 'Analogie et participation chez St Thomas d'Aquin,' *Etudes philosophiques*, 3–4 (1989), pp. 371–83.

[22] The point is made by D. Degrois, 'Dynamisme et unité: essai sur la recherche esthétique de S. T. Colerige (1804–34)' (Thèse de Doctorat d'Etat, Université de Paris III, 1979), pp. 333 *et passim*.

[23] Itself probably filtered through patristic reinterpretations, especially that of Origen. See E. von Ivanka, *Plato Christianus. Übernahme und Umgestaltung des Platonismus durch die Väter* (Einsiedeln: Johannes Verlag, 1964– ; French trans., Paris: PUF, 1990).

The Mists of Avalon:
A Confused Assault on Patriarchy

JAMES NOBLE

In her 1982 novel, *The Mists of Avalon*, Marion Zimmer Bradley sets the familiar characters and events of the Arthurian legend within the context of a pseudo-historical crisis, in which the androcentric theology of the fifth-century Christian Church is threatening to extinguish forever the pagan matriarchal tradition of goddess-worship sacred to the priestesses of the Holy Isle of Avalon and to much of the indigenous population of Britain. The challenge for Arthur as king is to prevent the eradication of goddess-worship by establishing a kingdom where there is 'room for the Goddess and the Christ, the cauldron and the cross' (p. 15).[1]

Needless to say, this contest between matriarchal Avalon and the patriarchal Christian Church affords Bradley ample opportunity to hold patriarchy up to careful scrutiny and to assess it for what it has historically meant for the Arthurian legend in general and for the women of the legend in particular. On the surface of things, patriarchy seems not to fare very well under the scrutiny to which Bradley subjects it. Time and again its values and traditions are shown to be wanting, especially as compared to the matriarchal traditions of Avalon. As I shall argue in this paper, however, Bradley's assault on patriarchy in *The Mists of Avalon* is at best a limited success, since she ultimately acquiesces in and (apparently without recognising that she is even doing so) valorises the very belief-system she thinks she is condemning.

The primary targets of Bradley's assault on patriarchy are the priests of the Christian Church, whom she sees as having long been instrumental in suppressing the rights and freedoms of the Christian faithful in general and the female Christian faithful in particular. Consistently, the priests in *The Mists of Avalon* are portrayed as ignorant, intolerant, mean-spirited individuals bent upon imposing Christianity on all the people of Britain. Reflecting upon her romantic feelings for both Accolon, her stepson, and Lancelet, the son of her foster-mother, for example, Morgaine remarks to

---

[1] All quotations from Bradley's novel are given in parentheses within the text of the essay.

herself: 'But they are too close kin to me only by the laws made by the Christians who seek to rule this land . . . to rule it in a new tyranny; not alone to make the laws but to rule the mind and heart and soul' (p. 583; cf. p. 783). The tyranny of Bradley's priests is reflected in their narrow intolerance for any faith but their own. Archbishop Patricius, for example, is described as fanatical (p. 263) in his determination to rid Britain of its 'heathen' practices and superstitions (pp. 260, 262). When the Merlin suggests to Patricius that his intolerance for the religious traditions of the Druids makes him harsher than Christ himself, Patricius replies: 'I think too many people presume to read the divine Scriptures, and fall into just such errors as this . . . Those who presume on their learning will learn, I trust, to listen to their priests for the true interpretations' (p. 260).

The impact of patriarchal Christianity on the faithful of fifth-century Britain is to be discerned most readily in Bradley's novel in the characterisation of Gwenhwyfar, who is portrayed from the outset as a victim of the patriarchal culture Archbishop Patricius and his priests are so intent upon imposing on Arthur's subjects. Gwenhwyfar is introduced to the reader as an exceedingly timid young woman raised in an atmosphere of oppressive paternalism and living with a father who insists she must trust him to know what is best for her, even as a young woman facing the prospect of marriage: 'That's what I'm here for,' Leodegranz informs his daughter, 'to look after you and make a good marriage with a trusty man to look after my pretty little featherhead' (p. 256). Bradley's Gwenhwyfar is an individual so conditioned by the patriarchal value-system instilled in her at home and in the convent where she has been educated that she is incapable of thinking of herself as anything but a 'featherhead' whose duty it is to conform to the expectations of the dominant male culture (Gordon-Wise, p. 144). When, for example, she finds herself fuming about the fact that she is being packed off with her father's horses to marry a man who is more interested in her dowry than he is in her, Gwenhwyfar immediately reproaches herself for daring to question the value-system of patriarchy, a value-system which, as the following passage is intended to suggest, was designed to make and keep women silent and subservient:

> Gwenhwyfar thought she would smother with the rage that was choking her. But no, she must not be angry, it was not seemly to be angry; the Mother Superior had told her in the convent that it was a woman's proper business to be married and bear children . . . she must obey her father's will as if it were the will of God. Women had to be especially careful to do the will of God because it was through a woman that mankind had fallen into Original Sin, and every woman must be aware that it was her work to atone for that Original Sin in Eden. (p. 268)

Gwenhwyfar, however, is not the only woman in Bradley's novel to experience the stranglehold of patriarchial injunctions designed to keep women suppressed and subservient. As the wife of Gorlois, whom she describes as a man 'too filled with his Roman dignity to show much tenderness to a young wife, and with nothing but indifference for the daughter who came in place of the son she should have born him' (p. 8), Igraine experiences in her life at Tintagel the fate of women born into a patriarchal culture. Raised in Avalon to think for herself, Igraine finds herself at Tintagel in an environment that is hostile to women who dare to question patriarchy's values and traditions. Her every movement subject to the watchful eye of Father Columba, Igraine finds herself the object of ready censure by her house-priest and married to a man who has little time or inclination to listen to a woman's opinions about anything, especially about matters relating to statecraft or religion; in Gorlois's mind – which is to say, in the mind of patriarchy – these are matters about which only men are qualified to make judgements and express opinions (pp. 60–1). As if being intellectually marginalised by her husband were not enough for her to bear, when he comes to suspect Igraine of having encouraged Uther to love her Gorlois repeatedly subjects his wife to both physical and sexual abuse in an attempt to force her to submit to his will. His treatment of her leaves Igraine feeling 'humbled . . . beaten down utterly' (p. 71), and when Gorlois later imprisons her in his castle, theoretically 'for her own protection' (p. 76) but actually so that Uther will have no access to her or she to him, Igraine feels herself 'shut like a rat in a trap' (p. 77), not the wife of Gorlois but someone with no more rights than a slave or servant (p. 77).

That women in a patriarchal culture are too frequently treated as the equivalent of mere chattels is further impressed upon Igraine when she learns that even a man who loves her is prepared to decide her fate without ever having consulted her. Upon hearing that Uther has approached Gorlois with the proposition that he divorce Igraine so that Uther might marry her, Igraine rages 'that even Uther should think of her as a woman to be given away without her own consent . . . Was she a horse to be sold at the spring fair, then?' (p. 70). Igraine's response to her treatment by Uther is echoed by Morgaine later in the novel, when Balan suggests that she is well past the age when Arthur should have given her to some man in marriage. In her mind, the only environment in which it is safe for her to do so, Morgaine responds to Balan with the statement, 'And why should it be for the King to give me, as if I were one of his horses or dogs?' (p. 312).

As Lancelet informs Morgaine, however, Gwenhwyfar is a woman forced into marriage under precisely such conditions: 'She was given to Arthur like something bought at market, part of a purchase in horses because her father would have kinship with the High King as part of the price!' (p. 481; cf. p. 272). Despite the fact that Arthur soon comes to love Gwenhwyfar and to accord her a degree of gender equality she had never enjoyed in the home of her father, Gwenhwyfar proves incapable of transcending the patriarchal value-system that has been so much a part of her upbringing. As a Christian wife and queen, she feels herself duty bound to bear Arthur a male heir and to persuade him to renege on his oath to the pagan folk of Avalon (pp. 329–30). When she finds herself incapable of carrying a child to term, Gwenhwyfar becomes convinced, under counsel from her priest, that God is punishing her and Arthur with childlessness because Arthur's commitment to preserving the religious traditions of Avalon is preventing him from becoming a truly Christian king (pp. 551, 553–5).

Using the only tools available to her, Gwenhwyfar resorts to pleading, petulance and tears in an unrelenting assault on Arthur that ultimately proves successful. With a sureness that astonishes the people of Avalon, Britain gradually becomes a land in which there is no longer any place for the traditions of goddess worship: the Beltane and Midsummer fires cease to burn (pp. 578, 681), the sacred groves are all cut down (p. 692), and an irrevocable shift in consciousness takes place in the land: as Kevin the Merlin puts it, 'There seems to be a deep change in the way men now look at the world, as if one truth should drive out another – as if whatever is not their truth, must be falsehood' (p. 726).

That Gwenhwyfar is at least as much to blame as Arthur for the changes that have taken place in Britain by the end of Bradley's novel is testimony not only to her strength of character, but also to the insidious potential of patriarchy to victimise those who strive to perpetuate it. Described by Niniane as 'a creature of the priests' (p. 469) and by Nimue as someone who is 'fanatically, mindlessly Christian' (p. 788), Gwenhwyfar is a figure who, by virtue of her upbringing and an indomitable will, succeeds in justifying her personal insecurity as a woman by imposing upon her husband and his subjects the very value-system that has made her so desperately fearful and unhappy.

Although Bradley would have us see Gwenhwyfar's triumphant championing of patriarchy over matriarchy as both a present tragedy for the people of Avalon and an event that will adversely affect humankind for centuries to come, one does not have to look very closely at the matriarchal culture she holds up as an alternative to the patriarchal Christian tradition championed by Gwenhwyfar to see that the two are not fundamentally very different. Whereas in patriarchy, for example, it is the woman who is regarded as an expendable commodity and who is expected to defer to the will of her father, husband or priest, in the culture of Avalon it is the man who is so treated. Viviane, for instance, admits that 'no man had ever been more to her than duty, or a path to power, or a night's pleasure' (p. 194; cf. p. 161). The child sacred to the matriarchal culture of Avalon is the female child, who is customarily denied knowledge of her father on the grounds that no man should claim fatherhood to a child of the goddess (pp. 16–17). She is reared in Avalon, where she is afforded an education of the type typically reserved for males in a patriarchal culture (pp. 5, 440) and where she is also trained in herbal medicine and the mysteries of the goddess religion. A daughter of Avalon grows to maturity believing herself answerable to the goddess and her human agent, the Lady of the Lake, but to no man. When Mordred, for example, accuses Niniane of having allowed Arthur to become too familiar with her, she replies: 'But I am Niniane of Avalon, and I account to no man on this earth for what I do with what is mine – yes, mine and not yours. I am not Roman, to let some man tell me what I may do with what the Goddess gave me' (p. 849).

Decidedly less privileged are the male children born to the priestesses of Avalon; at birth they are sent off the island to foster-mothers, only occasionally to be summoned back to Avalon to visit their birth-mothers. Just as a female reared in a patriarchal environment of the type experienced by Gwenhwyfar may grow up to resent the indifference with which she was treated by her father, in the figure of Lancelet we see a male who is exceedingly resentful of the fact that the matriarchal traditions of Avalon have robbed him of the maternal affection he has always longed for: 'I would rather have a loving mother,' Lancelet tells Morgaine, 'than a stern Goddess whose every breath bids men live and die at her will' (p. 144).

As the human representative of the goddess on earth, the Lady of Avalon wields a power that is absolute. To her and her alone are the destinies of the goddess's subjects revealed, and to her is delegated the responsibility of seeing to it that those destinies are fulfilled. Thus it is Viviane who arranges for Igraine to be married to Gorlois and who, only a few years later, arrives at Tintagel with the news that Igraine's fate is now to bear a child to Uther Pendragon, the future king of Britain. Similarly, it is Viviane who arranges for Morgaine to make the Great Marriage to the land with Arthur at the time of his kingmaking, and who invests Arthur with Excalibur and exacts from him an oath of allegiance to the goddess.

In the execution of her duties, Viviane is expected to act without thought for her own feelings or the feelings of those in whose lives she feels obliged to intervene on behalf of the goddess. The consequences of this blind obedience to the will of Ceridwen are frequently painful for all concerned, since, as Viviane explains to Morgaine upon her arrival in Avalon, a life of service to the goddess is 'a hard life and a bitter one' (p. 136): 'Morgaine, Morgaine,' Viviane laments on this occasion, 'I would you had been my own child, but even so I could not spare you, I must use you for her purposes as I was myself used' (p. 136).

As Morgaine is soon to discover for herself, the experience of being 'used' by Viviane on behalf of the goddess is one that too often results in feelings of bewilderment, pain and anger (p. 183). When she discovers herself pregnant with Arthur's child, Morgaine bitterly upbraids Viviane for having known this event might well transpire but done nothing to prevent it (pp. 211–12). Igraine likewise feels victimised by Viviane for having been pressured into a loveless marriage with Gorlois (pp. 16–18), and, on her deathbed, confesses that she had sent Morgaine to Viviane for training 'even though I knew well how ruthless Viviane could be, that she would use Morgaine as ruthlessly as she used me, for the well-being of this land and for her own love of power' (pp. 358–9). The ruthlessness to which the agent of the goddess is sometimes obliged to resort is something Morgaine herself comes to experience when she re-commits herself to the service of Ceridwen. Having agreed to concoct a love potion for Elaine that would encourage Lancelet to love her, Morgaine justifies her personal betrayal of Lancelet by reflecting that 'Viviane had been just as ruthless as this . . . this too is for the good of the kingdom' (p. 536). Similarly, having commissioned Accolon into service on behalf of Avalon and the goddess, Morgaine acknowledges that she has 'used him . . . as ruthlessly as ever Viviane did me' (p. 674).

Surely what Bradley is offering to her readers in these details of the Avalonian lifestyle is a definition of a matriarchal culture that amounts, in the final analysis, to nothing more than patriarchy in disguise. Viviane and her priestesses emerge as the female equivalents of Patricius and his priests, women as committed as are their male counterparts to perpetuating a power-structure that is essentially phallocentric. If, as Jane Gallop has argued, phallocentric power is 'power that is unified, has a single direction, and is wielded by one [either an individual or an institution] in the masculine ideal of self-sufficiency' (Fuog, p. 81), there is little indeed to differentiate the female power-structure of Avalon from that which Bradley defines in her novel as the male power-structure of the Christian Church. Because both groups have a single leader, both are designed to accommodate a singleness of power. Both have a single purpose or direction: to perform the will of the god or goddess to whom they have committed their lives. And, finally, both groups seek not only to be self-sufficient, but also to influence those over whom they wield power.[2] That one group is as ruthlessly tryannical as the other in exercising this power is a phenomenon to which Bradley's text bears too ample testimony.

If the power-structure of Avalon is essentially phallocentric, in its definition of gender roles it is also essentially patriarchal. Indeed, Bradley has done little to alter the gender symmetry of patriarchy whereby woman is considered to be the complementary opposite, albeit not the equal, of man. All Bradley has done by way of altering this traditional model is to afford the women of Avalon a privileged status of the kind enjoyed by men in a patriarchal culture. As a result, the gender-roles of patriarchy remain essentially intact in Bradley's novel, and the two sexes remain in competition with one another for power and privilege (Fuog, p. 86). Even

---

[2] Fuog (p. 83) applies these criteria in assessing the matriarchal culture of Avalon; I have simply expanded the application to include the patriarchal culture of Christianity as the latter is defined in Bradley's novel.

in their sexual practices the women of Avalon are merely imitating the predatory sexual rites of males in a patriarchal culture: the only difference is that it is men, as opposed to women, who become objectified for the purpose of satisfying sexual desire or engendering offspring.

Because of the gender symmetry that prevails in Bradley's novel, moreover, virtually all of its women end up finding in their sexual relations with men what amounts to a patriarchal sanctioning of their individual worth as human beings. Igraine, for example, discovers in her lovemaking with Uther a sense of having 'been reunited with some hidden part of her own body and soul' (p. 105). Similarly, Morgaine confesses that 'she had never been so happy in her life' (p. 180) as when Arthur initiates a voluntary sexual encounter with her on the morning following the Great Marriage. Later in the novel, Morgaine confesses to having been 'healed' (p. 417) in her lovemaking with Kevin and brought back to life by virtue of her sexual relations with Accolon: 'Or is it only that when he touches me, speaks to me, I feel myself woman and alive again after all this time when I have felt myself old, barren, half-dead in this marriage to a dead man and a dead life?' (p. 587). To an even greater extent than is the case with any other woman in the novel, Morgause's sense of personal identity is firmly grounded in her power to lure men into her bed. When old age robs her of her sexual allure and she finds herself rejected for the first time ever by a would-be lover, Morgause immediately feels herself totally disempowered, as though 'the whole weight of life seemed to descend on her in deadly weariness' (p. 859).

In summary, then, while Bradley's assault on the patriarchal world of the Arthurian legend is one that aims in good directions, it is an assault that ultimately falls disappointingly short of its mark. In her depiction of patriarchy's attempt to impose itself upon the people of Britain through the vehicle of the fifth-century Christian Church and in her skilful representation of female characters like Gwenhwyfar, Igraine and Morgaine, Bradley scores more than a few sound hits at her target. In modelling the matriarchal order of Avalon on the order of Christian patriarchy, however, she ends up creating an alterity to patriarchy that is essentially false and that ultimately valorises the very phenomenon she had set out to discredit. Ironically, in short, some five hundred years after Malory's, Bradley's version of the medieval legend of Arthur attests to the fact that patriarchy continues to wield a very powerful sway in the mythic realm of the Once and Future King.

Works Cited

Bradley, Marion Zimmer, *The Mists of Avalon* (New York: Ballantine Books, 1982)

Fuog, Karin E. C., 'Imprisoned in the Phallic Oak: Marion Zimmer Bradley and Merlin's Seductress', *Quondam et Futurus: A Journal of Arthurian Interpretations*, 1 (Spring, 1991), pp. 73–88

Gordon-Wise, Barbara Ann, *The Reclamation of a Queen: Guinevere in Modern Fantasy* (Westport, Conn.: Greenwood Press, 1991)

The Arthurian Legend in the Cinema: Myth or History?

SANDRA GORGIEVSKI

Tracing the trajectory of the oral, then literary myth of King Arthur – initiated by Geoffrey of Monmouth with his *Historia Regum Britanniae* (1136) – entails travelling through the distorting mirrors of history, which reflect the various modes of thought and imagination specific to each period of time, cultural era or individual. It also involves a complex voyage through forms and genres, each of which retains its own codes and dynamic principles. This particularity does not preclude influence, exchange, borrowing or competition among the multiple settings of the myth, which include romances, poems, ivories, tapestries, stained-glass windows, paintings, operas, plays, novels, comic books, cartoons, films and more. Indeed, all these variations feed on one another and are enriched by the reflections of former centuries or decades, which recall the time when Arthurian literature flourished, yielding a canvas of very intricate patterns. This process bears witness to the anonymous and 'creative virtue' of myth,[1] which lends itself to metamorphosis from one formal system to another, sometimes losing its own identity in the process.

This paper will focus on a single syncretic form, the cinema, which blends images, sounds and narrative continuity into a homogeneous whole. My intention is not to survey the entire cinematic production linked in any way whatsoever to the Arthurian legend in order to label it 'historical film', 'epic' or 'fantasy'; least of all do I wish to tackle the thorny problem of Arthur's historicity and the transformation of an allegedly historical hero of the sixth century into a legendary, then mythical one.[2] Rather, what interests me is the deep-rooted and universal fascination which this legend in particular (and the Middle Ages in general) holds even today, as reflected in its diverse representations on the screen. Except

---

[1] See Mircea Eliade, 'La vertu créatrice du mythe', in *Eranos-Jarbuch*, 25 (1965), pp. 59–85.

[2] On the transformation of history into myth, see Mircea Eliade, *Le mythe de l'éternel retour* (Paris: Gallimard, 1969–92), pp. 48–64. See also H. M. and N. K. Chadwick, 'Myth is the last – not the first – stage in the development of a hero', in *The Growth of Literature* (Cambridge: Cambridge University Press, 1932–40), iii. p. 762.

for some films indebted to it but transposed into a different historical setting (the contemporary world or even science fiction), the Matter of Britain has always been associated with the Middle Ages, a historical period defined in terms of imagination rather than by strict historical landmarks. Its two major film references in the English-speaking world are *Excalibur* by the British director John Boorman (1981) and *Knights of the Round Table* by the American Richard Thorpe (1953). Although both screenplays claim to be based on Sir Thomas Malory's *Le Morte D'Arthur*, the films represent two divergent perspectives, and must be examined in the broader context of their historical and cinematic framework. The degree to which each is contaminated by other myths (whether medieval or contemporary) must then be assessed.

Cinematic frameworks as frames of mind

When we consider the way the Matter of Britain was and is still perceived and represented in popular imagination, and more specifically on the screen, we see that it is inseparable from the appearance of the Middle Ages in the history of the cinema. Thus, we become aware that our perception is influenced, indeed conditioned, by a prior series of representations. The screenplay of Thorpe's *Knights of the Round Table* draws prominently on Malory's text, so that the narrative discourse follows rather closely the rise and fall of the Arthurian world and illustrates its major themes and characters. Yet it actually lies within the framework of a particular, well-defined, even rigid genre: the swashbuckling film of the Hollywood tradition. Significantly, Richard Thorpe directed two other 'medieval' swashbucklers – *Ivanhoe* (1952) and *Quentin Durward* (1955) – with the same actor in the title roles, Robert Taylor, who also features as Lancelot in *Knights of the Round Table*, thus completing a famous trilogy produced by Metro Goldwyn Mayer (MGM) in the early fifties. Together they offer a Hollywood portrayal of the Middle Ages which relies more on nineteenth-century interpretations of the worlds of romance than on the medieval romances themselves.

A close look at the history of the genre is enlightening. The swashbuckling film brought to life in the American imagination the heroic dreams and romantic fancies at the heart of nineteenth-century England. Indeed, its thematic origins can be traced back to the age of Romanticism, with its fantastic imagination and mysticism, its taste for chivalry (Malory was reprinted three times between 1816 and 1817), its exaltation of the past in the form of ancient myths and legends and its fondness for historical novels. Alexander Dumas's and Walter Scott's tales of gallantry and heroism were influenced by chronicles and romances but also by popular ballads, folk-tales and legends. They thus reactivated collective archetypes and laid out the motives to be found in melodramas and modern medieval epics, and, much later, in westerns. Ironically, this movement, which was initiated against the formalism of the Enlightenment, turned out to develop its own formalism of rules and rituals in swashbuckling novels and plays.

At the turn of the century, with the appearance of the silent screen, a whole imagery was set up in the USA which lasted until the sixties. Its mainstays were gorgeous costumes, lavishly designed stunts, spectacular group sequences, codified, stereotyped actions and easily recognisable characters devoid of psychological depth and individuality, as if to compensate for lack of sound. Between 1910 and 1930 four Arthurian films were produced, three on Robin Hood and two on Ivanhoe, examples of the 'medieval' genre, and designated as such regardless of the historical period concerned.[3] Other escapist figures and heroes replaced them until the great Arthurian revival in the fifties. This time, because of the crisis in Hollywood provoked by the McCarthyist witch-hunt in the film industry, it was in England that MGM produced its trilogy with Richard Thorpe and Universal and Columbia shot low-budget swashbucklers. They advertised their films as an attempt to restore to England its own cultural heritage. They had drastically remodelled this past, contrary to the Arthurian literary production of the time, which was more indebted to the medieval literary tradition than to any Hollywood imagery. Four Arthurian films were shot, only three on the Robin Hood legend, and three historical films – about Richard the Lionheart, Richard III and Joan of Arc. In the meantime the growth of television as mass entertainment encouraged the British to shoot cheap, black-and-white, pocket-sized versions of the great originals, which they exported to the USA.[4] But the portrayal of the Middle Ages in these adaptations, aimed at a particular public, remained the same, albeit suffused with touches of exotic, 'true British' elements.

The most striking characteristic of these films is the dazzling swordplay of the central hero, enhanced by a selection of stars who often ended up being typecast in the role (Robert Taylor is a perfect example). The hero belongs to the knightly class or, in the case of Robin Hood, climbs the social ladder and exhibits better morals than the upper class does, as a testimony to the values of the democratic era. Such heroic values are embodied in the chivalric code, as illustrated by Malory's definition:[5]

(the king) charged them never to do outrageousity nor murder, and always to flee treason; also, by no means to be cruel, but to give mercy unto him

---

3   See filmography by Jaques Durand, 'La chevalerie à l'écran', in *Cinémathèque 22. L'avant-scène Cinéma*, 221 (février 1979), p. 39.

4   The British tried to impose their own TV star system; for instance, their Ivanhoe was played by Roger Moore (*The Saint, James Bond*).

5   The chosen reference here is the Caxton edition to be found in paperbacks, e.g. *Le Morte D'Arthur*, ed. Janet Cowen (Harmondsworth: Penguin, 1969), as we are dealing with popular culture, and as Boorman and Thorpe had no access to scholarly editions of Malory. The numbers respectively refer to Caxton's division into Books and Chapters.

that asketh mercy (. . .); and always to do ladies, damosels, and gentle-women succour, upon pain of death. Also that no man take no battles in a wrongful quarrel for no law, ne for no world's goods. (iii. 15)

The historical setting is stylised rather than realistic, relying on opulent period sets, obviously unhindered by major historical and geographical anachronisms. Thorpe followed in the wake of this genre, its Camelot castle and armour being reminiscent of the Norman Age, whereas accuracy would have demanded a representation of the Merovingian age. But had not Malory done just the same in the fifteenth century, and Tennyson and the Pre-Raphaelites in the nineteenth century?

In any case, the adventures of the heroes are in fact fictional exploits of archetypes rather than actual adventures of historically defined individuals. They consist of a series of ritualised themes, as if not to deceive the standard expectations of the audience, contrary to other popular genres which have evolved towards greater complexity (consider, for example, the influence of psychology and psychoanalysis on the western and the detective film). Arthur's adventures as retold by Thorpe can be compared step by step with those of Richard the Lionheart. The motives in both are the king's loss of power (Arthur threatened by Mordred and Morgana, Richard the Lionheart by his brother), followed by battles and a quest for power (the Grail in the former, the intervention of Robin Hood in the latter), then finally the restoration of order and the punishment of evildoers (Mordred's death and Galahad's reassertion of chivalric values, or the return of the king). Other compelling items of this stylistic composition are the siege of a castle, a tournament, a ride through the forest and the rescuing of the maidens (Guenevere and Elaine, or Marian). Thorpe thus conjures up an image of Arthur as the ideal monarch, belonging to a familiar, coherent yet anachronistic period of history which the Hollywood myth-making industry has turned into an ideal past, still fascinating to us and arousing in us childish bewilderment and pleasure. The Middle Ages are thereby but a fictional and imaginary world.

But are these mainstays of the swashbuckler sufficient to convey the essence of the Arthurian myth? In fact, three major instances definitely run counter to it. First, Thorpe exercised a rationalisation of the supernatural. Merlin is reduced to being Arthur's military strategist and friend, which is in accordance with Malory,[6] his prescience and magical powers expelled. He wears anonymous armour instead of the traditional sheepskin or hood which would identify him immediately as a necromancer. Like a helpless old man, he is treacherously poisoned by Morgana and Mordred (a heresy!), in sharp contrast with the mystery of his disappearance

---

6 Malory insists on Merlin's control of events: 'For the most part of his life he (Arthur) was ruled much by the counsel of Merlin' (iii. 1), and more specifically in Book I, with such words as 'advice' (i. 5; i. 10; i. 14; i. 15), 'counsel' (i. 3), 'providence' (i. 6), 'provision' (i. 11) and 'devise' (i. 3; i. 14).

and its ontological undertones in the legend, whether he is entombed in the earth or under a large stone by the magical powers stolen from him by the girl Nimue (iv. 1). Stonehenge, known as a place of sacred magic where the human and other worlds come into contact in the Celtic tradition, is turned into a profane platform where political issues are discussed. This violation reaches an extreme when Arthur asks his knights to 'vote' for or against the war. As for the Grail, it is hardly shown, since Galahad is *said* to have *heard* voices by the voice-off which creates an effect of distance from any overt depiction of the supernatural. This time Thorpe could not but make some small concession to this cumbersome but compulsory element of the legend; yet the spiritual dimension involved in the Grail Quest is left aside, and its discovery is secularised.

Moreover, the decline of earthly chivalry, the sense of impending doom and failure so present in Malory's last books, is here totally obliterated. In the optimistic final sequence Galahad finds the Grail and Lancelot has killed the wicked Mordred and will be forgiven, thus demonstrating that the age of chivalry is to be redeemed. Thorpe thus complies with the Hollywood tradition of the happy ending, representing the unflinching supremacy of Good over Evil, in concurrence with the Cold War mentality.

Finally, Hollywood censorship weighs heavily. There is a conspicuous lack of some of the most powerful and disquieting motives of the myth. Incest between Arthur and one of his sisters (i. 19) has been expunged, as their incestuous son, Mordred, is simply said to be one of the kingdom's barons. Adultery is only hinted at: Guenevere gives token proof of her love (a scarf) to Lancelot, and comes to his chamber in a sequence loaded with sexual connotations, in which Ava Gardner gracefully takes off her cloak but no more. In a way this might be interpreted as being in accordance with Malory's biased presentation of the entrapment scene, although departing from his knowing understatement: 'And whether they were abed or at other manner of disports, me list hereof make no mention, for love at that time was not as is nowadays' (xx. 3). The last combat features Mordred against Lancelot, not Arthur, thereby avoiding the ultimate confrontation between father and son and the issue of patricide. Heavily bowdlerised, *Knights of the Round Table* loses its universal impact in order to fit into the mould of the swashbuckler.

Thirty years later,[7] Boorman's *Excalibur* signals the return to fantasy and visual pleasure, such as can be found in the popular heroic-fantasy

---

[7] The swashbuckler did not exactly vanish, but in the sixties its audience turned to its related genres – historical epics such as Viking films, biblical epics or even martial arts pictures, *samurai* standing for knights. The seventies, an age of re-evaluation, dealt a severe yet salutary blow to the dying medieval genre, reviving Arthur and even Robin Hood as the targets of parody, and deconstructing myths in *Monty Python and the Holy Grail* (1975) and Richard Lester's *Robin and Marian* (1976). In France however, two authentic transpositions of the legend were released: Robert Bresson's *Lancelot du lac* (1974) and Eric Rohmer's *Perceval le Gallois* (1979).

genre to which Boorman is clearly indebted, and which was applied in the eighties to films, novels, posters and comic-strips. It is an almost exclusively American product which revives the tradition of the swashbuckler yet tries to reactivate the old spirit with new settings and an updated taste for legends and lost civilisations: a hybrid genre, as its aesthetic universe is inspired by German, Celtic, Oriental and Byzantine mythology, with a renewed interest in magic.

Magic is usually thought of as the elementary force which man manipulates without assessing its true power. In the cinema the weapon, not the man, is endowed with supernatural powers and confers on the warrior his heroic status, so that it becomes identified with him and gives him an unearthly, mythic stature. This myth of the weapon more powerful than gold is but a reworking of many European myths depicting the symbiosis between man and weapon – Caldalbog (the Celtic ancestor of Excalibur), Mjöllnir (Thor's hammer), Gram (Siegfried's sword), or Durandal and Hauteclère in the *Chanson de Roland*. In Boorman's film, Excalibur's supernatural powers kill Mordred, a feat which no human weapon could have achieved. Excalibur is sacred, as it symbolises the king's legitimacy; transmitted from Uther to Arthur (thus replacing the many swords to be found in Malory), it deprives Arthur of his identity as king when he embeds it between Lancelot and Guenevere. 'A king without a sword; a land without a king,' Lancelot laments. Its modern avatars include the sword of *Conan the Destroyer* (a perfect illustration of the heroic-fantasy film) as well as the invincible laser-sword of Luke Skywalker in the last section of the science fiction trilogy *Star Wars*. It is not by chance that the posters for all three of these films display the swords brandished upwards in the foreground.[8]

The heroic-fantasy genre is at the same time keen on historical verisimilitude. Historical and archeological studies in the seventies[9] had shed light on Arthur's Romano-Celtic origins, so that, with his superb muscles, he fits into the newly fashionable image of the sixth-century barbarian depicted in heroic fantasy. He continues the tradition of the muscle-men of epic films, like Charlton Heston in William Wyler's *Ben Hur* (1959) who later appeared in Anthony Mann's famous swashbuckler *El Cid* (1961), or like Kirk Douglas in *The Vikings* (1958) by Richard Fleisher, who also directed Arnold Schwarzenegger in *Conan the Destroyer*. Thus the cinematic appearance of the Middle Ages approximates to a kind of primitive prehistory. The first part of *Excalibur* lies within the scope of Conan's universe. The film opens with the remote, fantasmagorical world of 'the Dark Ages', as they are called, enshrined in the obsessive rhythm and primitive force of Siegfried's Funeral March from Wagner's opera

---

[8] Richard Fleisher, *Conan the Destroyer* (1984); the *Star Wars* trilogy: George Lucas, *Star Wars* (1977), *The Empire Strikes Back* (1980) and Richard Marquand, *The Return of the Jedi* (1983).

The Ring. All-pervasive violence is to be found in events – war, lust, breach of contract, ambush, treason, murder, rape – as well as in images. The gnarled armours of the knights and the horses' harnesses suggest a reptilian, antediluvian world, the castle of Tintagel peering over the steep cliffs is dark and oppressive, the sea is wild, the forest is dark and untamed, war-fires blaze everywhere. It is an age of chaos, the dawn of time, when man emerged from nature.

Sometimes, heroic-fantasy films emphasise an element of horror, creating an aesthetic of violence and gore, perhaps intending to highlight the savagery of the Middle Ages, yet often undermining the overall quality of the film. One might be tempted to associate *Excalibur* with this aesthetic, especially as Boorman displays a predilection for violence in other films, such as in the unforgettable and unrelenting shots of a farmer's corpse transfixed with an arrow in *Deliverance* (1975), or the horrific make-up of a demon girl digging in the hearts of her victims in *Exorcist II: The Heretic* (1977). But in the case of *Excalibur*, is the violence not dictated by the medieval texts themselves? Medieval use of hyperbole, rather than a taste for raw brutality, is evidenced in Malory's narrative. Frequent bloodbaths, far from being realistic, underline the corporeal and the violence inherent in knightly deeds: 'They tamed their helms that the hot blood ran out, and the thick mails of their hauberks they carved and rove in sunder that the hoot blood ran to the earth' (iii. 10). Boorman recaptures this dimension when the Duke of Cornwall is impaled on a range of spears, or when the sword Excalibur inflicts terrible wounds on its opponents, just as in *Le Morte D'Arthur* the king shortens a giant's legs and cuts off a Roman's head lengthways down to the breast (v. 8). A crow surreptitiously plucks out the eye of one of the Grail knights hanged on a tree, in a sequence strongly reminiscent of François Villon:[10]

> La pluie nous a bués et lavés
> Et le soleil desséchés et noircis
> Pies, corbeaux nous ont les yeux cavés
> Et arraché la barbe et les sourcils.
> Jamais nul temps nous ne sommes assis ;
> Puis ça, puis la, comme le vent varie,
> A son plaisir sans cesse nous charrie,
> Plus becquetés d'oiseaux que dés à coudre.

The cruelty of the last battle, culminating in patricide, is an exact translation to the screen of the Malorian text, with the roles reversed:

> Then the king gat his spear in both hands, and ran towards Sir Mordred, crying, 'Traitor, now is thy death day come.' And when Sir Mordred heard

---

9   See the research work of Leslie Alcock, John R. Morris and Geoffrey Ashe.
10   'L'épitaphe de Villon en forme de ballade', in François Villon, *Oeuvres* (Paris: Garnier, 1951), pp. 152–3.

Sir Arthur, he ran until him with his sword drawn in his hands. And there King Arthur smote Sir Mordred under the shield, with a foin of his spear, throughout the body, more than a fathom. And when Sir Mordred felt that he had his death's wound he thrust himself with the might he had up to the bur of King Arthur's spear. And right so he smote his father Arthur, with his sword holden in both his hands, on the side of the head, that the sword pierced the helmet and the brain pan. (xxi. 4)

Contamination by other myths

Both cinematic frameworks, the swashbuckler and heroic fantasy, have created their own 'mythologies', in Roland Barthes's words,[11] further playing on the existing mythologies surrounding the actors themselves. Some more profound influences, however, underlie Boorman's film, such as the other medieval myths of Tristram and Isoud, or Siegfried.

In Malory the Tristram section functions as a parallel motive to the Lancelot–Guenevere relationship, and works through comparison and allusion. As early as in Book V, Lancelot is 'wroth' because Tristram is allowed to join Isoud in Cornwall whereas he must leave Guenevere. In the Tale of Sir Tristram (viii to xii in Caxton's edition), we are constantly made aware of the progression of the love between Lancelot and Guenevere: Isoud writes to Guenevere (viii. 31) while Tristram writes to Lancelot (ix. 5); Morgan le Fay, the 'enemy of all true lovers' (viii. 34) sends a magic horn to test Guenevere's loyalty, but it is Isoud who is eventually put to the test (viii. 34); they exchange rings (viii. 12, xx. 4); Isoud sends a message to Guenevere which makes the parallel even clearer: 'there be within the world but four lovers, that is, Sir Lancelot du Lake and Queen Guenevere, and Sir Tristram de Liones and Queen Isoud' (viii. 31). The title of 'Queen' strengthens the motif of divided loyalties to the King (whether Arthur or Mark). The castle of Joyous Guard shelters both Tristram and Isoud (x. 52) and Lancelot and Guenevere (xx. 6). All these parallels point to the ill-fated character of both couples' love, beset by secret meetings, adultery and tragedy within a courtly-love system.

In *Excalibur*, Boorman points to this myth of eternal love through the use of Wagner's opera *Tristan und Isolde*, which, according to D. de Rougemont, represents the culmination of the myth as a temporal absolute, a desire for eternal unity only achieveable in death: *La musique seule peut bien parler de la tragédie.*[12] The Prelude can be heard each time Lancelot and Guenevere meet, during their first encounter at Guenevere's father's castle, when Lancelot escorts her through the forest to her wedding, when he avoids her at Camelot and goes into exile in the forest, and

---

[11] Roland Barthes, *Mythologies* (Paris: Seuil, 1957).
[12] 'Only music can speak thoroughly of tragedy.' Denis de Rougemont, *L'amour et l'Occident* (Paris: Plon, 1938–72), p. 251.

again when she joins him there, thus illustrating the theme of the voluntary flight to the utopian shelter of the desert-forest. Finally it is heard when they make love and are taken unawares by Arthur. The entrapment scene is a narrative reminder of the myth, and visually encapsulates this connection: it is directly borrowed from the French medieval texts, in which King Mark surprises the two lovers sleeping in the forest. As Tristram's sword separates them and their bodies lie apart, he prefers to believe that they are innocent. He renounces slaying them, and embeds his own sword between the two bodies as an omen: *l'acier froid de l'épée brillait entre eux.*[13] In *Excalibur* Arthur does the same, but this time as evidence of their fault as well as of his forgiveness, since the two lovers, naked, sleep in a tender embrace.

Despite adultery, it is actually the royal couple who rework the myth of eternal love in this film. In *Knights of the Round Table*, as in Malory (xxi. 9), Lancelot pays a last visit to Guenevere in the nunnery where she has taken refuge after the kingdom's downfall. The choice of the two stars (Robert Taylor and the sex-symbol Ava Gardner) makes it clear that it is this couple which has survived in popular imagination, whereas the actor Mel Ferrer (as Arthur) cuts a pathetic figure and appears as a wishy-washy king. In *Excalibur*, however, the lovers are not destined to meet after the entrapment scene, for it is the ageing Arthur who comes to the nunnery to forgive and be forgiven, his dignified yet humble bearing being more convincing than Lancelot's unflinching, fanatic assertion of his love. Arthur evokes 'the hereafter' of their lives and the possibility for reconciliation: it is the royal couple whom we will remember. Moreover, Boorman makes use of a Malorian episode to Arthur's advantage: Lancelot was made knight by both King and Queen, dubbed by Arthur with the same sword Guenevere had given back to him after he had lost it (xviii. 7). In the film it is Arthur who, formerly dubbed by Sir Uriens, owes his identity to his wife when she returns Excalibur to him in the nunnery.

Once more Wagner serves as an auditory link with Germanic mythology, this time with Siegfried's Funeral March. Rather than the hero himself, it is the sense of doom arising from this recurrent musical motif which pervades the whole film. Indeed it actually structures the film, as it singles out the key moments of the legend – Uther's death and the prediction of Arthur's reign; the creation of the Round Table; Arthur facing treason without Merlin; the last combat against Mordred; and finally the moment when Excalibur is thrown back into the lake and the prophecy of Arthur's return is delivered. The Funeral March (from *The Twilight of the Gods*, the last part of *The Ring*) also marks the disappearance of the old gods and the crumbling of the Valhalla. In the Prologue the thread of

---

13 'The cold steel blade was gleaming between them.' *Tristan et Iseult*, translated from Old French by René Louis (Paris: Librairie Générale Française, 1972), p. 127.

destiny had been broken, symbolising the advent of the Age of Man.[14] Indeed, Merlin's disappearance in the film highlights the necessity for Arthur to take charge of his own destiny, no longer relying on Merlin's prescience and advice: 'I can tell you nothing more, my days are ended ... It's a way of things, it's a time for men and their ways.' The idea that 'the gods of once are gone forever', that 'the one God comes out to drive out the many gods' is in keeping with medieval reality and the rise of Christianity in the Western world, yet the idea of man mastering his fate alone is inherited from the Renaissance movement. Thus different historical world views are synthesised in Boorman's own interpretation of the disappearance of the Arthurian world.

No such references can be found in Thorpe's film, the American director instead returning to his own 'national myths' and to the legendary past specific to the new continent – the myth of the frontier and the western. At first we witness a visual contamination. A single sequence bridges the gap between two apparently opposed genres: a military attack by a horde of Picts, fraught with the intensity to be found in great Indian attacks in westerns. The 'wild' warriors ride down a steep gorge resembling canyons, yelling like the stereotyped 'wicked' Indian tribes, 'savagely' stabbing their enemies to death. This striking link is enhanced by the narrative voice-off, a commonplace device in westerns, such as *The Big Sky* by Howard Hawks (1952).

But it seems likely that cross-fertilisation has occured. Some motives are blatantly filmed in the manner of western clichés, which are themselves likely to be borrowed from romances. First of all they focus on the knight and his horse. The myth of the 'lonesome cowboy' who cannot find rest or home anywhere else but on his horse, the physical entity which both represent (a cowboy hardly ever walks on solid ground; rather, he rides) and the emotional link which binds them, are all inherited from romances. In Thorpe's film, on the eve of battle, men and horses stay up together by the fire in a snow-covered landscape reminiscent of the Wild West. In the final sequence Lancelot's horse plays a prominent role in the single combat against Mordred, as it saves his life twice by getting him out of quicksand. In fact it reawakens the symbiosis between the knight and his horse, especially in battle, to be found in Malory, *Sir Gawain and the Green Knight* and epic tales. Malory often mentions a horse's wounds as an objective correlative of its master's, and shows the knight taking care not to endanger it: 'When he saw his horse should be slain he alit and voided his horse' (ix. 4).

Male friendship is one of the supreme values in westerns, as well as in romances. In *The Big Sky* the two heroes, at first enemies, come to recognise each other's worth during combat, as do Lancelot and Arthur in

---

[14] See Eric Eugene, 'Le sens politique de l'anneau', in *Avant-scène Opéra*, 13/14 (1978), pp. 19–21.

Knights of the Round Table. This theme is best exemplified in Malory by Sir Bors, who is faithful to Lancelot 'whether in right or wrong' and, after the entrapment of the lovers, is ready to take 'the woe with the weal' (xx. 5–6). Male friendship can even be regarded as superior to kinship. In *Le Morte D'Arthur* brotherhood is of the utmost importance. Brothers are closely linked, and their names cannot be dissociated, as the use of assonance and consonance underlines – Balin and Balan, Blamor and Bleoberis, or the four brothers Agravain, Gawain, Gareth, Gaheris, the sisters Lynet and Lyoness and the sister and brother Elaine and Lavaine. But the Round Table serves as a more binding brotherhood. Gareth's loyalty to chivalric service takes him away from his brother:

> There was never no knight that Sir Gareth loved more so well as he did Sir Launcelot . . . And ever for the most part he would be in Sir Launcelot's company; for after Sir Gareth had espied Sir Gawain's conditions, he withdrew himself from his brother Sir Gawain's fellowship. (vii. 34)

This love intensifies the dramatic irony of Lancelot's inadvertent slaying of Gareth (xx. 8), 'for Sir Gareth loved Launcelot above all men earthly' (xx. 9).

Another common legacy is the female stereotype, to be found in the pure, ingenuous child (Olivia de Haviland as Elaine in her pale blue, virginal dress, just as in *Ivanhoe*), or the *femme fatale* (Ava Gardner as Guenevere). The codified behaviours, ceremonies, oaths and banners partake of both chivalry and cavalry as if the memory of the old continent had shaped the attitudes of the new one.

The Hollywood production history sheds light on this process of mutual influence. Throughout the fifties, Universal and Columbia resorted to western directors for their swashbucklers, with a cast reflecting the western's familiar supporting actors. At the same time, they selected title roles for their 'chivalric' appearance. Robert Taylor played in first-rank westerns just before and after the MGM trilogy,[15] and was no doubt chosen by Thorpe because 'he was the embodiment of the solid chivalric virtues, mature, upright, inflexibly honorable'.[16] In terms of the creative imagination, is not the conquest of the West the only possible Middle Ages for America?

Boorman, by contrast, seems less dependent on any fixed framework, and relies rather on an individual recreation of the Arthurian world, achieving his personal mythology by means of syncretic imagination and

---

[15] R.Taylor played in *Billy the Kid* (David Miller, 1941), *Devil's Doorway* (Anthony Mann, 1950), *Westward the Women* (William Wellman, 1952), *The Last Hunt* (Richard Brooks, 1955), *Many Rivers to Cross* (Roy Rowland, 1955) and *The Law and Jack Wade* (John Sturges, 1958).

[16] Director John Sturges, quoted by Jeffrey Richards in *Swordsmen of the Screen: From Douglas Fairbanks to Michael York* (London: Routledge and Kegan Paul, 1977), p. 94.

stylisation. To a certain extent *Excalibur* lies within the scope of the heroic-fantasy genre's affinity for the supernatural, and recaptures many of its elements, whether narrative or visual. This tendency is never gratuitous, but is in accordance with the demands set up by the Arthurian myth or the vision created by the director's own idiosyncrasies. For instance, Boorman does not yield to the new fashion of living bestiaries, be they monsters – such as the ghastly monster in Ridley Scott's *Alien* (1979) – or nostalgic counterparts in futuristic worlds like the puppet Yoda in *Star Wars*, or the elves of the fable *Dark Crystal* by Jim Henson (1982). Boorman's sole imaginary creation is the Dragon, which is spoken about but never seen in full view. The director favours the fearful dragon of Arthur's dream in Malory (v. 5), interpreted by a wise philosopher as an image of Arthur the Conqueror, which contributes to a coherent Arthurian world. In the film, it ensures the unity between the king and his land, just as the sword Excalibur does. Its breath (a fog) enables Uther to lie with Igrayne and to conceive Arthur, and it stands against Mordred's army in the last battle. It also presides over Arthur's initiatory night with Merlin, thereby becoming the emblem of Camelot. When Arthur relinquishes Excalibur he thrusts it not only between the lovers' bodies but also, symbolically, into the dragon's spine, thus renouncing his kingdom. The dragon is suffused with Boorman's fondness for esoteric symbols. It stands for the cosmic, primary forces of the earth described by Mircea Eliade: *l'involution, la modalité pré-formelle de l'univers, l'un non fragmenté d'avant la création.*[17] Merlin says that 'it is everywhere, it is everything', it is the place where 'all things are possible and all things meet their opposite'. Furthermore, it combines effectively the four elements of medieval cosmology, which is another compelling constant in Boorman's films:[18] it emerges from water, spits fire, breathes vapour and lives under the earth.

As for Merlin, he combines the traditional roles of friend, prophet, omniscient strategist and inspirer of the Round Table; and he is also Boorman's favourite figure. His films are filled with Merlin-characters: manipulators, such as the powerful businessman in *Catch Us if You Can* (1965), the estate manager Lazlo in *Leo the Last* (1970), Arthur Frayne in *Zardoz* (1973), who also act as metaphors for the film-maker himself as they pull the strings behind the curtains. Merlin is an embodiment of the shaman archetype, who also appears as Wanadi in *The Emerald Forest* (1985) and Kokumo in *The Heretic* (1977). Furthermore, he recalls the trickster figure as defined by C. G. Jung.[19]

In his recreation of the Middle Ages, Boorman devises his own fantasy

---

[17] 'Involution, the undifferentiated form of the universe, the non-fragmented whole before creation.' Mircea Eliade, *Le mythe de l'éternel retour* (Paris: Gallimard, 1969; Essais/Folio, 1992), pp. 54–60.
[18] See Michel Ciment, *Boorman, un visionnaire en son temps* (Paris: Calman-Lévy, 1985).
[19] C. G. Jung, *Four Archetypes* (London: Routledge and Kegan Paul, 1972), pp. 135–53.

world. His condensed vision offers multiple perceptions of the era, avoiding monotony while retaining coherence because each canvas corresponds to the particular narrative structure of the film. The age of Uther, depicted above as part of the heroic-fantasy imagery, is a period of chaos, out of which King Arthur arises as a new, unifying ruler. In visual as well as narrative contrast with this age of iron, the age of Arthur is one of gold and silver. It is a shining era which opens with a joust near a luminous waterfall, between two silver-armoured knights – Arthur and Lancelot, the flower of chivalry. The forest is clear and welcoming, providing food for Perceval and rest for Lancelot. Camelot nestles in a grassy valley and appears as an elaborate piece of fantasy sculpture, far from any identifiable existing castle, a *mélange* of Indian, Gothic and Roman. The interiors hold the golden Round Table, and are warmly lit and hung with rich tapestries reminiscent of Gustav Klimt's golden stylised frescoes. The kitchen swells with musicians, a puppet master, a jester, alchemists – a whole miscellany of medieval archetypes. 'There is no want,' the king boasts. It is an age of temporary stability, peace and plenty, yet carrying within it the seeds of its own destruction, for gold also portends vainglorious wealth.

Consequently the last part of the film, the Grail Quest, displays a bloody, muddy world, in the tradition of the Italian cinema, from the neo-realism of Vittorio de Sica to P. P. Pasolini's social concerns in his medieval films *The Decameron* (1971) or *The Canterbury Tales* (1972). We have moved from the enclosed, courtly world of chivalry to a poverty-stricken, plague-ridden peasant world. The land becomes sterile and the forest is devastated, objectifying the decay of chivalry and the king's illness in a kingdom which can only be a waste land. Boorman takes up the theme of moral and spiritual failure, choosing realistic details for their symbolic significance. He was influenced in this respect by Pre-Raphaelite paintings, though he does not recapture their dream-like, ethereal atmosphere.[20]

The director moves even further away from pseudo-historical references, and plays with science-fiction imagery. Knights wear full-dress, solid-metal, shining armour which reminds us of the diving-suit imagined by Jules Verne, the golden robot in Fritz Lang's *Metropolis* (1920) and the first space-suits. The parallel is even more obvious in group sequences, when knights ride together in search of new adventures, swearing oaths under the stars, thus suggesting a mythical fellowship which is in no small way akin to the spirit of the space conquest. Science fiction combines the themes of the exploration of unknown worlds with medieval imagery,

---

20 What also prevents us from drawing further comparisons is that the depth of field gives space to his sharp-eyed actors, whereas Rossetti's and Burne-Jones's mystic characters, for instance, seem to move on a shallow, rectilinear plane. See also William Morris's 'Queen Guenevere' (1858) or Frederik Sandys's 'King Pelles bearing the Vessel of the San Grael' (1861).

interstellar space replacing the medieval forest. For instance, the space-ship in Stanley Kubrick's *2001: A Space Odyssey* (1968), in which human adventures are held in camera, suggests the enclosed, outlying castle of ancient legends. It is of interest that the Arthurian subject gave rise to other manifestations in science-fiction literature and cinema, as is revealed in a close analysis of the *Star Wars* trilogy screenplay.[21]

The legend of the once and future king still catches the popular imagination, answering perhaps the spiritual yearnings of a disillusioned era, proving its continuing relevance. The Middle Ages still fascinate us because they are both mythical and imaginary, as George Duby said: *Un Moyen-Age qui fonctionne comme une mythologie, qui se situe simplement 'bien loin dans le temps' et assez obscur pour qu'on y projette librement ses fantasmes présents, en leur donnant consistance de l'épaisseur du passé.*[22] Both Thorpe and Boorman have created a world onto which the viewers can project themselves, thus playing on the collective imagination and on potent symbols rather than on history. As opposed to Thorpe's film, which is a perfect product of the dream factory Hollywood was in fifties America, Boorman has proved to be more personal in recapturing the great Arthurian motives while working from his own motivations, thus satisfying the quest for a genuine appropriation of the myth, enabling its ultimate survival.

Works Cited

Lacy, Norris J. (ed.), *The Arthurian Encyclopedia* (New York: Garland, 1986–95)

Le Goff, Jacques, *L'imaginaire médiéval* (Paris: Gallimard, 1985)

Girouard, Mark, *The Return to Camelot: Chivalry and the English Gentleman* (New Haven and London: Yale University Press, 1981)

Buache, Freddy, *Le cinéma américain 1971–1983* (Lausanne: L'âge d'homme, 1985)

de la Breteque, François, dir. 'Le moyen-âge au cinéma', in *Cahiers de la cinémathèque*, 42/43 (1985)

Elley, Derek, *The Epic Film: Myth and History* (London: Routledge and Kegan Paul, 1984)

Richards, Jeffrey, *Swordsmen of the Screen: From Douglas Fairbank to Michael York* (London: Routledge and Kegan Paul, 1977)

Viviani, Christian, *Le western* (Paris: Artefact, Henri Veyrier, 1982)

---

[21] See Renée Hein and Catherine Saisset, 'La chevalerie dans les étoiles', in *Cahiers de la Cinémathèque*, 42/43 (1985), pp. 167–70.

[22] 'The Middle Ages which function as a mythology, which are distant enough in time and obfuscated enough so that one can freely project one's own fantasms onto them, while giving them the potency of the past.' George Duby, quoted in *Cahiers de la Cinémathèque*, 42/43 (1985), p. 171.

Franklin Pierce College Library

0 0 1 3 0 2 9 4

DATE DUE

DEC 2 1 2004	

GAYLORD

PRINTED IN U.S.A.